ORIGINAL RUDE BOY

FROM BORSTAL TO THE SPECIALS
A LIFE OF CRIME AND MUSIC

NEVILLE STAPLE
WITH TONY McMAHON

FOREWORD BY PETE WATERMAN

Aurum

First published in Great Britain
2009 by Aurum Press Ltd
7 Greenland Street
London NW1 0ND
www.aurumpress.co.uk

This paperback edition published in 2010 by Aurum Press

Photographs: p.iii, courtesy of Redferns/Getty Images; p.xi, courtesy of Pete
Waterman; p.192, courtesy of UrbanImage/Adrian Boot; p.230, *The Face*, April
1982, courtesy of Bauer Media; p.342–3, courtesy of UrbanImage/Adrian Boot

Every effort has been made to trace the copyright holders of material quoted in
this book. If application is made in writing to the publisher, any omissions will
be included in future editions.

A catalogue record for this book is available from the British Library.

ISBN 978 1 84513 542 3

1 3 5 7 9 10 8 6 4 2
2010 2012 2014 2013 2011

Text designed and typeset by Saxon Graphics, Derby
Printed by CPI Bookmarque, Croydon

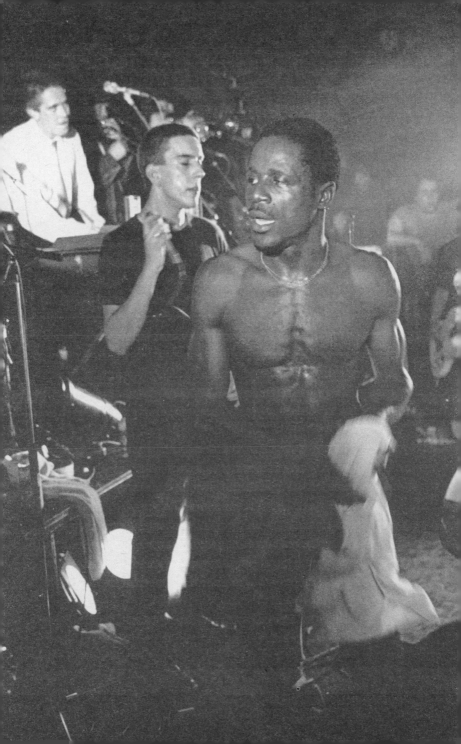

Dedicated to Katherine Brown Staple
– my mother
1933–2008

CONTENTS

FOREWORD
BY PETE WATERMAN

Way back in the late 1960s and early 1970s, if you'd been blessed with a crystal ball you'd probably have thought it was on the blink.

Had you been able to see what the future would hold in relation to what was happening at a Coventry nightclub called the Locarno – it would have stretched the imagination beyond credibility.

As a DJ at that same club, my job – as I saw it – was just to entertain. In truth, to me it was always about the music and involving the audience in that experience. I always searched out new sounds and ideas, and I always had a superb rapport with the audience – the kids who paid to come in.

Looking back now, nearly 40 years on, I can see that in what was a relatively intolerant society, we were quite a unique little organisation and yet nobody really talked about the diverse cultures that were involved. It was just accepted.

One of the kids I befriended was this cheeky West Indian who had a twinkle in his eye, was full of mischief and was passionate about music. His enthusiasm, and ability to actually back that enthusiasm with talent, gave me the opportunity to feature him regularly on stage as a 'toaster' and a dancer.

He was also instrumental in bringing me new sounds. Not all, as I seem to remember, were great – but some tracks did become huge audience pleasers.

Later, when I joined the record industry as an A&R scout and then as a young record producer, the initial success I had actually put me off the business. I had to return to Coventry to get my feet back on the ground in the real world.

It was when I had a job on a building site that I found myself listening to the rehearsals of a punk/ska band that at the time called themselves The Automatics. Because an American band had the same name they had to change theirs – and were to be known thereafter as The Specials.

I became their first manager. Once again, I found myself involved with Neville and just as he had been an asset to me as a DJ at the Locarno – he was an asset to me in this new role. Neville's involvement with The Specials was just that little bit different from the ordinary.

I remember well us all piling into a van one Sunday and going down to Berwick Street Studios where we recorded 'Too Much Too Young', 'Jay Walker' and 'Concrete Jungle'. The Specials went on to achieve amazing success and ska became a culture all of its own.

No crystal ball could have ever told from those Monday nights at the Coventry Locarno, that both Neville Staple and Pete Waterman would hitch their wagon to a star and achieve such fame – we were just two rude boys in a world of wonder.

Tone Records/Chrysalis Records (© EMI)

INTRODUCTION

2 Tone tour poster.

Neville Staple, *personal collection*

As usual I'd just started to have a mid-afternoon kip on the sofa – round about 2pm. Years of being on the road with The Specials – often touring in cramped conditions – had acclimatised me to the sofa over my bed as a place to sleep. I'd smoked my very large roll-up, was thoroughly chilled out and looking ahead to some gigs at the weekend.

That's about the moment that my front door came crashing down. Nine heavily uniformed coppers charged through the opening.

'Stay where you are! Do not move!' My gob half-open in disbelief, I watched as the boys in blue began ripping my skirting boards off, overturning all my furniture and flashing torches into every dark corner. I had no idea what they were up to.

'This yours?'

'Yeah…' The copper sniffed the small plastic bag, half full by now. "… it's for personal use.'

That didn't wash with the forces of law and order.

'You have the right to remain silent…' And so on. After four or five hours in a police cell, the local constabulary decided that I wasn't the drugs overlord of the city of Coventry and could be safely let out on to the streets again without posing a threat to the general population.

I cursed myself on the way home that I'd left an illegal substance on the coffee table. But I'd been distracted the night before by three young women who'd come round after a gig to keep me entertained. They'd left some other shit on the table that was far worse than my drug of choice. I hadn't cleared any of that crap away – but then I was hardly expecting the front door to come flying off its hinges.

This event didn't happen when I was in The Specials or Fun Boy Three. It happened barely a year ago.

It's symptomatic of the two sides of my character. One is the Dr Jekyll side. The public persona as the vocalist in two seminal pop bands. A face regularly seen on *Top of the Pops* or beaming cheekily from the front cover of *Smash Hits* or the *NME*.

The other is Mr Hyde – a Neville Staple that is a creature of the streets. A man who has burgled houses, been thrown in borstal and fought skinhead gangs with knives and chains. A Jamaican-born rude boy who knew all about ska music and the feelings of frustration and anger that inspired that music long before The Specials made it the sound that kicked off the 1980s.

It's often said that there were two distinct and very different halves to The Specials. A well-educated art school set versus the uncouth rude boys. Those rude boys were me and my two buddies Trevor Evans and Rex Griffiths, who were officially the band's roadies but really my mates – and in Trevor's case a fellow borstal inmate.

We ended up in a band with the art students, a rockabilly, a soul guitarist and a white punk. It may have looked like the chance throwing together of a bunch of people who, against all expectations, produced the greatest songs of their era but, as I'll reveal, the emergence of The Specials was no accident. It evolved from a music scene in Coventry that stretched back to the 1960s that I was very much a part of. A scene that most people know very little about but was vibrant, edgy and sometimes mixed with extreme violence.

My upbringing was a world away from those of the musicians I shared stages with in Europe, the United States and Japan. There was warmth and security in their childhoods, while there was none in mine. They obeyed the law as good, middle-class kids – while me and my mates resorted to house breaking, dope dealing and extortion to make ends meet.

As pop stars, these guys abhorred the trappings of fame, as well as the easy sex, limos and a powdered hooter. I lapped it all up, secretly worried that the good times might not last.

You have to get to grips with my life if you're going to understand how an out-of-date Jamaican beat, fused with the punk ethos, creating a distinctive sound that burst out of Coventry, of all places, at the end of the 1970s. From this unpromising town, still getting over Hitler's bombs, emerged a musical movement that gripped Britain in the run-up to the explosive riots of 1981.

Me and my mates Trevor, Rex, Bookie, Scuff, my brother Franklyn, and others you'll meet in the next few pages, lodged a bit of Jamaica in the heart and mind of Coventry. And not just the music and style of that unruly tropical island – its uncompromising attitude as well.

In a few short years, I went from being an ex-jailbird to a regular on *Top of the Pops*. Then, just when the ska wave receded in the UK – it stormed back stronger than ever in the United States, giving birth to bands like Unwritten Law, No Doubt and Rancid, and making me a ska elder statesman on the other side of the pond.

This isn't a book that will drearily list a series of boring 'muso' facts about 2 Tone. Instead, this is very much my story. I suppose I should apologise to some people in advance for the sex, drugs and rock clichés that I indulged in, and which are recounted in the chapters ahead. But it makes for a better read and, as many people will tell you, some with disgust, it all happened.

I will reveal how the original rude boy sound and ethos helped the British music scene break free from the death agonies of punk. How the music I helped create became the soundtrack for those turbulent times. And how a very fractious group of blokes from Coventry went on to conquer the global pop scene before needlessly tearing each other apart.

THE CITY CENTRE CLUB
Tower Street, Coventry

proudly presents

THE
SPECIAL A.K.A.
and SUPPORT

on TUESDAY, 31st JULY 1979

Advance Tickets £1.25   On the Night £1.50

Limited Admission

Live on stage 10 p.m.

BRUNEL ENTS PRESENTS

THE SPECIALS
Plus THE SWINGING CATS
Wednesday, 8th Oct., 1980
SPORTS BARN   Doors open 7.30

Tickets : £3.00

Hammersmith Palais
242 Shepherds Bush Road, W6

TUESDAY 22nd
FEBRUARY

at 8.00p.m.

ADMISSION £4.00
Inc. V.A.T.

№ 1404

TO BE GIVEN UP

Hammersmith Palais
Box office open 12-6 Mon-Sat
Telephone: 748 2812

TUESDAY
FEBRUARY 22

at 8.00p.m.

HEAD MUSIC presents
Fun Boy Three

№ 1404

THIS PORTION TO BE RETAINED   (PTO)

Me (*left*) and Lynval Golding, guitarist with The Specials, sharing a rude boy moment.

Neville Staple, personal collection

1

JAMAICA TO RUGBY
– THE EARLY YEARS

In my early teens.
Neville Staple, personal collection

In rural Christiana they hear whips cracking in the night and slaves moaning, crying out for mercy, normally near the caves. Everybody hears it – I can't think of a person who lives round there who says they haven't – but nobody actually sees any of these slaves.

Well they have been dead for a long time.

My grandmother lived in this area her entire life until her death at nearly a hundred. She had a keen memory for her mother country under British rule. Granny spoke an impenetrable creole that most of you would find near impossible to understand. And she talked about things you'd find even harder to believe if you didn't have any roots in this Caribbean island.

One story stands out above all the others. It was a cloudy, starless night in the 1920s and my grandmother was a young woman. For whatever reason she wandered in to a deep cavern near her home and clambered around for a while. Local people always warned you not to go into that dark hole, as if you went too deep you would never be seen again. That didn't deter my grandmother.

She claimed all her life that she saw a mermaid swimming in a pool, deep inside the cavern. In the pale, shimmering waters below was a female figure – but only half human.

Confronted by this bizarre spectacle, my grandmother ran to the police. In no time, the cave was visited by the colonial-era cops and a British official – who had probably come out of curiosity. Maybe he muttered under his breath about the crazy stories these Jamaicans tell.

But we're a people who believe in spiritual things. I know because many years ago I saw something just as incredible. Until the age of five I lived in Jamaica and my memories of those times are a bit strange and random – out of the ordinary even. But one memory sticks out more than any other.

I was coming back from nursery school, as a very little boy, walking along the edge of a field full of some sort of tropical vegetation. This part of Jamaica was mountainous and the crops cultivated by the landowners were usually bananas and coffee, as well as oranges and grapefruit. The sun was partly blocked out by the foliage and I could hear the wind rustling the leaves. Then I was aware of a much louder noise growing in volume.

All of a sudden, a huge beast roared out of the field and for a moment stood in front of me. Shaking with terror, I gazed up at its long head, blazing eyes and strong muscular form. I was awestruck, as I never have been before or since. In the middle of its head was a long horn. For a few seconds that seemed like an eternity, the beast stared down at me, flaring its nostrils, then it galloped off.

To this day, nobody believes I saw a unicorn. They say I must have drunk some of the sensimella tea that was freely available in Jamaica. A marijuana infusion that plenty of folk drank at home. Well I didn't – I was only five after all – and I know what I saw.

From that moment – I knew my life was going to be a bit different. Other people in Christiana have nodded at me knowingly when I've told them that story.

'The rolling calf.' That's what they call that creature out there. People talk about the rolling calf as if it is the most natural thing in the world you could see. In fact, they'd be more surprised if I hadn't seen one.

Which brings me back to those slaves. Not only do people in Christiana see the rolling calf, they hear the cries for mercy of those slaves who used to work the plantations. Tormented in life and condemned to walk the earth in death. If you questioned this you'd be regarded as deluded.

The part of Jamaica I was born in was littered with English names. My birthplace was the parish of Manchester in the county of Middlesex. There was a town near where I spent my childhood called Battersea and another called Waltham.

The parish capital was Mandeville, with its imposing nineteenth-century courthouse. It still looks more English than a lot of villages in England itself, apart from the coconut palm trees, blistering heat in summer and the majority of black faces. There's even a village green, a quaint church and everybody is into cricket. But it is definitely Jamaica.

Norman Washington Manley, one of Jamaica's seven national heroes, was born in this parish. He fought for votes for everyone and set up the People's National Party which took power after independence in 1962. The main airport in the Jamaican capital Kingston is even named after him.

I grew up in that parish before the new flag went up in 1962. The island was still part of the British Empire, as it had been for 300 years. So my whole life – apart from a few years in California – has been spent living under the Union Jack.

I spent my childhood in a village called Sawmill, which was named after the factory chopping up trees nearby. Me and my twin sisters, Fay and Dawn, and my younger brother Franklyn lived with my elderly grandparents, as my dad had left Jamaica shortly after I was born to find work in Britain. First in London, then Coventry and finally Rugby. I didn't see the old man for the first five years of my life, until we got the call to come and join him when he got a job and a house in this strange place called Rugby.

Strictly speaking, Franklyn was my stepbrother as he was the child of a woman called Rita, and born a couple of months after me. My dad liked playing the field and wasn't married to either my mum or Franklyn's mother. As you'll see, this is a behavioural trait that I've picked up from his genes.

My mum was always referred to as my 'auntie' back then and, as she'd been quite young at the time of my birth, it was felt our grandparents should bring up me, Fay, Dawn and Franklyn. At least until Dad got his act together in far-off Britain.

Eventually, Dad contacted my grandparents and said it was time for me, Franklyn, Fay and Dawn to come and join him in England. This would have been around 1961 when I was five or so. A female cousin of ours would chaperone us over to Rugby and I would see the father I hardly knew.

My 'auntie' said goodbye and I had no idea then that we wouldn't see her again for twenty years – not until I was in The Specials. By then I would have found out that she was my mother and I had the money to get back to Christiana and find her. But two decades would have to pass first.

What music there was in small-town Jamaica came from the radio or the church. In far-off Kingston, things

were a lot different. The streets would be taken over by huge 'blues' parties with DJs like Duke Reid, Sir Coxsone Dodd and Prince Buster. They would play to massive crowds that sometimes had to be controlled by the police.

It always struck me how Jamaica's DJs used old British titles like 'sir', 'duke' and 'prince' and mockingly took those titles for themselves.

Sir Coxsone Dodd was a Kingston-born record producer who was integral to the development of ska. He had a huge sound system run by people like Lee 'Scratch' Perry, U-Roy and Prince Buster. Years later, Coventry's very own Pete Waterman would bring the music of Lee 'Scratch' Perry to audiences in the UK while I would play cuts by U-Roy in my very own sound system. As for Prince Buster – his influence on Coventry's 2 Tone sound is well documented.

But I'm leaping way ahead here. All that excitement was nowhere near Mandeville or the small house I grew up in. And the radio only gave you a small taster of the musical revolution Jamaica was pioneering. The young Neville Staple had to find other ways to entertain himself.

Animal cruelty was one running theme in my childhood. I remember catching mongooses with other kids. These creatures looked like otters but weren't particularly cute. To us they were gigantic rats and were seen as a pest in Jamaican farmyards. So we tried to teach them a lesson not to come back and stalk our chickens. Me and my friends would take a can of kerosene, hold the mongoose steady while they got a good covering of the strong-smelling liquid and then toss a lit match at the drenched creature. They'd dart off like a four-legged ball of fire emitting some very odd noises.

If we were very unlucky, the mongoose would decide to head for a field of sugar cane – and that spelt big trouble. These fields were highly combustible. Next thing, you could see a spreading orange and yellow colour as the sugar turned to caramel and the crop was destroyed. We'd stand there powerless with our mouths open, the box of matches still in my little hand.

'Oh shit.'

'We're done for.'

If setting fire to mongooses was off the menu of childhood sadism for a while, then we'd take to shooting down birds with catapults. Even as a toddler I was a good shot. I'd see a bird tweeting in a tree and my catapult would be raised. In seconds, a stone would knock my target off its perch and to the ground. If it was lifeless, that was what we called a result.

Before I move on from my time in Jamaica, I should point to a musical sound that had seized the country in my childhood – but would be regarded in just a few years as 'old man's music'. Ska was everywhere. In the early 1960s Jamaicans couldn't get enough of it. This being Jamaica, nobody could really tell you who had started it and everybody had their own story.

One theory, from reggae historian Steve Barrow, says the aforementioned Prince Buster was in a recording session and told his guitarist to 'change gear, man, change gear'. By emphasising the second and fourth beats in the bar, ska was created.

Also present at this ska nativity scene was the trombonist Rico Rodriguez. A respected figure in the late 1950s Jamaican music scene, Rico and I ended up sharing a tour bus and many stages around the world with The Specials.

Others would point to the late and legendary 'godfather of ska' Laurel Aitken who, like me, moved from Jamaica to the UK Midlands to find a better life. Coventry soul singer Ray King told me that Cuban-born Laurel had a bebop-style band, which was the main sound of the post-war era. One day he went to the studio but his usual guitarist hadn't shown up. So he got another guy, but he couldn't play bebop and so just strummed a simple beat. Everybody agreed on it and, more by accident than design, we ended up with ska.

Ray – who will pop up in my life as a big guiding influence – used to call Laurel Aitken 'The Emperor'. That makes it clear who he thinks kick-started the ska revolution. Not only did great musicians like Jimmy Cliff take up the ska beat, but also bands like Jimmy James and the Vagabonds – who in 1964 moved to England and recorded 'Ska Time' on Decca Records. There was also a certain Bob Marley – who Ray always likes to point out was dabbling in ska before he settled on the reggae beat.

Many of these musicians had to relocate to the UK to get the recognition and recording contracts they craved.

When the Staple kids got to England, it was like landing on the moon. This was a totally different place, but one I took to from the word go. The first thing I noticed, as I looked out of the car window on the way to Rugby, was the street lights. Everything seemed so bright. Some people think England was a dull place in those days, but to me it was incredible. I just kept staring wide-eyed at those brilliant street lamps, bright shop windows and car head-lights. I'd never seen so much illumination.

And then there was snow. I'd never clapped eyes on snow in my short life – Jamaica isn't exactly famous for it.

Unfortunately, the magic of the snow was somewhat destroyed when my dad made me stand in it and get doused with ice-cold water as a punishment for wetting the bed. But at the beginning, it was a gorgeous white coating on the landscape, making the country look like a gigantic wedding cake, as if tonnes of icing sugar had fallen out of the sky.

I had no regrets then about leaving Jamaica. I don't remember crying into my pillow or any shit like that. That wasn't the sort of kid I was. The young Neville lapped up all these new experiences and wanted to know everybody and everything about his new home. That unstoppable curiosity is something I've always carried with me.

I wasn't the sort of child that sulked. Spoilt children sulked, I just got on with living. My mother, when I got to know her properly, said I had a guardian angel on my shoulder that was forever lifting me up. On so many occasions when I have found myself in the doldrums over the years, my little winged friend certainly makes something happen to turn things around – as you'll see.

So arriving in England and being apart from my grandparents and so-called 'auntie' wasn't an event that threw me into a depression. I didn't need a social worker to come and psychoanalyse me. I saw it as the start of an adventure – a new chapter opening up in my life.

True, there'd be some tough times before I got into The Specials or Fun Boy Three – a stretch in borstal, for example. But the word 'regret' never fell from these lips. I took to England like a fish to water – it was almost as if coming here was in some way fulfilling my destiny. Me and my new mother country were meant for each other.

For my dad – it was a different story. He now found himself with four young mouths to feed as well as his own and, while he undoubtedly wanted us to come over, it put an unbearable pressure on him – which he dealt with violently.

The old man was a typical Jamaican disciplinarian. He beat me and Franklyn with a savagery you wouldn't believe. And when he beat us, it would be with the first thing he got to hand. That might be the poker, the wire for the curtain, his belt or a broom handle. What would amaze most of you was the violence and fury behind those beatings. Like he was having a full-on fight with his own children. It didn't matter how small we were. We were thrashed like runaway slaves. There was no mercy – no matter how much we cried out.

One night, still seared in my consciousness, he struck me with a broom handle over and over again, showing no sign of stopping. My hand was in front of my face to protect it and I could see my fingers swelling under the severe blows raining down. But I didn't scream. I couldn't scream. Not in front of my dad.

'Now you go to bed.'

When I closed the bedroom door, I allowed myself the luxury of tears but not before then. For him to see me blubbing would have meant defeat.

He was a frustrated man. The years he had spent in Britain had obviously brought with them all sorts of humiliation, poverty, disappointment and gloom. The mother country had not extended the warm embrace he had been expecting.

After leaving Jamaica, the old man worked on the assembly line at the Ford car plant in Leamington and before that, briefly, at the Rugby cement factory. He was one of thousands of Caribbean immigrants in the 1950s and 1960s who helped keep industry going in the Midlands. Job satisfaction wasn't important to his employers – he was cheap, keen to work and insecure in his new life.

So he transmitted the anger, which built up from the petty put downs he endured at work, on to his family. It was almost our purpose in life to be human punch-bags. Hardly surprising, then, that we took to pissing the bed. Dad would come home in the morning from a night shift and find our beds soaked with urine.

To solve this problem, he used to put a barrel of cold water in the garden and – especially in the winter – let it freeze. In the morning, he'd parade me and Franklyn outside, break the thin layer of ice on top and then douse us with the chilly liquid.

People would call that kind of thing child abuse now but it was the way a Jamaican family operated. We weren't unique. If you ask any other Jamaicans who grew up at that time, I bet they suffered the same kind of thing. A Jamaican father ruled his family like a king, like a tyrant – a slave owner even. His word was law and he could treat us how he wanted. We were his property and we were never allowed to forget it.

One of my sisters told me recently that sometimes, when we knew he was going to chuck that water over us, she would get down to the kitchen quickly, boil the kettle and try to warm up the contents of the barrel a little. Just to make the punishment a little less barbaric.

Eventually, even some of his relatives in Britain thought he was going too far. My great aunt was living nearby and she took him to task. His own parents hadn't punished him

like that, why was he doing it to us? If he didn't know how to look after his kids, he should send us back to Jamaica, she said. That calmed him down a bit for a while, but only for a while.

Two years ago Dad had a stroke. His hard life finally came to an end. In the last few years, like many sons who have had difficult relationships with their fathers, I tried to reach out and get some understanding of him. You don't want to leave your dad on bad terms. But for most of my life, this angry man had terrified me and my siblings and he's still trying to terrorise us today.

Like many Jamaicans, I believe in duppies. Bob Marley sang about them in 'Duppy Conqueror', Bunny Wailer sang 'Duppy Gun' and Ernie Smith 'Duppy Gun Man'. To understand what duppies are, you need to drop your cynicism and enter the Jamaican mind.

Duppies are spirits – malevolent ghosts of ancestors. Some might call them poltergeists, but they're not really the same thing. In Caribbean culture, there is a strong belief in duppies and I share that belief.

My father has come back to my family since his death and plagued us with his complaints. He hasn't had the balls to come back to me. But since he found out my mother was handing away his clothes, he's come back to complain to her in no uncertain terms.

My mum tells me: 'You daddy won't leave me alone – gimme problem.'

And I respond: 'Tell him to come to me, I'll sort him out.'

He's visited my sister and nephew, but so far he's steering clear of me. Well, he knows the mouthful he'll get if he turns up to have a moan.

My near lifelong friend and former Specials roadie Trevor Evans, having been born in Jamaica, understands our belief in duppies. He says that if the Catholic church employs priests to do exorcism, then why can't we believe in duppies? Trevor is often visited by his dead mum. 'I can look you in the eye and tell you she visits me', he says. He knows that plenty of people in Britain would find that claim hilarious but we know these things happen.

Trevor often says that if any place in this country is crawling with duppies then it's the city of Coventry. So many houses were blasted to smithereens by Hitler's bombs and the families inside didn't get a proper burial. It's as if they were trapped in limbo – their screams silenced in a second. Anybody who comes from Coventry will know what I mean – thousands of souls were snuffed out in those days and nobody can tell me and Trev that they're not still in torment.

As I pointed out before, my dad wasn't married to my mother when she gave birth to me. In England, that would have been a scandal in the 1950s but in Jamaica, it was par for the course.

Dad did eventually marry the woman I was forced to call 'auntie' when I was younger. They were both old by then and Mum came over to live with him for three short years before he died. After that, she returned to Jamaica where I still go to visit her these days. Dad spent most of his time in Britain living with a woman called Adassa, an evil stepmother who was a constant source of torment for me. But more about her later.

At school in Rugby, I got on with everybody – especially if they were female.

Some of my old school mates have been in touch lately and I've published their letters on my website. They tend to confirm that my rude boy tendencies evolved early. Brian AKA 'Eitey' summed me up nicely: 'You was no angel was you Nev?' He remembered me getting six of the best for smoking by the terrapins and another caning for attacking some teacher called Mr Long with a broom. Apparently I also 'assaulted' an art teacher in the supply cupboard, but that's long since slipped my memory box.

A girl – now a woman of course – called Lynda remembers a teacher called 'Glob Harris', not his real name I'm sure, often bellowing out my name in the corridor. No doubt just before yet another encounter between the bamboo and my palm or arse. At lunchtimes, I would try and teach Lynda to dance. However there was always an ulterior motive. She remembers that I used to laugh at her short skirts and knickers – that wasn't so much a laugh as a cackle full of dirty intent. Just to make it clear what my real motives behind the dance lessons were, I gave her the nickname 'Mersey Tunnel'.

I think Lynda has since figured out what lurked behind my innocent grin.

I've always preferred the company of women to blokes, they're just a lot more interesting in so many ways.

In one lesson at school, a teacher lost the plot when I was spotted playing with the long blonde hair of a girl sitting at the desk in front of me. I was just fascinated by her long, golden tresses. None of the women in Jamaica – except perhaps the British ambassador's wife – had hair like this. It shone in the sunlight coming through the grubby classroom windows.

'Staple – leave them alone!'

The girl didn't seem to be objecting at the time.

As a very young kid I sucked my thumb. But that cute image belied a very different reality. What teachers remembered me for was being continually mischievous – which earned me several trips to the headmaster for a sound caning. They clearly hoped they could beat the rude boy out of me, but bamboo canes were no match for my natural instinct.

In photos there was always a smile or a smirk on my face as if I'd just hatched an evil plot. The endless refrain I got used to hearing from exasperated school staff was: 'Staple – you again!' Or 'Staple – get to the headmaster's office!'

When I got bored, which was quite often, I'd take to disrupting the class. This normally involved kidding around and making the other kids laugh – which I now look back on as part of my formative training as an entertainer. I just loved an audience reacting to me. But that wasn't appreciated by the teaching profession:

'You always have to be the centre of attention, don't you!'

Eventually, at around junior school age, my fooling around got much more amorous in nature. At eleven, I lost my virginity. I sloped off with a girl to some fields near the school, as I had done many times before. Already I'd been in double trouble for snogging and being out of bounds. But that day, things went one stage further. Instinctively, I got on top of her and having begun the day as a boy, ended it as a man. At least, that's how it felt at the time.

There was racism in the playground in those days but nothing like some kids of my generation experienced.

Maybe because I was quite popular I didn't get a stream of abuse, though I appreciate that a lot of other black kids did.

You have to realise that this was a time when the television was full of racist stuff. Sitcoms like *Love Thy Neighbour*, with the main black character being called a 'sambo'. Millions of people tuned in to watch the *Black and White Minstrel Show* on the BBC – strangely one programme from the 1970s that Auntie doesn't repeat. These sorts of programmes would be beyond the pale now but this was the 1960s and 1970s when the sun had only just set on the Empire.

I do remember one kid in the playground unwisely deciding to refer to me as a 'wog'– and he certainly lived to regret using that word. This unsuspecting kid saw a side of me that probably sprang from my father – the ability to dish out a violent response and not know quite when to stop. Just after the kid said that word, the playground bell went.

But neither of us went back to class – not until I'd taught him a lesson he wouldn't forget in a hurry. He was going to be beaten like an un-submissive slave on a plantation.

I chased him round the school field to start with. My now-terrified classmate was probably hoping I'd give up, but I was like a thing possessed. As with my stage performance in later life, I showed no sign of fatigue while others around me wilted. My eyes were wild and my breathing heavy. There was no thought process as I pursued this child racist, just raw anger and fury. When I got hold of him, he'd be in severe trouble.

We ended up back in the school playground and that's where I finally captured the bastard, now covered in sweat and smelling of fear. Down he went on the tarmac with a thud. Then I grabbed his head and started banging it off the ground – over and over and over again – like I was bouncing a ball. I didn't care what the end result would be, whether he was alive or dead. I just wanted to keep smacking his cranium off the hard surface until I felt vengeance had been served. Luckily for him, salvation was at hand. My uncontrollable violence must have been glimpsed from a window because next thing, three or four teachers were trying to prise me off this kid who wasn't moving very much by now.

I'd lost it completely. It took me a while to calm down and get a grip on myself. But now the whole playground knew that Neville Staple was not a 'wog', a 'coon' or a 'nigger'. In true and uncompromising Jamaican style, I'd delivered a lesson in racial tolerance. And if any other kids weren't sure about the message, I'd put them right in no uncertain terms.

It was in my early teens that I first ran in to Trevor Evans, who became one of my little gang. Trevor arrived in England from Jamaica in 1966, which was a very good year to ship up in Blighty. The place was a buzz after the recent World Cup win. Especially as the beaten team was Germany – after all, this was still only twenty years after the Second World War.

But unfortunately for Trevor, any happiness he was experiencing soon faded away. His mum died suddenly, six months after arriving on these shores. I think that made him look outside his home for companionship.

'There was no love in my life then,' he often says of those times. Both of us were instantly united by a hatred of our stepmothers. Like characters from fairy stories, we had wicked witches for mothers and neither of us found it much fun. At least I could harbour the hope of one day seeing my real mum again. Trevor had no such consolation.

After finishing junior school, Trevor and Franklyn went to Fareham High School in Rugby while I went to Newbold Grange. As a secondary school kid, I soon established a reputation behind those school gates and across town for being a hard fucker. Don't take my word for it. There are plenty of kids who grew up with me who'll remember that I was physically stronger than a lot of my white contemporaries and had an uncompromisingly violent streak. I wouldn't start fights for no reason but if I was pushed to breaking point, I'd make somebody regret it.

Trevor once said that if somebody at his school was told 'Neville Staple is looking for you' – it was enough to reduce them to tears. In fact, they'd shit themselves. I've no doubt that Trevor and Franklyn used me as a kind of shield. If they were in trouble at their school with other kids, they'd say I was coming down to defend them and that ended the problem.

It wasn't that I was a thug, but I learnt early on that in those more brutish times, you had to establish some rules. Boundaries, you could say. Other kids had to know when they'd overstepped the mark. And as I'd realise when I did time behind bars later on, you had to look confident and in control to survive as a young black man in the 1960s and 1970s in Britain. Any sign of weakness invited potentially fatal aggression.

Like all Jamaican families at that time, church wasn't a voluntary thing. It was compulsory and in mega doses. We were sent to praise Jesus whether we liked it or not. Three times on a Sunday – morning church, afternoon church and night-time church. And as if that wasn't enough praying to the Lord, there was the Young People's Evening (YPE) on a Monday night and a midweek church session on a Wednesday night. God and Satan, heaven and hell, and all the angels were crammed down your throat 'til you were sick of it.

My father couldn't imagine a world without Jesus and his archenemy down below. He was almost a fundamentalist but in a very Jamaican way. This was part of his inability to connect with England. Other new arrivals to this country had the same problem – they'd take refuge in a religious zeal that Trevor jokes was like being Amish.

He clung to a fire-and-brimstone Jamaican Christianity where there wasn't much by way of the milk of human kindness. One incident in church showed how a supposedly forgiving God could be successfully distilled with the ultra-disciplinarian attitude typical of all Jamaican dads.

I pissed about during the services – I was a little kid at the time, not really thinking about how the adults around me would react to my bad behaviour. Nowadays, kids are given a lot of leeway to express themselves – quite loudly even – but not then. A badly behaved child in the eyes of a Jamaican congregation was as good as a possessed child. Especially if you were being naughty in their church, so I was immediately on a par with the spawn of Satan.

Faced with such ungodly disobedience from a small child, my dad decided I was in need of some stern and forthright Christian discipline. He beat the living daylights out of me in front of those good Christian people and not one of them batted an eyelid as I screamed for mercy.

The only reason we turned a cheek in the Church of God was because the other one had been soundly

walloped and it was the reverse cheek's turn for the same treatment.

One time at home, my dad did something that would have landed me in care if it happened now – and probably had him in court. He jammed a piece of cutlery straight in to my small head – as if it was a marshmallow.

I was in the kitchen at home, messing around again, when I felt this incredibly painful sharp jab. My dad had actually managed – with not inconsiderable force – to stick a fork into my bonce. You couldn't credit it now but I was scarpering out of the kitchen with a piece of stainless steel jutting out of me. I was more frightened than those mongooses I'd set alight and chased years before.

My sister Fay still remembers this incident and says he threw the fork at me like a javelin, narrowly missing my jugular. I'd apparently been questioning him while he was telling Fay off for something. For once, as he looked at the fork sticking out of the side of my head, he was horrified at his own actions.

Not for nothing did me and Franklyn take to calling Dad the 'Indian Chief' – a tribal overlord who beat first and asked questions later.

In some ways, Dad wasn't so different from other Jamaican fathers. Children were to be seen and not heard. While white families had long ditched all that Victorian crap, our families embraced it with vigour. No rod was to be spared when it came to bringing us up. Our colonial masters on the plantations had always beaten us and we were going to continue that fine tradition – preferably in the name of Jesus.

As for buying sweeties, my dad wasn't going to waste any money on that sort of nonsense. I'd stand there and watch him put a fiver into the collection plate – a lot of money back then – while telling me and Franklyn that he couldn't spare a penny for bubblegum.

There was also the question of shame in our parents' minds. Trevor and I often talk about how they lived in constant fear that we would somehow show them up in front of the community – especially in church. It was all about keeping up appearances – wearing the right clothes, not being dirty and keeping quiet. If my dad thought anybody was dissing me or Franklyn, he'd take it out on us for being the cause of that bad mouthing – not the person running us down. We would be punished for embarrassing him.

Trevor calls our dads 'black Hitlers'. I kind of know what he means, though it's a bit harsh.

There was a thing about Jamaicans though. We were the hardest people in the Caribbean. If I look at somebody like Ranking Roger, lead singer of The Beat and big friend of mine, he's a lot milder in temperament. Roger's family were from Saint Lucia, another Caribbean island, where people just seem to be more laid back than in Jamaica. His theory is that the British used to send the most rebellious slaves to Jamaica to be tamed with the whip and the lash – and that's how we got our bad boy attitudes.

My ancestors were wild animals, in the eyes of their owners, who had to be broken – sometimes literally. It is true that Jamaicans scared a lot of white people in the past with their general demeanour – and maybe still do today. We're just more uncompromising in the way we speak, even about quite mundane things. I know that in The Specials, when me, Trevor, Rex Griffiths and Lynval Golding used to talk excitedly and slip into our hard-to-understand, thick patois, the white members of the band thought a fight was about to kick off. But we might just be talking about the weather.

Trevor thinks that as I've got older, I've started to turn into my dad. 'You see Nev, you see his dad, he's a carbon copy'. I suppose it's one of those cruel and unexpected ironies of life that I should end up reminding a lot of people of the bane of my childhood – the now departed 'Mr Staples'.

I might even end up coming back like Dad does in duppy form, hounding those who did me great wrongs in life. I can already think of a few people I'll be visiting in the music business.

Returning to our experience of church – it was enough to turn any right-thinking person into an atheist. Of course, my dad had to be affiliated with the most full-on version of hellfire-and-damnation Christianity you could find in Jamaica, let alone the Caribbean community here in Britain. The Church of God was one of those ultra-evangelical religions where women dropped down to the floor, shaking and talking in tongues:

'Habalalalalalalalalalah!'

Men stepped forward to pull some of these ladies' skirts up as they got carried away and their legs were wriggling in the air as they went off on one. I would often be caught trying to suppress my laughter.

'Staple!' Some church bigwig would glare down at me, 'behave yourself!'

You really can't avoid smirking when a large lady in her Sunday best is on the floor in front of you foaming at the mouth and giving you a full view of her underwear.

I knew there were only two paths open to me when it came to the Church of God. Total acceptance or total rejection. They didn't allow for a middle way and that was OK by me. I opted for total rejection. My sister Fay went the other way. So much so that she never came to see me perform in The Specials because of her deeply held church views.

Basically, me, and lots of Jamaican kids of that generation, got way too much religion crammed into us 'til we gagged. Either you had to cave in or run away from it.

Another sad aspect of the colonial mindset of our parents was the limited expectations they had of their children. Our folks didn't push us at school because they didn't expect great things. It was almost like they colluded with the system to ensure we didn't amount to much.

As I said, Trevor was at school with Franklyn. He often bemoans the fact that Franklyn could have made something more of himself. He was always excelling at sports – particularly cricket and football. But instead of my dad looking at him as the next Cyrille Regis or Laurie Cunningham, he got him sent to approved school instead to toughen him up.

At around fourteen years of age, I was sent to a young offenders' institution – a sort of school where you were locked up at night. It gave me my first taste of incarceration and all the other kids were white. Now this could have worked against me in all sorts of ways but, luckily, I seemed to have a kind of novelty value. Far from getting it in the neck from the other kids who'd been thrown into this place, we all got on like a house on fire.

That said, nobody likes to be locked away and far from home. And it gave me a preliminary taste of my time in borstal and prison that lay ahead.

When I returned to my dad and our home, things just slid downhill. My stepmother had a key role in getting his temper up and directed at me. She was only going to be satisfied when I was gone – out of her life. After all, I wasn't her flesh and blood.

We called our stepmum Adassa – though her real name was Eugenie – and she was always threatening me and Franklyn that when Dad came back, she'd rat on us.

'Wait till your father comes back.'

That was no empty threat. Whereas white kids in the same situation might expect a verbal reprimand from their dad and maybe no dinner, we had something far worse to look forward to. So Franklyn and I would try our hardest to please her during the day – doing little chores, while giving her a weak smile, and avoiding getting under the old bat's feet. But none of this worked. The moment the imposing figure of my father came through the front door – Adassa was shit stirring.

She addressed Dad as 'Staple':

'Staple – talk to Neville – him rude! Them no listen to what I tell them.'

His eyes would blaze with anger and we knew that the evening would be the fiercest hell on earth. The belt or curtain rod or whatever would be in his right hand. You have to wonder what our neighbours thought of the resulting commotion.

I know my dad must have endured endless humiliation and frustration both in Jamaica and here in Britain – but it can't justify what him and other Jamaican dads did to their kids. Nowadays, if my kids mess about I tell them there's no PlayStation for a week. But back then, we came away with cuts and bruises.

As I turned fifteen, one murderous row led to me fleeing the house. He was going to kick me out anyway at some point. We were both resigned to seeing the back of each other. I was on the pavement outside and nobody was asking me back in. That was it – the end of life at home. Not so much leaving the nest as being tipped out headfirst.

As night fell, I tried to sleep in a couple of broken-down, abandoned cars but it wasn't comfortable. So I found the cemetery and bedded down under a hedge, but got scared and a bit freaked out by the nearby company of the deceased. Finally, I curled up under a hedge in the front garden of my cousin Jen's house. I didn't want to ring the bell as it was very late. The next morning, they found me snoozing there:

'Staple beat you again?' Jen asked. I just shrugged my shoulders.

Jen's brother, Alvin, was a cousin I liked. He now runs a taxi firm in Rugby. When Dad had gone too far and turned really violent, Alvin would appear to stick up for me. On one occasion, he even had a scuffle with the old man to reinforce the point that he couldn't pummel me the way he did and get away with it. In case you're wondering, I supported my cousin's action a hundred per cent. Alvin was more than able to hold his own against my dad as he was an amateur boxer and only needed to land a few decisive punches to keep my father at bay.

I was fifteen and Alvin was about twenty-eight. It was Alvin who introduced me to the whole world of sound systems – the gigantic wooden constructions black guys built to blast out reggae and dub music at parties in the 1970s. These sound systems all had names and his was called The Messenger.

I couldn't stay at Alvin's for long and needed to get some independence, a place of my own. I was still at school but, mentally, I had already left. So in my mid-teens, I rented a room in a house in Rugby from a family called the Ruddocks. Mrs Ruddock charged me 2s. 6d for an upstairs room and I did some shoplifting to make sure she got the rent on time.

Stealing became a way of survival. I was stealing to eat and for my school clothes. In the evenings, I would hang out with my mates in town – and just to show Mrs Ruddock a little consideration, I would sneak back late at night by climbing up the corrugated kitchen roof and slithering into my bedroom through an unlocked window. Entering properties like this would become a big part of my life in the future.

At the age of fifteen, I already had a secret hiding place at home for my ill-gotten gains. Behind a loose brick in the outhouse I squirreled away the gear I'd got my hands on. A bit like Fagan in *Oliver Twist*, I'd pull that brick out and there'd be a regular treasure trove behind it.

The local grocery store was one of my targets for about six months. How the owner didn't work out who was behind this grand larceny is anybody's guess. But I was filling my pockets and walking out of there week after week with free food and sweets – anything I could spirit in to my pockets with my light fingers.

At some point, maybe when one of them was having a shit, Franklyn found my stash behind the loose brick and started 'borrowing' from it. I had no idea for a while that my own brother and best mate Trevor were stealing from my hot property. Suffice to say, they had no intention of ever paying me back.

When I removed the brick one day and found my takings were inexplicably way down, I made a beeline for their school. I was mad, like a deranged bull, and I charged down there to beat the living daylights out of both of them. It was one thing for me to dent Woolies' profits through my larcenous activities, but quite another for them to bite into my bottom line. I was going to show them that you don't steal from a thief.

'Your brother's outside the school gates Franklyn.'

'He's looking very pissed off.'

Franklyn knew that taking me on in that kind of mood would be near fatal – for him. Even the two of them together wouldn't be able to hold me down. They'd taken my stash. So when the final school bell rang, they shot past me, running for their lives while I pegged it after them.

'Come back here ya bastards!'

While we were still at school, Trevor discovered some low-hanging fruit that could be picked very easily to boost all our earnings. We would bully younger boys for their pocket money – and once we started, we wondered why the idea had never occurred to us before.

Unlike most of the English-born kids in the school playground, Trevor and I stood out at our respective educational establishments. We were just harder and rougher. The reason is simple enough to understand. Before either of us left Jamaica, while we were still young kids, we had to do chores outside of school that adults would have found daunting in England. Drawing water from wells and carrying it back, moving animals back to their pens, cutting wood to heat food – things that sometimes had to be done before we could eat breakfast.

When Trevor came to England already aged about eleven, he had the strength of a fifteen or sixteen-year-old boy. We also knew more about life. There was no childhood innocence or wetness behind our ears. So the soft shits at school were easy to tap for their pocket money on a regular basis. In no time, Trevor was earning two bob a week, particularly from the Indian kids. He'd then give some of that money to Franklyn to do his homework for him so he didn't get a whipping from his dad.

School limped to its inevitable conclusion and I left without much remorse. It was time to get a job anyway. My first employment was as an apprentice TV engineer, for a company called Multibroadcast, which was pretty unmemorable. The second was for a local slaughterhouse and turned out to be infinitely more enjoyable. I really liked it. Sometimes, I'm asked if it put me off eating meat. But quite the contrary, I'm as a voracious a carnivore now as I've ever been.

It also has to be said that I'd never been anything approaching an animal rights campaigner – as my earlier mongoose torturing pastimes will testify.

In my new job, I cheerfully slaughtered pigs, cows and sheep – all succumbing to my sharp knife. Having seen animals killed in Jamaica when I was very little, I didn't blink twice when it came to dispatching the local livestock. Gentler souls might have had difficulty with the big eyes looking up or the odd 'moo' or 'baa', but not me. It was a job that had to be done to put a meal on the plates of the good folk of Rugby. If I didn't do this, somebody else would.

The big cows would lumber in, get stunned, bled, hung up, skinned and then carved up into joints. I'm not denying there was a surreal aspect to a big living creature strolling in at one end and leaving in bits at the other. But if I said it troubled me in any way, I'd be lying. It was a job, it was interesting and the pay was good for a young bloke in those days.

The other employees were mostly older guys who were only too happy to teach me their bloody skills – how to immobilise the animal, where to run the blade and how to quickly and methodically remove the hide. I'm often asked whether there was any smell and I honestly don't recall any stench that got into my nostrils. It was all really surprisingly odourless.

The main perk of the new job was to take home great hunks of meat – as my diet had sometimes been a bit protein deficient since leaving home and not having much money. So it was good to get big pork and lamb chops down me. It all went a long way to building the physique that would scale speakers at Specials gigs and leap down on to the stage below.

In spite of the joys of slaughtering, I started to get itchy feet. There wasn't much keeping me in Rugby anymore and I'd started to go clubbing at the weekend in a much bigger urban sprawl up the road.

Coventry was just thirteen miles away and as I got to know the place, I began to realise that Rugby was too small to contain Neville Staple. Little did I realise what a huge impact Coventry would eventually have on my life.

2

COVENTRY, THE LOCARNO AND BORSTAL

Rude boys make the pages of the *Coventry Evening Telegraph* in the early 1970s. The 'terror' refers to the Primrose Park battle. Rex Griffiths features in all three articles!
© Coventry Evening Telegraph

The Locarno drew me to Coventry like a moth to a light. Dancing and shagging – for a young bloke whose hormones were raging, that was a winning combination.

This massive ballroom venue was owned by Mecca. You might automatically associate them with bingo, but in the 1970s Mecca was more than just 'clickety click – sixty-six'. The owners of Mecca believed it was their sworn duty to entertain the working classes, seven days a week, with every age catered for.

Which was how on Saturday mornings in 1970, I found myself at their weekly matinees for younger teens. It was a bit like the old Saturday morning flicks, only instead of watching films we were dancing with each other. And as we were below the legal drinking age, there was no booze on sale – just soft drinks.

Up on stage was a black DJ called Dancing Danny, who it turned out was a miner. In between digging for coal, he was master of the decks at the Coventry Mecca Locarno. Danny was a tall, skinny bloke who earned his nickname by the way-out manner of his dancing moves.

We all gathered around the stage or strutted our stuff on the dance floor while he belted out the chart-topping tunes. At some point Dancing Danny disappeared off the scene and we had a new DJ to keep us bopping – step forward Pete Waterman!

The man who would bring the likes of Rick Astley and Kylie Minogue to British pop fans in the late-1980s was our very own DJ at the start of the 1970s. Pete would have been about twenty-five years old at this time. Unlike most other DJs, he'd already taken a keen interest in Jamaican music – but for the oddest of reasons.

Pete was – and still is – a massive train enthusiast. He's even done programmes on the telly about the history of the railways. As a kid, he'd noticed that lots of the old steam engines were named after parts of the British Empire. So you'd get an old boiler called the 'Windward Islands', for example.

When West Indian families started arriving in the Midlands after the war – like my dad and then us – most white people's first reaction was to keep their distance. But Pete says he went straight up to the new arrivals and started pestering them for information about these places they came from that his beloved steam engines were named after. Almost accidentally, he then came into contact with the sounds of the Caribbean. In other words, Pete got into reggae because he's a bit of a train spotter.

We soon struck up a mutual appreciation society. Even as a young teenager, I fancied myself as something of a connoisseur of Jamaican music. I'd begun to nick some very good records and started sharing them with Pete – although he had no idea he was handling stolen goods. At the time he had his own record store in town – Soul Hole Records – which of course I never stole from.

Soul Hole was part record shop and part drop-in centre for the local youth. It was rammed with kids asking to buy a record – which would then be passed over everybody's heads while the money went in the opposite direction.

Pete gave away free coffee and we'd sit in Soul Hole Records every Saturday – and Fridays when we bunked off school. He only opened the shop on those two days.

Back at the Locarno, Pete would play the pop charts stuff as well as some nods towards reggae like Desmond Dekker, The Upsetters and Johnny Nash. The Upsetters was Lee 'Scratch' Perry's band and this was Johnny Nash before he drifted away from his reggae roots. With the contacts he had made in Jamaica, Pete was probably the only DJ in Britain playing Jamaican music that had only just been released over there. To say that Pete Waterman had his finger on the pulse of what was going on in Kingston would be putting it mildly. His musical antennae were finely tuned to everything that was coming out of my home country.

At some point, Pete would suddenly stop everything. He'd put on a track called 'The Horse' and yell:

'This is for Nev and the Boys!'

Which was our cue to get up and dance. That was me, Trevor, a bloke we'd met in Coventry called Rex Griffiths and a girl called Michelle Harris. Everybody would gather round and we would do our little routine. That involved everything from the splits to throwing ourselves in the air.

This being the Mecca organisation, which ran dance halls all over Britain, I suppose it was inevitable that we would catch somebody's eye. A Locarno employee suggested that Nev and the Boys enter the Coventry heat of Mecca's national dancing competition, which we did and, to my amazement, we won!

Next thing I was with Trevor, Rex and Michelle on an all-expenses-paid trip to London. We arrived at Marylebone train station and, not really knowing where we were going, somehow found our way to the Grosvenor

House Hotel on Park Lane. Just for pissing around at the Locarno, we now found ourselves in a deadly serious competition with adult couples who took their dancing very seriously. You have to remember that Mecca invented *Come Dancing*.

Suffice it to say, we didn't win the national competition, but it gave me my first real idea that just maybe I had some real ability as an entertainer.

Pete started to let me up on stage to 'toast' to the records. I had no idea as a teenager at the mic, doing my thing to his reggae records, that in a few short years I'd be standing in the same place with a band called The Specials and another band called The Stranglers backstage. All that was yet to come.

I loved the limelight. More than that, I loved seeing an audience enjoying what I was doing. There I was at four-teen or fifteen, belting out some words over a beat and I could see the Coventry teenagers really liked it.

We were a mass of youths, dressed in those early-1970s flared suits, gyrating around. Just to make our clobber even more garish, we'd do things like cut a V-shape in our flared trousers and insert luridly coloured bright blue or orange silk cloth. As we moved to the rhythm, you'd get these flashes of blue or orange appearing and disappearing.

It was DIY fashion because we couldn't afford top of the range stuff. Some kids would do the same to their jackets, making loads of vents with coloured material in between and a silly number of pockets on the outside.

As each Saturday matinee wound down, we were all asked to make our way to the exits. There was only one place me, Trev and our mates could go after a morning of

dancing – Woolies! Now bust, back in 1970 the department store chain was the ideal venue for post-Locarno comedowns.

Pumped up with adrenalin from a morning of dancing and chatting up the girls, we went to the café upstairs in the local Woolworths, just to cause trouble. We'd arrive around midday, put our feet up on the Formica tables and spend as little money as possible.

The bane of our lives was a store detective called Harry who took it upon himself to sort us out.

'You can't hang around here – go on, get out.'

'You can't say that to us,' we'd pretend to be very offended and indignant, 'we've paid for our coffees – what's the problem mate?'

'Go on – shove off – I know what you're up to.'

Of course what we were up to was psyching ourselves up for a little shoplifting downstairs. Woolies in those days was infamous for the ease with which you could stuff your pockets with sweets and walk out without paying. Not so much Pic 'n' Mix as knick 'n' mix.

Our God-fearing and authority-respecting parents would have been horrified at what we were doing, but rules and regulations were there to be broken in our eyes.

While Woolies offered rich pickings for thieves like us, the more upmarket Marks & Spencer wasn't so easy to work over. But we'd still give it a try occasionally. There was always a better class of goods on offer. Then those stolen goods had to be off-loaded and we'd try and do it as quickly as possible. We'd either sell it off to our mates or second-hand shops at knock-down prices. It was low-level criminality, but it put some cash in our pockets.

Sometimes, Trevor and me just drifted into M&S and instead of stealing anything just stuck our fingers in as many of the posh trifles on display as possible. There was no reason for making those desserts unsellable to the general public, it's just that we were bored out of our minds. So destroying ten trifles gave a few minutes of our day a little lift.

As we got older and entered our late teens, Saturday mornings at the Locarno had to be left behind – it was now Monday nights for us. That was the big sixteen to nineteen-year-old night and if you missed it, you might as well have just given up living.

Worse than missing a night though, was to be barred by the bouncers. These big lumps of meat in bow ties knew they had power over us. Some of them were a bit dodgy on the race question, although the Locarno was a lot better than most clubs in terms of letting black kids in. I'd go further and say it was almost progressive for the time.

However, there was one bad incident involving some of the bouncers when reggae star Nicky Thomas played the Locarno around 1975. The man who had a hit five years before with 'Love of the Common People' – later covered by Paul Young – had a stormier reception than he might have expected. Far from experiencing any love, the common people were kicking the shit out of each other that particular evening.

The whole thing degenerated into a riot and before long police sirens could be heard outside. It all kicked off because the bouncers refused to let in some die-hard reggae fans who weren't taking no for an answer. Not when their hero Nicky Thomas was in town. For once, the

bouncers got a hiding – from a furious crowd. The whole thing ended up in Birmingham Crown Court with some of those involved being put away.

Pete Waterman still recalls a big fight at the Locarno – it may have been that same night. The police turned up, let a load of Alsatians loose inside the ballroom and then bolted the doors. Presumably the idea was to wait outside 'til everybody was huddled against the walls, cowering in front of those snarling beasts, and then waltz in and make their arrests. Not what you would call community policing, but this was a different era.

Monday nights were good for the music, but they were also good for the girls. I never stopped pulling in that place. Pete once said I was 'more of a lover than a fighter' and he was right. The Locarno was huge and had many levels, so there was no shortage of dark corners to get down to it. Sometimes they'd block off the balcony areas with a sofa thrown across the stairs.

Upstairs would be pitch black with the coffee bar closed and no lights on – perfect shagging conditions. I'd leap over the sofa with some girl and we'd disappear into the dark. I wasn't the only person up to this but I was possibly more regular than a lot of guys my age. My sexual appetite took a lot to satisfy.

As the Locarno was by far the biggest music venue in Coventry, it also played host to the supergroups of the day. The Who played there; Pink Floyd in 1969 and Led Zeppelin in 1971. Then when punk came along, the supergroups gave way to the new leaner and meaner combos like The Stranglers. Inevitably, the Locarno would one day play host to The Specials.

But for now, the only member of The Specials at the microphone in the Locarno was me and my toasting skills – which had been duly noted by DJ Pete Waterman.

It was at the Locarno that I met Ideta – some would say the love of my life. My brother Franklyn started seeing her sister Cordelia at the same time. And just to show you what a small world Coventry's black community was – Cordelia already had a kid by Silverton Hutchinson, the first drummer with The Specials, later replaced by John Bradbury.

Ideta's family were originally from the Caribbean island of Nevis and she was petite and very good looking. She couldn't possibly realise that she was committing herself to three decades of life with a man who has a loving streak but also had an eye – and still does – for other ladies.

Basically, I couldn't and can't keep my cock in its lair. She would often fly off the handle when my womanising got out of control.

'You're a bastard!'

Ideta was fiery. An Aries, if you don't mind me bringing her star sign into the equation. As we argued over the years, she would always stand her ground. Rex Griffiths – one of my dancing buddies in Nev and the Boys – went to school with her and says she wasn't fiery in class. Possibly, living with me made her fiery!

I had two children with Ideta – Byron and Melanie. Byron was born when I was in my mid-teens – barely out of Saturday matinees. Melanie was born later in the 1970s. Let's just say that The Specials song 'Too Much Too Young' described my lifestyle more than anybody else's in that band.

At one point, I was seeing Ideta and two other women at the same time. One of them was Carmen, who I had my son Darren with, and a white girl called Yvonne, who I had my daughter Andrea with. Darren is now the lead singer with a California-based reggae band called Dreadstarr.

But even before this there'd been another Yvonne in my life, just to confuse things, who I had my daughter Sheena with. That was back in Rugby before I was sixteen and legal. Sheena will pop up later as a big part of my involvement in the American 'third wave' ska scene. And I shouldn't neglect to mention Paulette, with whom I had Tara and young Neville.

Just to show you that I haven't slowed down in my middle age, the latest addition to the Staple family is three-year-old Amber (at the time of writing in 2008) whose mum, Tracey, lives in Liverpool.

A grand total of eight children then. As you'll see, I've always been supportive of my big family over the years. Throughout my misspent youth, I just have to say that me, women and making babies happened as easily as falling off a log.

In my years in Coventry ahead of The Specials, it was Ideta who got the lion's share of my attention. She and I had an ongoing relationship throughout The Specials, Fun Boy Three and the 1990s, and it's only quite recently that we called it a day. She was a kind of constant presence while I carried on with many, many other women.

There are those who say that Ideta was my soul mate, a rock in my life. They're right, but as I got propelled into the whole pop scene, as it was back then, I could not resist temptation. Friends may say I should have said no to all those women who threw themselves at me after gigs, but instead, I said yes, yes, yes…

It may be hard to believe now, but Coventry in the 1970s was a magnet for black youth from all over the Midlands and beyond. The music scene was vibrant and the club scene was excellent. There was a growing Afro-Caribbean community that had begun to arrive twenty years before to work in the car factories. Although Pete says he could see the troubles ahead for the motor industry, to people like our parents and many Coventrians, it still seemed like a boom town in the early 1970s. Pete would eventually be proved right, though.

There were houses owned by black guys in Coventry that you knew you could crash out at, get something to eat, party and gamble. This was part of the community network that had developed over the years.

One guy, Henley Gordon, had a bedsit on Wren Street, right opposite the Binley Oak – a pub The Specials would one day use for rehearsals. Young men from Northampton, Leicester, Oxford and even London would come up to go clubbing and then crash out in his flat. Although, 'flat' is a rather grand description. All I remember is a single room and a communal kitchen which served the entire building. But if you wanted to feast on corned beef and dumplings, filched from the local grocers by one of us, that was the place to go. You could even take a girl back there. Henley wouldn't bat an eyelid.

Another local, known as Baggy, ran a gambling house on Grafton Street where we often crashed out. Baggy features strongly in the history of the city's sound system

scene. He'd moved most of the furniture he owned to a back room and the modest living room was turned over to poker and black jack sessions, with blokes coming in to play and bet from who knows where. He still lives there now, in his late sixties.

Baggy would sell food – stuff like chicken, rice and peas, soup and, of course, dumplings – a dish dear to the hearts of all Jamaican guys. As young kids, Baggy's place was our lifeline. Somewhere to kip, somewhere to eat, somewhere to gamble.

The opportunity to move permanently to Coventry came when Trevor's dad bought a house in the city. According to Trevor, it barely cost a grand. In fact, he ended up having two houses in Coventry for a total of about £2,000. The house he lived in was on Kingsway and as he was hardly ever there, with the hours he worked in the factory, I moved my stuff in. Without a second's thought, I left Rugby behind and became a resident of a city that I still live in today.

A lot of black guys lived on and around Kingsway, which was in the Hillfields area of Coventry. There were flats around there where black guys were crammed in with maybe up to fifteen people living in one place – literally kipping in the cupboards or anywhere they could find to lay their head. These were guys who had come to Coventry looking for jobs or had been kicked out of home by a dad like mine.

Me and Trev were still in our teens and some of these guys we started hanging out with were older – in their twenties and thirties. They were rootless and ruthless. When we were able to draw the dole, they would trick it out of us. We'd be in one of the gambling dens and would lose the lot at the turn of a card. Then they'd order us to go out and rob food for them, but then not give us any of it.

There seemed to be a time in the early 1970s when everybody was stealing to get by. Certainly me, my brother and many of my mates got into being right, regular tea leaves (rhyming slang for thieves, in case you didn't know). The point was – we were completely and utterly skint. All the time, twenty-four seven. So in order to look good, scoff some decent grub and have a Saturday night out, we had to nick for it. Simple as that.

Stealing was an important part of my teenage life. I stole clothes. I stole food. I stole records. I stole jewellery. I stole stuff for my sound system. And I eventually graduated to burglary.

Making ends meet involved a mixture of social security, robbing homes and shops, and selling weed at the blues parties where we would play our sound system – more on that in a moment. We'd also sell weed in bars round town, but never at the Locarno. That hallowed place was solely for pulling birds and having sex on the dark balconies, not for making money.

Phone boxes were a good source of loot as so many people still had no telephone at home and would have to queue at the red phone box, then provided by the nationalised GPO, down their street just to have a natter. You might get three or four people standing by those big, red, solidly built metal boxes waiting to have a chat to a relative or a friend. They'd always be tapping on the glass to encourage whoever was on the phone ahead of them to get a move on. Then went the ten and fifty pences into the meter as they yacked and yacked. Once the queues died away, we moved in to jemmy our way to the cash left behind, filling our pockets with a huge stash of silver.

Some of my mates had thieving down to a fine art. I was particularly impressed by the ingenious way of removing deposits from the allegedly secure money containers they used to have outside building societies. The method of extraction involved a coat hanger and a piece of chewing gum and out came the bank notes.

As I embarked on a life of petty crime, the gang of mates around me expanded – my new Coventry rude boy posse. The first new addition was Rex Griffiths – who I mentioned earlier – a member of our Locarno dance troupe, Nev and the Boys.

Rex came from Coventry. After he left school, he became an apprentice draughtsman at GEC for about £12 a week, which meant he didn't get involved in the thieving.

Rex was small and when he was younger, he had a pit bull quality about him. This was useful as we started to get into big fights with his former skinhead buddies. Compact and capable of violence when the circumstances demanded it, Rex would bite the ankles of our enemies first and then us loftier boys would move in for the kill.

'He'd throw rocks and bricks and bottles,' Trevor recalls, 'but physically, he wasn't as imposing as the taller blokes.'

He was one of seven brothers and a sister – a typical big Jamaican family. Along with Trevor, he'd eventually end up being a roadie with The Specials and part of the gang on the 2 Tone tour bus.

He didn't know many black kids and so ended up hanging out with skinheads. In fact, his first girlfriend was a skin. Rex, the skinheads and the suedeheads would be walking round in the same clothes that 2 Tone would later adopt – trilbies, Sta-Prest jeans, Ben Sherman shirts and so on.

They'd all go to the same bars and pubs and listen to reggae – particularly Desmond Dekker. That's not to say all was peace and love between young blacks and skinheads, because it wasn't.

Ranking Roger of The Beat told me that, like Rex, he used to hang out with skinheads as a sixteen-year-old black punk growing up in Birmingham.

Roger had loads of mates from Yardley, which was a notoriously racist area of Birmingham at that time. One day he was strolling along with his skinhead chums when one of them casually blurted out: 'I really hate black people.' Then, realising what he'd said, added: 'But you're alright Roge.' That was the sort of schizo mentality some of these guys had towards blacks.

Rex can remember being in clubs and finding the skin clique on one side of the dance floor and the black guys in a huddle on the other. The black guys would normally be outnumbered and Rex would stick out like a sore thumb as a black guy who was dressed like a skin.

For the record, I have never believed all skinheads are racist. Many of them were – and are – decent enough blokes. But it was very easy for many of them to get caught up in the street violence that often had a racial undertone. This was even more the case in the late 1970s when the National Front started actively recruiting skinheads and unemployment shot up. But at this time, in the early 1970s, the line between us was more blurred.

That's why, with 2 Tone, we tried to bring the two sides together. After all, we were all just working-class youth trying to get by – some of us white and some of us black.

Rex recalls first seeing me and Trev walking by wearing our jeans hitched up high to show off our red socks. Trev says that Jamaicans always wore bright red socks to spell out the word 'danger' to anybody thinking of taking us on. The jeans were Lee Cooper or Wrangler and we must have looked a sight. Rex probably looked smarter but then he, unlike us, had a job.

As Rex often points out, in the early 1970s, the skins were better turned out than the NF-led revival around 1979. They would be in their Doc Martens and Harringtons during the day going to the footie match for a ruck. But in the evening they'd be kitted out in Prince of Wales checked suits and looked extremely smart. They were a million miles away from the fascists who turned up at Specials and Selecter gigs at the end of the decade.

Amazingly, Rex would even hang out in the Mercer Arms – the main skinhead boozer where most of us didn't dare set foot. But the skins knew Rex and kind of accepted him for a while – although that was soon to change. It was Rex's initial proximity to the skinheads that eventually made them hate him more than any of us.

As he gravitated towards the new arrivals – me, Trevor and Franklyn – he saw less of his old skinhead buddies. Some of them in turn began to notice his skin colour, when it hadn't been an issue before. Maybe they felt rejected or maybe, more likely, they didn't like Rex's sharp tongue. Rex was always good with words and that upset blokes who didn't like a black guy who could answer back. It's not surprising that Rex is now a lecturer in a London college – still sounding smart.

Other black guys were drawn into our orbit. Dennis Willis was somebody who moved into our circle and played an important part in our various illegal fundraising activities. He was known to us as 'Scuff the Hustler', on account of the scuffles he got into with skinheads and his unsurpassed ability to hustle money out of the most unlikely people.

Like us, Scuff had been taken out of Jamaica and dumped in the UK. He'd arrived here a year after Trevor and was a bit younger than the rest of us, though not by much.

Scuff felt that people like us had nothing much to live for – not an untypical point of view among the black youth at that time. Our parents had brought us over from the Caribbean and as good as forgotten about us. We'd essentially been left to fend for ourselves on the streets.

In part, that meant dealing with the cops who were on our case all the time. If they saw a group of us walking down the street – and we walked in groups back then for good reason – they'd assume it was going to be trouble. Scuff used to get annoyed that we were pulled over by the police all the time. The only thing that calmed him down was Rasta music – which was becoming more influential in the late 1960s and early 1970s. It gave young black guys a sense of purpose and spiritual wellbeing. Scuff also adopted the dietary regime of Rasta and still doesn't eat pork today.

Before hanging out with me and the lads, Scuff used to keep company with Desmond Christie, older brother of the Coventry boxer Errol Christie. The family lived in the Radford area of the city. All the Christie boys were handy with their fists and Scuff already had a reputation for being able to duff up a skinhead if he had to. He also knew from day one not to get on the wrong side of me and regarded me as a sort of street celebrity by this stage.

There was also a guy in our ever-expanding group called Johnny Stevenson. He came to England from Jamaica when he was fifteen or sixteen. He was a great poet and writer – a really talented guy who reminded Trev of Pete Tosh, the late and great reggae artist.

We first met him at the Locarno and kept bumping into him in all the pubs that played live music in Coventry at that time – the Penny Black, Eagle and so on.

At some point, he decided to go and live in London and experience what was assumed to be the high life. Endless clubbing around Soho, living in Ladbroke Grove and dealing drugs. Then in the 1980s, he eventually returned to Coventry when I already had my musical career in full flow with Fun Boy Three. Things didn't end well for Johnny.

He always had a knack for sniffing out and getting his hands on big chunks of money – a talent we greatly appreciated. During the yuppie boom of the late-1980s, he took this talent to new heights and got involved with drugs in London – brown sugar and charlie. You could say Johnny was half pusher and half cultured aesthete. In spite of the way he made his cash, he was never aggressive and kept on penning songs, poems and the like.

But his weakness for hanging out with gangsters eventually got the better of him. Having returned to Coventry, someone who had a grudge against Johnny snuffed him out. His head was battered in and they found his body somewhere in Hillfields, the no-go area of Coventry, slumped on the ground in a tower block called Pioneer House.

That was the end of our mate Johnny.

There were a lot of black guys we hung out with in Coventry in the 1970s who came to similarly sticky ends in the 1980s or after. If the way you made a living brought you into contact with the criminal underworld, you always ran an outside risk of ending up dead.

As I pointed out with regards to Rex, there was an uneasy truce between many of the skinheads and young black guys. Some of the skins and suedeheads were OK. They liked Jamaican music and appreciated where their fashion had originated from – the streets of Kingston – but some skins were complete dickheads and had to be dealt with accordingly.

There was always something bubbling away below the surface in Coventry. You'd be in town and there would be a gang of skins on one side of the road and a big group of, say, fifteen black guys opposite. Sometimes nothing would happen, just a bit of abuse maybe. But then a black guy would get his head kicked in somewhere, so then a skinhead would have to get his head rearranged in a revenge attack. And so it went on.

There came a point where the violence started to escalate. I don't know why. One day I was outside the Holyhead Youth Club and four white guys strode up to me, pumped up with aggression. You could just read it in their faces and their stance. Thumbs tucked into the top of their tight jeans and swaggering from side to side trying to look rock hard.

I had enough street knowledge to realise that in a situation like this, the underdog – me – had to act quick and decisively.

'Where d'ya thing you're goin'?'

'In there,' I pointed with a calm assurance that hid my real feelings.

Then, without a word more, I lunged forward and grabbed one of the youths by the throat, and squeezed hard. I lifted him slightly, which was difficult as we were about the same height, and started marching towards the club. His head was cocked upwards, eyes bulging a bit now, as he struggled to breathe. There was a slight gurgling sound from the moron as we moved along. The other three were taken too much by surprise to react and just kind of stood by with shocked expressions.

I took four or five big steps and my victim was on his tiptoes trying to keep up. The only thing going through my mind was that I had to keep a firm grip 'til I got to the club door. At the window, I could see my mates. Once I got to the door, I could let go and bolt inside. If I let go before then, I'd be kicked to fuck – jumped in seconds by the group and booted round the floor like a football.

Sure enough, my master plan went like a dream. I got to the entrance, wheeled round with my skinhead prey still gasping in my right hand, then let go and ducked through the door. But not before I issued a little threat:

'Any of your friends come looking for me – I'll kill 'em. Right?'

The hapless skinhead was bent double, clutching his throat and taking deep breaths. Once more I'd had to show the less intelligent life forms in Coventry that any bullshit like that was not going to be tolerated.

I should point out that my ability to squeeze the living daylights out of somebody by grabbing their throat would come in handy backstage on one occasion in my musical career – to silence a mouthy guitarist who thought he was the dog's bollocks. A talent for squeezing a throat never leaves you.

Skinheads like that were bad enough, but the West Midlands constabulary was one step beyond. We played constant cat and mouse with them and there was no doubt they viewed black kids like me as nothing more than trouble.

My nemesis in those days was an Irish detective called Seamus. He used to drive around Coventry keeping his beady eye on us. In my memory, he's the archetypal 1970s beat copper – constantly on the lookout for trouble and always on your case. To try and catch his prey, Seamus had even gone to the trouble of learning what he took to be Jamaican patois. He would suddenly appear in his car driving along slowly next to me:

'Hey Neville, you blood, what ya bopping for?'

I'd smile politely and turn down the first side street.

Seamus was always trying to make a friend among Coventry's young blacks to see if he could get an informer singing for him. Needless to say, to my knowledge, he never got one. Not because we'd have killed such a weasel necessarily, but because they'd have been an outcast.

Back then the West Midlands police were famous for their somewhat negative attitude towards black people. They didn't trust us, and we didn't trust them. As far as we were concerned they wanted nothing more than to get your black ass in to the local cop shop and stick your head down the toilet – or whatever else passed for an 'interview' in those happy days. Their bad reputation was the talk of the country, though half of Britain would probably have approved of their conduct in those times.

From when I was a small kid, I can remember being stopped and searched even before the notorious SUS (short for on 'suspicion') laws were introduced. Those were the laws that led directly to the 1981 riots in the inner cities.

The cops thought nothing of using the n-word when they saw a black kid. When it came to arresting us, there was always far more aggro because we'd struggle more. We'd also shout a lot more. You could say it was down to our culture and the way we expressed ourselves. There was no stiff upper lip – we kicked and hollered all the way to the station and the police then obliged in kind with their boots and clenched fists.

My dad once took me and Franklyn to a police station in Rugby – to show us what a terrible place it was and how we should never get into trouble. That lesson didn't work, as the next episode in my life only illustrates too well.

As the violence on the streets just got worse and worse, I started to think that we had to do something to get the streets back under our control. If we didn't sort the skinheads out we would be under an effective curfew. That was never going to happen.

Coventry had become a war zone – with gangs fighting for control of the city street by street. If we lost an inch, we felt it. So as the skins were getting more organised and aggressive, we had to respond in kind. The only response that was going to get through to them was the bloodying of noses and more besides.

One day we were all playing football in Gosford Green Park, when in the distance we saw a bloke called Nasty Norman – one of the local skins. In spite of his menacing name, all the skinhead girls loved him. That day he was turned out well – white Fred Perry shirt, Sta-Prest jeans, polished loafers and trilby hat. The best-looking skinhead in early 1970s Coventry – and he was about to get his head kicked in.

Somebody in our team, possibly Rex, shouted: 'Norman!' Then him and Henley Gordon – who owned that bedsit we used to crash at when we first came to Coventry – dashed off after him. They caught him on the Walsgrave Road and Rex was first in as usual to soften up the target, before Henley gave him a complete hiding. Unfortunately, Norman took particular exception to this duffing up as it was his birthday – hence being so well turned out in gleaming Fred Perry shirt and shiny loafers.

Now the skins were on a war footing. A couple of our mates got the treatment so I decided we had to think big. This was how one of the great events of my youth came about – the Battle of Primrose Hill Park.

Don't bother looking in a history book because you won't find it. Primrose Hill Park was a grassed-over gulley with bushes on the ridges above, like a small valley and a perfect ambush site. What we needed to do, I decided, was to lure a load of skins into the middle and then rush down on them from all sides. The bushes would hide us 'til they arrived.

To get them in the park, we needed bait. Who better than Rex – their former mate turned archenemy. We would have to send Rex into the Mercer Arms. He'd only have to say 'Hi, mine's a Double Diamond', and they'd come bounding at him. Poor Rex would be like Daniel in the lions' den. Then my little buddy would have to move as fast as his legs could carry him to the park, where we'd spring the trap. If Rex fell over, he'd probably never get up again.

So the day of battle arrived and we sent Rex into the Mercer Arms knowing full well what the reaction would be.

While he wandered off on his dangerous mission, about a dozen of us black kids took our positions in the park – battle lines you might say. There was the gulley, raised banks and bushes – a terrain that we were very familiar with.

We were pretty sure that as the enemy weren't the sharpest crayons in the box, they could be relied on to fall for our plan. All we had to do was lure then into the trap. We all waited while Rex departed on his dangerous mission – a small solitary figure heading towards the Mercia. He had balls, I'll give him that.

As it turned out, none of us needed to worried about our plucky hero. It couldn't have gone more like clockwork. The door of the Mercia swung open and he smiled nervously at the punters inside.

'There's Rex Griffiths – the black bastard!'

Within a few seconds, his familiar figure was pegging it towards us like he was trying to break the world speed record. Behind him was a small army of tanked-up skins in Doc Marten boots, tight jeans and green bomber jackets. I knew most of their names: 'Nasty Norman', sporting a real shiner of a black eye, the even more aptly monikered 'Hatchet', Bri Falconer, and so on.

We were heavily outnumbered – twelve versus an entire pub – but we had a determination born of necessity.

Me and the gang waited, like Zulu warriors about to wipe out a passing British regiment. As Rex shot past, we charged down the banks to greet a now horrified bunch of skinheads. Any cockiness they had about their superior numbers was soon eradicated as we delivered a sound beating.

'You fucking cunts!'

Blows rained down and blood ran from noses and the corners of mouths. I'd be lying if I didn't admit it wasn't all perversely pleasurable – we were killing machines without feelings.

In those days when knives were used – as they were – it was to 'wet' your opponent. Slash him so the blood ran, not stick it in to kill him. Today's youth take note! We just wanted them to remember us when they looked at their pretty scarred faces or limped because of a stab to the buttock. Now it almost seems naïve, compared to what goes on in this century.

At some point, the altercation reached a natural conclusion. It kind of petered out. Like the aftermath of a battle, the wounded staggered away and we got ready to proclaim victory. That was, until somebody noticed that one guy was still on the ground. And he wasn't moving.

I didn't know at first who stuck the knife into Bri Falconer but it transpired later this was Trev's handiwork. Faced with the grim and frightening prospect of somebody going deceased on us, our response was predictable enough – we pegged it as fast as our legs could carry us back to what we thought was the safety of our homes. Nobody hung around to administer first aid.

The important thing now was to be as far from the scene of the crime as possible and put a mighty big distance between ourselves and this potential corpse.

That evening, the cops started to come round to our homes. Knocking on the doors of black families round the

streets where I lived. I could almost hear them getting closer as they finished with one house and moved on to the next.

From some houses, they'd lift a guy and put him in the police van. Others they'd walk away from empty handed. It was clear the skinheads had grassed us all up. They knew who we were and where we lived – and all they had to do was give a list of names and addresses to the West Midlands Police. Coventry wasn't a big enough place to hide away unnoticed, especially when something like this had happened. It was a time when a stabbing like this didn't seem like an everyday occurrence.

Bri Falconer had survived Trev's knife wound but the cops were now on red alert. The fight with the skins in Primrose Hill Park had gone just a little bit too far for the standards of the day. It was clear that examples would have to be made of us. Several of us were arrested, including me, Rex, Trevor, Franklyn and Rex's older brother Alcutt.

Shortly after being hauled into the cop shop, Trev grassed himself up: 'C'mon Trev – no need to deny it, all your mates said you done it'. Trevor said yes and that was that – he was going down. But there might still be hope for the rest of us.

A big fuss was created around the trial with even the Commission for Racial Equality sticking its oar in on our behalf. A deal was worked out and if Trev owned up and went down, the rest of us would plead guilty to causing an affray and get a judicial ticking off.

We agreed.

The magistrate, Dr Frederick West, banned us from going anywhere near the park. Ironically we were also banned from entering the Mercer Arms.

Amid a shower of words from Dr West about how wicked he'd been, Trev was sent to a young offenders' institution. His place of incarceration was the Eastwood Park Detention Centre, near Bristol.

The regime at Eastwood would have gladdened the heart of any *Daily Mail* reader. Trevor says it was like being in the army. For three months, he got the short sharp shock treatment. Marching every day and then doing the most brain-deadening work you could imagine – something called 'bed bashing'. This involved taking old iron bedsteads apart and, armed with chisels and hammers, the inmates had to cut them to pieces. I can't imagine what the din must have been like with a room full of angry guys trying to dismantle those beds. If they did five of them in a day, they got 30p. For Trevor, the experience was like a trip back to the Dark Ages.

In the aftermath of the battle, a lot of people had difficulty walking for a few weeks – with the amount of knife wounds in their butts. Several people needed stitches on their arses.

Scuff wasn't at the battle for one reason or another, but he tells me that the event grew in notoriety – to the extent that there were regular 'mini-Primrose Hill Parks'. Black kids all over town were setting up traps for skinhead gangs who fell for it every time. One kid would walk up to them, get chased and other black kids would be waiting round the corner to ambush them.

Day to day, our stealing ways continued. We'd stuff eggs and flour under our coats and go home to make dumplings. People still had bread and milk delivered to the door in those days so we walked off with that as well. On occasion, we'd have a real stroke of luck and make off with some catalogue goods that had been left on a doorstep by the postman.

But stealing to eat wasn't good enough. I had to steal to look good as well and that was going to take a bit more than mere shoplifting. I needed stylish clothes – the look and feel of tailor-made jackets, shirts with the right cuffs, narrow trousers, well-made leather shoes and gangster headwear. There could be nothing worse for a rude boy than to look shabby in public.

The route to top of the range threads and the best-looking girls at the Locarno became only too obvious – burglary. And that took stealing into a different league. It was time to graduate from the shelves of Woolies to the jewellery boxes in the bedrooms of the Midlands' semi-detached homes.

Franklyn was already involved in doing over family properties – along with our mates Trevor, Johnny Stevenson and Bookie. I'd been hesitant to go down this route but I soon had a big reality check. There were the boys returning from shopping trips to the King's Road in Chelsea with mod-style tonic and mohair suits, and coats looking as dapper as fuck. They were proving that the road to style passed through the jemmied windows of suburban homeowners.

If the boys couldn't get into the homes proper, they'd get in the basements where the coin-operated meters for gas and electricity would be situated.

They were going down to Chelsea with £120 in their pockets, while all our dads were earning maybe £30 a week in the factories. This was serious money. The trouble was – it was often in ten and fifty-pence pieces from the meters that had been prised open. So Franklyn would go into the post office dressed very smartly and ask to change this inexplicable amount of coinage into notes. Then the boys would go shopping.

They'd go to shops on the King's Road and sometimes Carnaby Street that seemed really cool in the 1970s, shops like Take Six. There was no Armani or Ralph Lauren back then. Shoes were from Sacha or Ravel – and seemed like the height of fashion.

I could only watch Mr Evans and the lads coming back in blue, green and brown tonic suits for so long before deciding I had to throw in my lot with them. Crime wasn't just paying, it was like a lottery win every week for those guys. I'd sometimes watch Bookie and Trev counting out the money they had stolen over the kitchen table in Trevor's dad's house and the sight made me green with envy.

All I had to do now was get a masterclass in how to burgle.

For some reason there was one particular town in the Midlands which produced a lot of skilful burglars – and those guys were only too keen to pass on their nefarious talents to us eager and impressionable Coventry boys.

Northampton, it seemed, was the global centre for burglary. The boys from that town would turn up in Coventry on the hunt for girls and then eventually settle in Cov and impart their trade to wannabe housebreakers like ourselves. They'd even have the decency to take Trevor and the lads over to Northampton to show them how it was done on houses they knew were a walkover. Bookie had been one of these Northampton burglars and as we became friends, we also became his apprentices in crime. He used to say he was the 'stray that led us astray'. Very apt.

Over and over again, I pestered Trevor, Franklyn and Bookie to take me on one of their jobs. It seemed unfair that they'd got in on this act and were doing so well. I wanted to know what a burglary was like as well – it just seemed very exciting.

As a young man curiosity seemed to burn inside me. Two years later, it was the same insatiable curiosity that would have me following The Specials around 'til they finally accepted me as a bona fide band member.

Anyway, after some persuading, the lads let me in on the act.

In total, I got involved in about fifty or sixty burglaries. My first one was on Swan Lane in Coventry and I was looking forward to creeping round the house while the occupants snored their heads off in bed. But the guys decided that as this was burglary number one for me, I should stick around outside and keep watch.

Needless to say, I was a bit disappointed. Especially as I'd brought my own stocking to stick over my head, which I duly did – to guffaws from the others. Unfortunately, I'd neglected to cut eyeholes in it so I couldn't see.

'What? What you looking at?'

'You don't need that Nev!'

Well, I'd watched *The Sweeney* enough times to know that burglars always had stockings over their heads. It was an obligatory sartorial requirement. And as I hadn't nicked a balaclava, the lady's lingerie went on – with two hastily cut eyeholes and the legs drooping down either side of my head like limp antlers.

Our burglaries took us out of town quite a bit. After all, it was a bad idea to burgle your immediate neighbours. So I'd find myself back in my hometown of Rugby or up the road in Birmingham. The good thing about doing over homes in Rugby was that me and the lads had a pretty good idea of which ones to target. In fact, we did so conspicuously well out of Rugby that other homebreakers decided to follow suit. And inevitably, they fucked it up for all of us by getting caught or setting off alarms – all because they didn't know the lie of the land.

We'd drive to most of our burglaries in some clapped-out old banger that I bought for a crazily low price. Me, Trevor, Bookie and Franklyn crammed in.

I'd been driving this old standard 8 car for a little while. The tyres were bald, it had no lights, it made curious noises, there was no tax disc and I didn't have a licence. We couldn't have been less legal on the road. On one occasion, a copper did stop us while I was driving this heap of junk.

'What are you doing?' he said.

'Driving,' I answered.

'Get that wreck off the road – and if I catch you again, I'm going to nick you.'

Nowadays, he would have nicked me on the spot, but in the 1970s there must have been a lot more people driving round in bloody awful cars than there are now. As it turned out though, it was a shame he didn't force me off the road because that lousy car would be my undoing.

Burgling a house is probably one of the biggest thrills you can get. You knew the type of person who was going to keep all their wealth in the bedroom. Very often they were self-made Asian families who liked to keep their assets liquid and accessible – which meant in cash and jewellery, and usually under the bed. To get our hands on all this filthy lucre, we'd end up creeping round on all fours in the dark while husband and wife were obliviously snoring away.

If they stopped snoring, you stopped moving. When they resumed, you started up again.

It was always better to burgle when the owners were in the house because you could be virtually a hundred per cent sure the burglar alarm would be switched off. As I knew the neighbourhoods, we could be pretty certain about which houses didn't have dogs – whether big guard dogs or yappy little things.

If the owner did wake up – and worse still reached for some makeshift weapon they kept under the bed – you ran for it. Asian families were always the most protective of their wealth and if you had an Indian guy in hot pursuit, you really were running for your life.

One person who was noticeable by his absence on our burglary trips was Scuff the Hustler. He didn't have any truck with this line of work. You could say he objected on moral grounds. As far as Scuff was concerned, shops were fair game but people's homes were out of order. They'd worked for a living and we had no right to walk off with their possessions. Scuff worked hard at convincing me and Trevor that the burglaries had to stop – unfortunately, as events unfolded, we didn't listen to him soon enough.

While Scuff objected to burglaries, he nonetheless lived up to his hustler reputation by 'taxing' known burglars. It sort of fitted in with his moral objections to housebreaking. He would effectively punish those who had taken from decent, honest, working-class people. So Scuff took Trevor on his taxing expeditions.

They'd stand outside the Locarno on a club night and approach guys they knew had just done a job. Scuff took huge self-righteous pleasure in going up to these blokes and demanding a fifty per cent split with menaces. If they didn't comply, they'd get a very good and thorough kicking. Scuff, as I pointed out earlier, was a polished fighter.

He even resorted to turning up at houses where he knew the ill-gotten gains of the previous night were being counted out and demanded a cut. This may all seem a bit hypocritical, especially as Trev himself was involved in burgling, but such philosophical considerations were low down on our list of concerns – way below trying to make ends meet and buying decent clobber.

My burgling carried on even as I moved in with Ideta, who'd managed to get a council flat, what with having Byron to bring up. Our other child Melanie was born in the late 1970s, but this was 1972. In one room there was a spare double bed, which became a crash-out space for the boys after a night of clubbing. It wasn't unusual to find several rude boys snoring on top of it, typically Johnny Stevenson, Bookie and Rex.

Ideta knew Rex because she'd been to school with him, and over the years she would phone up to confide in him. At first she didn't know about my other women – and other kids – but then found out the awful truth.

That, along with my allegiance to music and the rude boys over her, as she saw it, would cause Ideta a lot of pain over the years. I wish I could turn back the clock and change a lot of things, but my life was always spinning out of control in those years. And just as Ideta thought we had a chance at some domestic bliss together in that flat, I went and ruined it all with my next burglary.

Me, Trev, Bookie, Johnny and Franklyn drove to our proposed target – a house owned by an Asian family in

Rugby. As usual, the car made all its customary growling noises as I jerked the gear stick around to get it moving at a respectable speed. We arrived and forced our way into the house.

In the middle of the burglary, the lads were creeping around on hands and knees, moving slowly while the home owner snored like an elephant – when he suddenly stopped breathing. Total silence. The lads froze. It was at that moment they could see his eyes were wide open.

The look on his face said he was going to cut us up into little pieces if he could get hold of any of us. Asian fathers would do anything to protect their property.

Franklyn, Bookie and Trev charged down the stairs, while Johnny Stevenson wrapped himself in the living room curtains and dived through a patio window. The rest followed and I was outside trying to get the car started. Over and over again I turned the key in the ignition, but it was becoming obvious why this car cost so little. In what seemed like an instant, police sirens filled the air and I was dragged out of the car by the cops. Bookie tried to run off but was caught very quickly. Trevor and Franklyn, however, got away and found themselves walking along the railway line in the direction of Coventry, hoping they wouldn't get nabbed. All night they followed the tracks 'til they got back.

Eventually, the cops caught up with them. Franklyn was lifted from a gambling house on Cambridge Street – a place where blokes sat around playing cards all day and eating whatever food was made available. Incredibly, Trevor was sitting right next to my brother but the police officers didn't arrest him. So he went on the run to Leicester. An older guy called Prince smuggled him out of the city and he tried to make himself scarce.

Once in Leicester, Trevor took the opportunity to learn a new trade. He was taught how to rob Omega and Seiko watches from the local jewellery shops – so his time there wasn't completely wasted. He would walk into one of these shops, dressed well and talking in a posh accent, and ask to see some of the watches. Then by sleight of hand, he'd half-inch them when the shop manager's back was turned. This kept him in funds for a couple of months.

Eventually Trevor came back to Coventry – nobody really wants to be on the run forever. When he did, he got caught. Apparently the shoe prints in the house were an excellent match for Trev, so he had no way of beating the rap.

As Franklyn and Trevor had disappeared into the night after the burglary backfired, I'd been handcuffed, read my rights, head forced down and bundled into a wagon. All within sight of the delighted home owner.

This was no joke. I knew – as did the others – that we were facing a stretch inside. I wouldn't see Ideta, my small kids and all the other women in my life for months, maybe years. We wouldn't taste freedom for quite a while.

After the shortest of court appearances, I was stuck in Brockhill Prison on remand.

Ending up behind bars is a discomforting experience, to put it mildly. Everything you've ever known is cut off from you. You feel lonely, but not necessarily scared, and you just don't have any idea how long you're going to be in there.

When I walked into Brockhill, I put on my brave face – as I would do afterwards in borstal. You couldn't show any sign of weakness, worse still, fear and to let anybody take the piss out of you early on was fatal.

I was processed in the usual way: clothes off, medical exam of sorts, welcome to prison, then off to a cell. Cells are as bleak as you've ever heard they are. All the clichés of prison life turned out to be true. People tapping morse code messages on the pipes to each other and shouting stupid things out of the small windows:

'I used to be a werewolf but I'm alright nowooooooooh!'

Swinging sheets out of the same windows, cigarettes, money or contraband concealed within. And even back in those days drugs seemed to move freely from cell to cell. Ideta would visit and bring things like toiletries that would make life a little more civilised. She was a picture of misery as you can imagine.

After Brockhill, it was like I ended up doing a tour of England's remand centres. Winston Green for a couple of months was horrible. Windows had been smashed in all over the prison and left broken. The attitude of the screws seemed to be that if we wanted to sit in the cold, that was fine by them. After that I ended up in the infamous Wormwood Scrubs for another couple of months. Finally, I was sent to Hewell Grange borstal for just under a year.

Borstals don't exist anymore and to describe them is to go back to a different era. They were youth prisons staffed by old timers who were supposed to teach us skills like woodwork, planting vegetables or painting and decorating. Like prisons they had governors. They were split up into 'houses' like public schools – probably to try and give us a sense of belonging, but nobody wanted to belong to a borstal.

The houses in our borstal were named after English royal dynasties. So I was in York house, Franklyn was in Lancaster and Bookie was in Tudor.

Security conditions were surprisingly open, though that didn't mean we could just walk out. Hewell Grange was an open borstal and would not have been impossible to escape from – there was no barbed wire – but you'd have only been hauled back and had your sentence extended. There was no option but to endure and make the best of a shit situation.

Discipline could be harsh – borstals were graded to fit different types of individuals. In extreme cases there was solitary confinement, but normally you'd be hauled before some official – maybe the governor – to account for yourself. This happened to Bookie when he was falsely accused of smuggling in aftershave. The reality was that his family were a little over enthusiastic in the amount they were giving him and he ended up with several bottles. But the screws weren't buying that.

He was hauled off to spend the night in 'the tower'. This was an imposing Victorian structure that wouldn't have looked out of place in a Hammer horror film. Bookie had to sleep in a cold, dark room – as did all inmates who were to face the governor the next day. I don't know what the reason for this was, but I assume it put you in a certain state of mind by the time you got flung in front of the prison boss.

The next day Bookie, looking a little dishevelled, was taken in to see the governor and was asked how he would plead to the accusation of smuggling.

'Nolo contendere,' he said in his finest latin. I do not wish to plead, it means. Bookie had paid attention in latin classes at school.

The governor gave him a look of complete blank incomprehension.

'I'm sorry?'

It was a sad reflection on the management of our prison service that Bookie's knowledge of the language that has framed our laws for 2,000 years was better than the governor's. He was found guilty and is still complaining about that judgment to this day.

In borstal, we wore blue shirts and heavy-duty overalls or trousers – all a far cry from tonic suits and Ben Sherman or Harrington clobber. Borstals were not high on style.

I opted straight away to work in the kitchen. I can't remember how I convinced the powers that be to hand me this cushy number. It wasn't as if my culinary skills were particularly amazing. But I took charge of preparing our meals pretty quickly and I surprised myself by becoming something of a stickler for hygiene.

If I saw guys picking up food that they'd dropped on the floor and trying to sneak it into the pot for that day's dinner, I'd take issue with them on the spot.

'Put that in the bin – now. You'll poison somebody.'

Eager to make sure that I kept my designated role, I ran the kitchen with military discipline. I could have been a chef in a Michelin-graded restaurant by the time I left the confines of borstal.

Franklyn ended up working with an electrician, while Bookie was doing painting and decorating. It's really hard to believe that back in those halcyon days, they really did want to reform young offenders as opposed to just throwing away the key – and there were enough old timers around prepared to impart their skills.

Sometimes, I'd see Bookie coming along the corridor in the morning on the way to do electronics, looking a bit glum. I'd stick my head out of the kitchen hatch and dump a cup of sweet tea and honey on toast in his hands, telling him to scoff it as quickly as possible before the screws caught sight of my good deed. Little things like that made life bearable for us.

One day, I was serving up the well-prepared slop and became aware of a commotion in the shower block. One of the other inmates ran over and said breathlessly:

'It's Paddy – he's beating up one of the brothers.'

Suddenly I had a mental image of this big, thickset Irish guy pummelling one of the black guys. It was time for me to dispense some justice and put Paddy back in his box. I forgot all about my cordon bleu offerings and made my way to the shower block.

I found him on one of the landings looking very pleased with himself and just jumped on top of him. My fists rained down, but then so did his, striking me back over and over again. We were way too evenly matched and as we rocked backwards and forwards I couldn't see how this bust up was going to end.

So while we were on the floor, I began to manoeuvre him to the edge of the landing. My aim was to shove him over the balcony and send his body dropping down the stairs to the cold, granite floor below – where, with a bit of luck, his brainless head would crack open.

But it wasn't to be. As I got him near to the edge, caught up in my psychotic rage, the screws arrived and were suddenly pulling me in every direction. I was dragged off Paddy, my fists and feet still lashing out. Somehow the screws bundled me into 'the block' – solitary confinement – where I remained for a week. Just me, a mattress and a potty.

In spite of this experience, Trevor has never tired of pointing out that as an 'open' borstal Hewell Grange actually had a relatively lenient regime. That didn't mean it was a pleasant place to be but, having punctured Bri Falconer's lung, Trevor had put himself in a whole different category of prisoner and done time in a 'closed' borstal – the detention centre where he'd bashed iron beds.

The most upsetting thing about borstal was the visits from my dad. My sisters would come as well, but there was the old man across the table doing something I'd never really seen him do before. He was crying. His voice croaking with shame and sorrow, he'd try to make sense of what was going on in front of him. There were his sons – me and Franklyn – in prison uniforms.

'I tried to give you whatever I could... make you moral... took you to church... why have you gone off the rails like this?'

Whatever I thought of him, I didn't want to see the old man reduced to this. He was no saint, but he wasn't the devil either. Me and Franklyn resolved that after tasting freedom, we weren't going to end up inside again.

For me that meant knocking the burglary on the head, in spite of it being one of life's more exhilarating and lucrative felonies. Bookie carried on housebreaking and did more time, before finding an even more cash generative, but still extremely illegal, pastime.

3

JAH BADDIS – THE SOUND SYSTEM SCENE

A rare photo of the Jah Baddis 'house of joy' in the early 1970s.
(*Left to right*) Rex Griffiths, our buddies Robert, Oscar (*front*), Dixon
(*behind*) and Rex's brother Courtenay on the far right.
Rex Griffiths, personal collection

Black families like mine arriving in Britain in the early 1960s noticed a few things about the mother country that they didn't like. It was cold, the pubs closed very early, there wasn't enough black music around and you couldn't party 'til dawn. So the first generation started to put those things right and brought the sound system over from Jamaica with its associated 'blues parties'.

The original guys who brought over this taste of Jamaica were Duke Vin and Count Suckle in London during the 1950s. Then Count Spinner set up his sound system in Coventry and the city hosted several rival systems in the 1960s.

By the time my gang of rude boys were fighting skinheads in Primrose Hill Park, two sound systems dominated the Coventry scene – El Paso and DJ Baggy (Hi Fi). That's the same Baggy who had the house that was also a gambling den and a sort of restaurant.

But first, I better make sure you all know what a sound system is. I mentioned that when I was growing up in Jamaica, there were big blues parties in Kingston. Rival DJs would set up their sound systems and compete against each other. The idea was to play the best records by the top musical artists at that time.

Artists would ally themselves to a particular sound system and provide their chosen system with unique recordings called 'dubplates'. These were jealously guarded by the sound system. The 'selecter' would hand the dubplate to the DJ who would play it. The artist might even have done a unique vocal track on that recording mentioning the sound system by name.

The sound system might also have its own 'toaster' or, if not, the DJ would toast. Toasting was the direct forerunner of rapping and hip-hop. The first time people spoke over a recorded beat was on the streets of Kingston, Jamaica, in the 1950s.

Later, in The Specials, I'd toast over some of our most famous tracks. 'Bernie Rhodes knows don't argue' in 'Gangsters' for example. Or, on one recording of 'Ghost Town', I toast: 'The town that I come from it is a ghost town, somewhere in England they call Coventry'.

The inspiration for my 'deejay' style of toasting was Jamaican artists like U-Roy and Dennis Alcapone. Another influence was the 1970s toasting deejay I-Roy – not to be confused with U-Roy. There was also the very funny and talented Dillinger – who was born Lester Bullocks and wisely changed his name. His toasting was more risqué, with tracks like 'Crabs in My Pants', which doesn't leave much to the imagination.

To generate the best sound, the sound system would have a 'house of joy'. These would be massive, wardrobe-sized wooden constructions housing customised speakers, made to fit. The reason for this expensive way of making a speaker was that conventional speakers in those days couldn't accommodate the heavy reggae, ska or rocksteady bass beat we wanted to hear.

Our audio equipment on the Coventry sound system scene was made by two larger than life characters – Eddie

the African and Legs the Giant. Legs was a physically huge Jamaican guy who Trev would see in London – these guys were our version of Sony or wherever you buy your speakers from today.

The amplifiers were big valve amps that needed to warm up before they blasted the music out – transistor amps were too small and weedy back then. Valve amps also added a richness to the sound that the newer transistor technology couldn't match. To the eye, valve amps looked completely outdated – like something from the Second World War – but to the ear it was the only way to listen to the music.

The sound system crew would be like a small army with a DJ, sound engineers, or 'sound bwoys', somebody who could toast over the beat and the selecter, who picked the records. The preferred make of turntable was a Garrard and unlike today's DJs we would only use one.

DJ Baggy – or Sir Baggy – played the blues parties in Coventry and around the UK. Blues parties were basically a party in somebody's house that hundreds of people would turn up to. The pubs closed by 11pm at the latest and even when we were young the nightclubs kicked out at 2am. It was just too early.

Most young people wanted to carry on – particularly the black youth. The idea that this would upset the neighbours – or our parents – never really crossed our minds. It wasn't that we wanted to break the law, it was just that our feet had only just got going and they needed another venue to keep dancing.

So a house would be made available, the furniture shoved somewhere, a table slung across the kitchen entrance and Red Stripe and Heineken cans sold at exorbitant prices. Me, Rex and Trevor would go to blues parties all over England. The word would just get out that a 'blue' was on somewhere and off we went.

The sound system at a blues party might not necessarily involve a whole house of joy set up. The DJ might use something smaller – even a radiogram. Every West Indian house had a radiogram, a quaint forerunner of the modern hi-fi, which might even contain a drinks cabinet. Some of these would be stripped of most of the woodwork to just reveal the bare bones of the amplifier and speakers.

My first taste of the sound system scene was before I left Rugby. My cousin Alvin, who had squared up to my dad after he beat me, had a sound system called the Messenger. He would travel to blue parties all over the country and as a young teenager I was mesmerised. The sound, the parties, the atmosphere. I begged Alvin to take me with him to these parties and off we went.

Once we arrived in Leamington Spa on a cold and frosty night. We thought nobody would want to go to a blues party on a night like this. They'd be blue with cold, not the music. We pushed the equipment across the ice to the hall and opened the doors to find it stuffed with people. Fairy lights were everywhere as it was around Christmas. There was food, drink, dancing – a magical scene. It took my breath away and I knew I wanted to be a part of this.

It was with Alvin that I first got a taste of the ultra-violence that would pop up at other blues parties. At the Rugby Memorial Hall, while a blue was in progress, a fight broke out. Even as a fairly hardened fourteen-year-old, I was still shocked to see somebody get stabbed in the neck. I watched as blood spurted out. A similar

scenario would involve a member of The Specials in a different decade.

Alvin let me toast occasionally and that was when I started to hone my vocal skills. We would go to some places where people would warn us there were a lot of racists around – and we might have problems being black. Frankly, by the time we got going with the sound system, we proved – as I've shown over the years – that music is a force for unity. Alvin and I would play blues parties with mixed black and white audiences that danced, drank and ate together – as it should be.

Having left Rugby and the Messenger behind, me and my new Coventry gang were always on the hunt for the best blues parties around the Midlands and further afield.

Leicester was always a good destination. Outside of Coventry, they knew how to party. We'd go to a great club called El Rondo, driving down in Rex's car. He'd finally learnt how to drive after buying a Mini and then not doing anything with it for a long while – relying on me to chauffeur him until even his own mum screamed – 'Why you so worthless, got somebody else driving you around?'

Shamed, Rex got in the Mini – with no lessons of course – and overcame his fear of driving by just going for it. Though the sight of a cop would turn him to a jelly. Especially with me, Trev and others crammed into his little car, speeding to the bright lights of Leicester.

After El Rondo closed for the night, we'd go looking for a blues we'd been tipped off about. We knew all about the great sound systems in Leicester like Fat Man and Mister Blues. The DJ behind the latter sound system is now dead and his sons took over, renaming it Junior Blues – they're still going today. A lot of the action in

Leicester was in an area called Highfields – poor, edgy and multi-ethnic – that was eerily like our very own Hillfields area of Coventry.

The blues parties there could be pretty heavy. We saw a lot of people smoking very strong marijuana and every so often, somebody would drop to the ground totally out of it. They'd have to be revived with cold water unceremoniously tipped over their head.

Those blues were rammed and kept going till about 8am – or until the cops were called to break the whole thing up. If the police did show, nobody would admit to the booze in the kitchen being for sale. That would be in breach of the licensing laws. So the story was that this was a regular house party and the Red Stripe was, of course, free.

Our blues parties in Coventry were normally where you'd find Baggy doing this thing. His rival, El Paso, was more targeted at the hall-based events. Sir Baggy's sound was down to earth, while El Paso was refined. One night we might find ourselves cheering on Baggy and the next night El Paso. It was like supporting Tottenham Hotspur and Arsenal at the same time.

Trevor, it should be said at this point, got into the scene big time with Baggy, performing as his DJ. This was quite unusual at the time, as some of the older guys would tell us young upstarts to get lost. But Baggy was always very helpful towards us and keen to encourage our growing interest in the sound systems.

Rival sounds clashed all the time – mainly at the big hall events where up to four or five would turn up to do battle. Literally battling in some instances. The guys from rival systems would set up their big boxes first with the afore-mentioned valve amps inside – looking like rows of milk

bottles turned upside down. The more amps you had, the better the sound.

Everybody would get their system ready and then hastily cover their house of joy with a sheet. It was deemed essential to guard the secret of their sound system's success. If a sound system thought a rival had a better set up, there was only one thing they could do – cut the wires when they weren't looking. This was very, very common. Sound system battles could be a dirty business.

The risk of cutting the wires was that when the contest began, some poor sod's sound system might actually blow up. The valve amps were notoriously unstable and electrics weren't quite as sophisticated as they are now. If this happened, the owners of the damaged sound system would be looking for blood. Valve amps weren't cheap – they could cost about £800, which in 1973 might buy you a house. So bottles and fists flew at these contests as there was a lot at stake.

Sometimes there would even be a cup – like a sporting trophy – to be won. The venues for these big battles would be places in Coventry like the Police Ballroom or the Railway Club.

The Police Ballroom was always packed for sound system events or gigs. You could send one person in to open the ground level windows at the side of the building and let the rest of us in for free. Sometimes the fire exit would be open and twenty or thirty of us would pile in. But on other occasions the door staff got wise to what was going on and a little altercation would ensue.

The Railway Club in the Holbrooks area of town was one of the first venues to host reggae events in Coventry and the sound system there was Count Spinner – who is still going strong.

At the sound system battles, there was an official etiquette that wasn't always followed. What was supposed to happen was that one sound system played three or four records – not all the way through – and then gave way to a rival sound system. But sometimes, the sound system concerned got carried away and just kept playing. Then the other system would get pissed off and start playing their records at the same time. There would be a huge racket as the systems pumped up the volume to drown each other out. At some point, a voice of sanity would prevail and one system would yield to the other. Until it all broke down again.

From the moment I saw and heard a sound system, I knew this was my future. This was music I worshipped and I loved the toasting I'd done at the Locarno – and with Alvin's sound system back in Rugby.

The big question was: how would I get my own sound system and rule the Coventry scene? A scene still dominated by a previous generation of sound systems. For getting my house of joy off the ground I have to thank the intervention of Ray King – lead singer of the Ray King Soul Band.

Ray touched the lives of three of The Specials very directly – me, Lynval Golding and Jerry Dammers – but in very different ways. In my case, he launched Neville Staple on to the sound system scene as a DJ in his own right. Lynval became part of the well-established Coventry soul scene. Jerry I'll come to in a bit.

Ray King came to England from the Caribbean island of St Vincent and the Grenadines at the start of the 1960s.

He arrived just in time for Cliff Richard and didn't get him at all. What he liked was the sound of Emile Ford and the Checkmates – a Jamaican-led pop group that got to number one in the UK charts in 1959 with 'What Do You Want To Make Those Eyes At Me For'. Far better in Ray's view than Cliff's efforts.

Ray went from singing on the production line at a Morphy Richards iron factory in Northampton, to being talent spotted and propelled to fame in the 1960s, as leader of the Ray King Soul Band. After a long residency at the Playboy Club in London, performing for the likes of Frank Sinatra, recording an album there and dispensing singing tips to French crooner Johnny Hallyday, Ray came back to Coventry. He played to a bigger crowd at the Locarno than the Rolling Stones got around the same time.

And then he retired. Or took a rest. He'd had it good in the 1960s and was happy to take a back seat, until a bloke called Charley Anderson got in touch and said he wanted to get some funding together to set up a youth club, mainly for black kids, in Coventry. This would be the same Charley Anderson who went on to play bass guitar in 2 Tone band The Selecter.

Charley knew how to talk to the race relations people on the council and, ever the diplomat, got them to let us do up the basement of a building on the Holyhead Road and convert it into a youth club. Together with Ray, they got something like £3,000 sponsorship out of Cadbury. Which suited us fine.

Ray ended up being the boss of this new youth club, which was basically a derelict space. Instead of getting professional builders in, he found himself with a rude boy army ready and willing to make this club happen. Armed with paintbrushes and mops, we got to work. Me, Trev, Cedric, Bookie and guys I'll tell you more about later, like Rocky and Banacek. None of us had formal jobs in the real world, so this was great.

But I had another motive for throwing my all into this. Trev and I approached Ray with a proposition:

'When this place is finished, it's going to need a resident sound system. We are that sound system. We are Jah Baddis.'

Now, most sound system DJs, like Baggy and El Paso, were made up of crews of men in their thirties – older guys who had done their dues in the 1960s and knew the Jamaican scene well from direct experience. We were asking to be the first young, vibrant, home-grown sound system.

Amazingly, Ray said yes.

In fact, he did more than say yes. Ray listened to my first attempts at toasting and decided to throw me in at the deep end. His band was gigging again and he had a slot at Leicester University. At the last moment, Ray told me he was ill and couldn't make his own gig, but didn't want to disappoint the university students. I would have to go and toast over some sounds for them – entertain them and put myself out there. So I went for it. In front of a student crowd that looked very different from my usual audiences at the Locarno, I gave a virtuoso toasting performance. All kinds of I-Roy-type stuff – and they lapped it up.

So that was my baptism of fire. Next thing was to finish off the Holyhead Youth Club – my very own venue – and become the resident sound system. I was bursting with anticipation and, like a man possessed, I threw myself into finishing the job. But not everybody showed such selfless devotion to the great cause.

Above us, in the same building, was a gym with judo mats. Ray caught Banacek shagging a girl on one of those mats and banned him from the building for good. In fact, that's how Banacek got his nickname – because Ray 'banned' him.

For those too young to remember, *Banacek* was a detective TV series starring the A-Team's George Peppard, which ran in the early 1970s. I have no idea what our Banacek's real name was – lost in the mists of time I'm afraid – but after Ray slung him out the name stuck. A decade later Banacek would crop up again, this time with disastrous results for a member of Fun Boy Three.

With some of the money left over from Cadbury, me and Trev started to build our house of joy and the amps. I'd never have been able to buy them otherwise. The wood came from a local timber yard and while we paid for most of it, we weren't above sneaking in through a hole in the fence and filching a bit extra. Those old light-fingered habits died hard.

Then there was the small matter of what to play – I was desperate to get my hands on the best cuts coming out of Jamaica. Close at hand was Patel Records in Coventry, where Trev and I would go in dressed in long coats. Thumbing through the racks of vinyl, we'd wait for Mr Patel to be distracted at the counter before quickly stashing the records we wanted under our coats. I had nothing personal against the old man – who had been importing great Jamaican records for a decade or more. He used to have some great stuff, but Ray couldn't fund our lust for the top sounds and I had to be the best sound system in Coventry.

Often I'd bolt down to Brixton in London on a Saturday morning, buy up some new records and get back as quickly as possible to play them on our sound system in the evening. I'd always want to know what was coming out of Jamaica and where I could get my hands on it.

The Holyhead Youth Club opened for business with some dignitary from London coming up to cut the tape or whatever. Then the youth came flooding in. Bored and with nowhere to go – apart from the Locarno on a Monday night – they finally had their own place.

The venue was dark, like most blues parties. The women would be on one side waiting to be chatted up by the blokes. The walls were painted with a load of symbols including, if my memory serves me right, a Lion of Judah – a Rastafarian motif. Our system was set up at one end of the basement and we ruled the place.

Soon we were, without doubt, the best sound system in Coventry. Blaring out some wicked stuff from our warmed-up valve amps. Being the DJ and toaster par excellence, it didn't take me long to increase my shagging rate – much to Ideta's consternation. She just got more and more fiery.

There were rival young sound systems that emerged to challenge us. The most prominent was a mixed race crew called Sound City who we traded the usual insults with and competed against. So intense did our sound system battling with them become that we had a day of reckoning with Sound City many years after, when I was already a *Top of the Pops* veteran and in Fun Boy Three.

Ray had instilled in me a belief that the audience had to be energised. As if a switch had to be pressed. If they weren't electrified by the music, I was failing. I looked out

at those kids night after night trying to read their faces and see if they were really enjoying it. We worked hard to ensure that every person left the Holyhead feeling they'd had the greatest of nights.

Very soon, we started treating Jah Baddis as a kind of franchise for the Holyhead Youth Club. We set up Jah Baddis FC – a football team for the club – and organised the Jah Baddis tournament, inviting sound systems from all over England to come and compete against us.

This turned into a festival of sorts and with permission from the council we served food outdoors, set up a small football pitch and table tennis tables, and did our bit for the community. Kids from all over the Midlands swarmed down to be part of what we were doing. Trevor thinks this sort of event was eventually killed off by yardies getting involved – which is a sad thought.

Jah Baddis started to feel more like a movement than a sound system, with teenagers from all over England coming down to the Holyhead. I had to start looking in new places for the best sounds to keep our new fans happy – a search that took me to the St Pauls area of Bristol.

In 1981 – six or seven years after – this district convulsed with violence during the great summer of riots which would leave Brixton and Toxteth, Liverpool, in flames. But in the early to mid-1970s, Trevor and I went down there time and time again. It had a long-established black community – going back to when the city was a slave port – and unlike Coventry, they ran their own neighbourhood. If they wanted a blues party, they had one. And no neighbours went off boo-hooing to the courts or police.

The black community in St Pauls felt so in control of its own destiny that me and Trevor were a bit overwhelmed. There was an utterly different feel to the place, one I had never experienced before. At the Bamboo Club, a place we returned to many times, we first set eyes on the one and only Rico Rodriguez. The Jamaican ska legend, a musician I had huge respect for, would eventually become The Specials' trombonist.

It was in Bristol that Trevor and me really got to grips with the Rasta lifestyle. There was so much of it going on down there – guys with dreadlocks, talk about Haile Selassie, emperor of Ethiopia, being the new Messiah, a belief that all the trappings of western society were 'Babylon' and followers smoking lots of ganja in search of enlightenment through 'reasoning'.

As a rude boy who wanted the finer things in life, I was not going to go down that route. The ganja wasn't so much the problem – more the rejection of the world's goodies. However, the same could not be said for Trevor.

Ray King clocked the growing Rasta movement and hurried me, Trevor and Franklyn into the recording studio to do a kind of reggae thing. I think he hoped we might be the new Bob Marley & the Wailers, but it wasn't going to happen. I still remember the lyrics:

'No ball' head man
No clean face man
Can enter Zion'

Basically, you've got to have dreadlocks to get into heaven.

Meanwhile, Rocky had gone Rasta and set up a commune of like-minded people in what he called the

House of Dread. He invited people to join and made himself the leader.

He was older than us by about five years and he'd come up from London to live in Coventry in the early 1970s. He was a little prone to violence. We all knew that wherever Rocky went, he had a meat cleaver concealed on his person – normally hidden away in an inside pocket of his coat ready for action. With that in mind, we kept our distance from him – though Trevor unwisely got into an argument once and ended up having the cleaver held to his throat until he begged enough to make Rocky put it away.

While we were building the Holyhead Youth Club, Rocky had been involved and it was during that time he began to get an interest in Rasta. My first clue to where things were going was when I saw Rocky heating hair wax over the cooker at the youth club. Then applying it to his steadily lengthening locks.

Trevor joined the Rastas and I looked on in horror as he went to live in the House of Dread. Off to the chemist went my mate to buy beeswax for his Rasta barnet. Quite a community started to gather in that house – and blokes from all over the Midlands turned up to follow Rocky. He told them that betting was bad and there would be no more trips to the bookies – white English women were also to be avoided as part of Babylon – I couldn't believe Trev was up for this.

So me and Banacek took to appearing outside the house in the Holbrooks area of Coventry and shouting out to Trev: 'You won't last!' After all, he was missing loads of pretty girls in the Locarno every Monday night for this rubbish – and I was missing his company as a mate.

Things got even weirder when Rocky took to using a ouija board to summon the dead. Trevor tells me they were all in a house in Hillfields one night when the glass moved jerkily and spelt out Rocky's name, then flew off the table and smashed. Ten fully grown young men shat themselves. Some of them even grabbed coat hangers, fashioned them into crucifixes and left the building in a hurry – bearing their crosses as they went.

God knows what any locals who saw these crucifix-wielding guys would have made of the scene. Trev says some of the guys left Coventry and never came back. They even got a Catholic priest to go and exorcise the place afterwards!

In this sceptical rude boy's view, there was no way this nonsense could last. Sure enough, the cracks soon began to appear in the House of Dread. First it was the kitty. Everybody stuck a bit of cash in to buy food and ganja. One of the followers was sent off to Birmingham to go and score some particularly fine dope that would assist the 'reasoning' no end. On the way back to Coventry, he couldn't resist the temptation to smoke half of it himself.

Realising he might be lynched by his fellow Rastas when they found out, he decided to cut the remainder with tea, just to bulk up the bag a bit. He arrived still completely stoned and handed over the gear. Trevor says that no matter how much they smoked, nobody could get anywhere near as stoned as he was. Smelling a rat – Trev took a closer look at the weed and informed everybody that they were inhaling PG Tips.

That was one sign that things were going wrong. Then there was Rocky. It seemed that his stringent rules about not going to the bookies and having a flutter didn't apply

to himself. Neither, apparently, did the rule about shagging the local birds. In fact, it seemed Rocky couldn't get enough of Babylon. After that, Trev threw in the towel. There was no point in self-denial if even your glorious leader couldn't stick to the rule book.

Rocky went on a kind of pilgrimage to Africa and came back totally disillusioned. He'd expected to find the land of milk and honey, and found nothing of the sort. Drifting away from Rastafarianism, he got a decent enough job at the Belgrade Theatre in Coventry but then hit a bit of a downward spiral.

Rocky eventually came a cropper during a huge fight at the Locarno when the cops came, dragged him away and he got about eighteen months behind bars. He was too old for borstal so went straight to prison.

The Holyhead Youth Club continued to thrive, but maybe it was doing just a little too well. Our sounds kept the place packed, lots of girls showed up, drinking was repeatedly out of hours and regulations weren't followed. The police started to show up and read the riot act.

Then the council, who had funded the whole thing, got involved and started asking questions. No doubt unimpressed that people were smoking dope and gambling on the premises, they decided to call it a day. The club as we knew it was closed and its main use on a daily basis was for local bands to hire out and rehearse in.

The blues parties, meanwhile, were being shut down. Police and magistrates were fed up with us black kids having a good time so visibly. There was a new intolerance in the air – something we'd become more and more conscious of as the decade drew to an end and the 1980s loomed.

By 1977, I'd got myself a bedsit on the Holyhead Road, near the club. I wanted a place of my own and it was becoming clear that my capacity to remain monogamous was scant. I needed my own pad to do what Neville Staple had to do – entertain other women, mainly.

I still saw Ideta and Byron and eventually Ideta moved into my place, but that was a little while off. For now I was a typical rude boy out on the streets, on the look out for ways to make money and get some action in between the sheets.

One day I walked into the Holyhead Youth Club to have a mooch around. The sound system equipment was stored there and I might have been popping in to check on it. As I approached the basement door, I could hear a band rehearsing. The sound was unfamiliar, it wasn't a combo I'd come across before.

My curiosity was aroused and, never being too shy to introduce myself, I decided to interrupt them in mid-thrash. But for a moment, I paused behind the door to listen to them a bit longer. There was a bit of reggae and a bit of punk, and a guy with a deadpan vocal style. Without knocking, I pushed the door open and walked in.

I had no idea that my life was about to be completely transformed.

Me with a case full of records.
Neville Staple, personal collection

4

THE SPECIALS – THE RUDE BOYS ARRIVE

The photo shoot for our first album, 'Specials'.
© Chalkie Davies

The album shot that got away. Photos taken in Coventry's canal basin.

© Chalkie Davies

Me, Rex Griffiths and Roddy Radiation – just after joining The Automatics.

Trevor Evans, personal collection

Standing at the door of that rehearsal room in the Holyhead Youth Club, I found myself staring at five very different people – including a bass player called Horace Panter. He'd been nicknamed Horace 'Gentleman' by the guitarist Lynval Golding who was also present.

On drums was Silverton Hutchison, a guy from Barbados who had been going out with Ideta's sister Cordelia – so we were pretty much acquainted.

On vocals that day was a bloke called Tim Strickland – a sort of James Dean looky-likey who was reading the lyrics to the songs off a piece of paper. Terry Hall would soon replace him.

Finally, the leader of the pack was Jerry Dammers, on an old, battered Hammond organ-type contraption. He was yet to part company with his front teeth, which happened during an altercation involving some angry white bloke at the Domino club in Coventry – an upstairs venue were live bands used to play. Trevor actually witnessed this bloody event. To this day, Jerry has never had his teeth repaired and it's become his trademark look.

Together they were The Automatics – not yet the band that would dominate the charts from 1979 to 1981. This was 1977 and they were still struggling to get their sound and look right.

I instantly offered my services as a roadie. The usual, impulsive Neville Staple. I'd found something new going on in my neighbourhood and I wanted in. I had no idea what this combo wanted to achieve or what musical style they would settle on, but right then I was happy to hitch a ride.

Jerry was open to the idea of me being around. It didn't stop me doing the odd bit of sound system stuff or interfere with my other less-than-legal sources of income.

To understand how The Specials – sorry, The Automatics – would eventually bring together several disparate musical styles, it's worth looking at the musical backgrounds of everybody who was in the band at that point. Particularly Jerry, Lynval and Silverton.

Those three had been involved with the one and only Ray King before forming The Automatics. The man who had helped me set up Jah Baddis and build the Holyhead Youth Club had also been nurturing the talents of the future members of The Specials. To understand how, let's rewind to the start of Ray's career.

Through the 1960s, the Ray King Soul Band toured the world and played with Ike and Tina Turner, Marvin Gaye and Otis Redding. The brand of soul he pioneered was different in feel to its American cousin. As Ray says, the Americans were good with the hi-hat and snare drums – but the British liked a bigger beat and knew how to stamp their feet. It was a harder, edgier soul sound.

When Ray started performing in the working men's clubs of the Midlands, he used to get asked to sing Paul Robeson numbers. But he'd reply as politely as he could that there was no way he was going to sing 'Old Man River'. It was still a massive novelty for many British audiences to have a black guy singing there in front of them.

This was at the start of the 1960s when Cliff Richard, Billy Fury and Adam Faith dominated the British pop charts.

After forming his band, Ray was signed to Pye Records for a while. The Playboy residency followed, as did an album recorded at that famous venue. In the audience one particular night in 1968 were Lulu, George Harrison and Ringo Starr.

The Ray King Soul Band did a lot of gigging in France – where they were very popular – and Ray rubbed shoulders with crooner Johnny Hallyday and film star Brigitte Bardot. In Paris, Ray performed with a band called Steampacket, which featured Julie Driscoll, on vocals, as well as Long John Baldry and a certain Rod Stewart.

One of Ray's regular tunes was the song 'Stand By Me', which he once sang while supporting the man who wrote it, Ben E. King. Instead of tearing strips off him for nicking part of his act, Ben E. King asked Ray to come on stage and perform it again – this time with him.

In the mid-1970s, he started jamming with some young musicians including Charley 'H' Bembridge and Desmond Brown, who would later be in the original line up of 2 Tone band The Selecter. Along with Silverton on drums and Lynval Golding, they formed a soul combo called Pharaoh's Kingdom. The look was a million miles from 2 Tone – more Earth, Wind and Fire.

Into this soul equation walked an art student from Lanchester Polytechnic – now Coventry University – called Jerry Dammers. And if I had a mission to entertain, Jerry's mission was to soak up every bit of musical knowledge he could lay his hands on.

Ray had started jamming with Neol Davies, another figure who would loom large on the 2 Tone scene. He went on to be the driving force behind The Selecter, though was less of an army general than Jerry.

Neol introduced Ray to Jerry and before you knew it Pharaoh's Kingdom was no more and a new band called Nite Train had been formed – with one Mr Dammers, Neol Davies, Ray King and two brothers called 'the Smiths' on bass and drums. They got a contract to play some holiday camp in Tunisia and went off to perform Gladys Knight & The Pips numbers to some lucky sunbathers.

Coming back largely penniless, they decided to go about things a different way. They'd play locally – no more jaunts to Tunisia – and adopt the ska beat. Ray had always loved ska and knew Laurel Aitken, the so-called godfather of ska. This was the music of his youth in Jamaica and he wanted to see how his new combo would interpret such a distinctive beat.

They did some gigs at the Bantam pub in the Holbrook area of Coventry and along came Lynval and Charley, who gave the new sound a big thumbs up. You can probably see where this is all heading.

Slowly but surely, the soul sound Ray had espoused was giving way to something else – something new.

For those who like the theory that Jerry masterminded the creation of The Specials, the next bit of the story will add grist to your mill. Ray says Jerry told him to dump the Smith brothers – they weren't 'superstar material'. But Ray wasn't up for being an executioner and refused. So, one day, Jerry just didn't show up for rehearsal.

Instead he'd taken off with Lynval and Silverton to do things his way.

Finding himself in charge of his own band, Jerry cast around for the other musicians he needed and brought on

board a bloke he was at art college with – down at the 'Lanch' – Horace Panter.

Now Horace and I were probably the most different people in The Specials. Our backgrounds were so far apart we might as well have grown up in different universes.

Horace was your archetypal middle class, art school, intellectual, emotionally aloof musician who wanted to be in bed as early as possible. Don't get me wrong. He wasn't a bad person and I've worked with him on many occasions, but we would never have hung out together if it hadn't been for The Specials.

Horace was as far from the rude boy ethos as you could get. While I was being sent to an approved school or getting the living daylights beaten out of me by my dad, he was growing up in leafy Kettering, listening to pirate radio and playing on the allotment.

Horace did grammar school, I did borstal. I toasted to the beat at the Locarno or my sound system, while he worshipped bands made up of long-haired hippies in kaftans. I listened to Toots & The Maytals and he listened to Little Feat. I worshipped the giants of reggae and ska, while he worshipped American soft rock combos clad head to foot in denim. So we were a bit different.

But Horace's big plus was that he played the bass to perfection – he was the consummate professional musician. That said, Lynval still had to teach him how to play to a reggae beat, but once he'd been given his reggae tuition he never looked back.

Writing about that experience, Horace admitted that Lynval was the first black person he'd ever met. This doesn't surprise me, as black faces still weren't seen in large parts of Britain in those days. In many parts of the country you could be white and never talk to a black person in your life.

But Lynval and Horace were able to strike up a rapport as fellow musicians. They could bore on about chords and music theory till the cows came home. This was totally alien to the sound system scene from which I came. To Horace, I probably wasn't a real musician at all – and to be perfectly frank, I didn't want to be. My mission was, and is, to entertain.

However, the sound system scene was a huge part of the black musical experience in Britain – let alone Coventry – and it would become clear to one and all that the rude boy sound and look was going to be an essential component of The Specials. But let's just say it wasn't immediately obvious to some of the band.

When I first met The Automatics, songs like 'Do The Dog', 'Little Bitch' and 'Dawning of a New Era' had already been penned and the band had even done a gig using Ray King's PA. So the grand old man of soul had taken Jerry's departure from Nite Train on the chin and, as ever, was helping out.

The look of the band was still all over the shop. It would take until 1979 to nail down the 2 Tone image and the rude boy look that would then be adopted by millions of teenagers. The big fashion influence on young white kids in 1977 was coming from the punk explosion. Dinosaur rock and the hippy leftovers from the 1960s had been blasted away by bands like the Sex Pistols and The Clash.

This uncompromising revolution had thrown up some punk outfits in Coventry like The Flys, The Urge and The Squad. Those involved in the city's punk scene included future VH1 presenter Paul King, 1980s pop star Hazel O'Connor and Terry Hall – who was lead singer of The Squad.

For black kids, the punk attitude was something that infected us and we understood where that anger was coming from. After all, if white kids' lives were shit, ours were doubly shit. Unemployment was rising, the factories were closing and there really was no hope, no jobs and no future.

The Sex Pistols opened up a musical can of worms that made it possible for any bunch of teenagers to form a band. You no longer needed a university degree in music before you could take to the stage. The public school prog rock bands with their concept albums and half hour masturbatory tracks were junked. Rock 'n' roll was back thanks to punk.

For me, The Clash were punk's best product and I still love their music now. Those boys were able to mix punk and reggae in interesting ways – and it was reggae that most black youth still turned to at that time. Bands like Steel Pulse, Misty in Roots and Aswad – they expressed our frustrations and hopes.

As it happens, Steel Pulse once had the distinction of being canned off when they shared a stage with my very own Jah Baddis sound system. For the record, the problem was that a lot of the kids didn't want to mellow out to a reggae band – they were busting to dance to the more frenetic beats from the house of joy. Not every black youth wanted to embrace Jah Rastafari, least of all the rude boys. Any suggestion that the canning off was encouraged by supporters of Jah Baddis is still rejected (by me) to this very day.

However, if there is such a thing as karma in the universe, then that night rebounded on me later with my new buddies in The Automatics. While I was roadying for them in the early days, we all went to Birmingham to support Steel Pulse at a festival in their home city. Faced with a mainly black crowd, the nearly all-white Automatics took to the stage and played their ska-influenced numbers. They bombed, badly. But The Automatics weren't canned off. There was just a deeply embarrassed silence.

Some of my black mates shared the feelings of that Birmingham crowd.

'Blood clot how comes you jumping up and down with the white punk bwoys?'

They couldn't figure out why I was spending more and more time with this group – even if I was just roadying – instead of toasting or playing reggae.

That same year, 1978, saw Steel Pulse team up with some of the big punk acts of the time to play some huge Rock Against Racism and Anti-Nazi League events. The Clash also did their bit to stem the rising tide of racism in Britain at that time. There were two major carnivals in London as the fascist National Front party became more active and got more votes. In Coventry, like other big cities, you could sense an ugly mood developing on the streets. Sadly it would later spill over into some of the 2 Tone gigs.

The Automatics decided to move their rehearsals out of the Holyhead and over to a room at the Binley Oak pub – opposite where my old mate Henley Gordon had used his flat as a drop-in for black blokes in the 1960s and 1970s. I would go along to the rehearsals and every time there was a lull in the music, I'd pick up the mic and do what I did best.

I could see my occasional bouts of toasting were making an impression on Jerry. The mind that never stopped working was slowly coming round to the idea of a rude boy element in the band.

But first, there was the small matter of Tim Strickland. He got his marching orders shortly after I joined and his replacement was Terry Hall of The Squad. Terry's move to The Automatics was a smart one. Already, the 'grrrr' aggression of punk was starting to ring a little hollow. Some of the newer punk bands were complete crap and frankly, anybody who had an ear for music was already trying to work out what was coming next.

To me, ska made complete sense. There was a lot of resentment around and young people felt abandoned by society. I wasn't a massively political person. But what ska vocalists had always done was sing about everyday issues in a matter-of-fact manner. Back in Jamaica, it was like a musical newspaper. There would be songs that told you about everyday issues, like a local strike or the price of bread.

My vocals on songs like 'Ghost Town' were a good example of that style. 'This town is coming like a ghost town... government leaving the youth on the shelf'. Just like a Jamaican man talking about the current situation. We didn't need to paint the air blue with swear words like the punk bands – it was all about telling it straight, even a bit understated.

By adopting ska, The Specials – or The Automatics as they still were – began to veer towards our rude boy style. Dressing smart and stylish was always the rude boy way – even if we had to burgle fifty homes in the Midlands to afford it. A rude boy never looked shabby in public. The brogues, tonic suits, Ben Sherman shirts, trilbies, Harrington coats – this was all part of the rude boy uniform. The Specials didn't invent it but they brought it to a massive new audience – and gave it a new, 2 Tone spin.

'We gave white guys back to their mothers,' Trevor says. It's true. After years of safety pins and spikey hair we put these white boys back in suits – but cool suits. Tonic suits. We taught them how to dance and appreciate one of the best sounds that ever came out of Jamaica.

The band appreciated the Jamaican roots of their evolving sound and Jerry was very aware of the heritage he was adopting. He'd later include a famous figure from the first Jamaican wave of ska in the band and revised some good old ska classics.

Having discovered The Automatics, I brought Rex and Trevor on board. In the earliest days, Trevor had a go at being a manager of sorts, looking for venues and doing general sorting out. Together with the other guys, we just became one big happy family. As Rex says, those were the best days for the band.

Another new addition was Roddy Radiation on lead guitar. Roddy was in some rockabilly-cum-punk outfit called The Wild Boys when Jerry decided he needed to 'punk up' the sound of The Automatics. Roddy wasn't an obvious addition to a traditional ska band but he brought something different that appealed to Jerry.

This seemed to be our glorious leader's approach at this time. If he saw something he liked, he grabbed it. Whether he was working to a master plan is another matter, but Roddy – a rocker type who liked a drink – was in.

Now began our Luton van tour phase. Me, Trevor and Rex crammed into what looked like an old removal van

with Terry, Jerry, Lynval, Silverton, Horace and Roddy. Horace and Lynval drove with the rest of the band in the back. We'd arrange all the equipment so we could sit or lie comfortably on it and then charge off down the motorway to whatever gig we'd managed to get.

Sometimes in the summer, the heat would be so unbearable we'd have the back doors open as we sped along. Every so often we would go to a pub, see a nice comfy seat and take it back to the van to incorporate into our bedding arrangements.

In the back of the van, I found myself face to face with the new vocalist Terry Hall. I had seen him around town over the years and always thought he looked like a character out of *The Great Gatsby* – very stylish.

His parents both worked in the car industry. His dad was at the Rolls-Royce Parkside plant and his mum worked at Talbot's Canterbury Street plant. He had a job at a used stamp and coin dealers on Station Square.

I didn't reckon much to his previous band and his attitude to an audience was very different to mine. Terry had been known to perform with his back to the crowd in a sort of disdainful pose – very punk. I could never do that.

Still, for now, The Automatics didn't give me the chance to either please or piss off an audience. I was officially just the roadie. Trevor and me were still doing the sound system and Rex fitted in his unpaid roadying for the band around his new job at British Telecom. None of us were getting paid by The Automatics and the whole thing was a bit of a laugh for three rude boys in search of some fun.

In the course of some of our banter in the back of the Luton van on one very hot day – Rex put his foot right in it, so to speak. We were all starting to sweat with the stuffiness and Rex blurted out:

'This is the way the Nazis transported the Jews man... you know... sticking the gas pellets in through the top of the van.'

The colour drained from Terry's face. None of us knew his family was Jewish. In fact, the search for his Jewish roots has become of great interest to him in recent years. When Rex found out, he was the most embarrassed man in Britain.

The gigs we played in our Luton van days were of very varying quality. The worst one was in front of some Welsh sheep farmers. It's difficult to know or even recall how this gig was set up – but we arrived on some farm and started to set up the gear in what looked like a large sheep pen. Then the farmers started to turn up for their evening social not at all aware of what was about to assault them. The band got on stage and the rustic lugholes got an earful of the emerging ska sound. They pretty much paid Jerry and the boys to get off the stage and leave town immediately.

In contrast, there was Barbarella's in Birmingham – the city's main punk venue. The Automatics took the place by storm. This gig had been set up by local band promoter and DJ Mike Horseman. One person in the crowd was a certain Roger Charlery known to musical posterity as Ranking Roger. He went on to be the vocalist in fellow 2 Tone band The Beat, but at this point in 1978, he was a black punk rocker who loved the microphone as much as I did.

That night some fascist skinheads turned up at Barbarella's. Mike Horseman was doing a DJ set and Roger was toasting on stage as he often did. Most of the punks present – who knew Roger well anyway – were enjoying his performance. But the fascists were moronically chanting 'Sieg Heil! Sieg Heil! Sieg Heil!' at our man. Getting more than a bit pissed off with this, Roger began to chant back to their rhythm – 'Fuck off! Fuck off! Fuck off! National Front! Fuck off!' etc. Before long, fists and feet were in action, followed by pint glasses and chairs.

The Automatics were now making waves round our hometown, playing regular gigs at Mr George's and any other pubs and clubs that hosted bands. In the audience at one of the gigs at Mr George's was a young black female radiographer called Pauline Vickers with her boyfriend Lawton Brown. She would eventually emerge as Pauline Black, lead singer of The Selecter, but that was still a year away.

For younger people now, it's hard to paint a picture of how vibrant the pub music scene was. Bands that went on to be global giants like The Clash and The Stranglers experienced their first audiences in dark and smelly boozers. This was where they trod the boards and earned their creds.

It didn't take long for The Automatics to come to the attention of my old friend Pete Waterman. He's sure the first place he saw the band perform was in the General Wolfe pub in Foleshill Road. Amazingly, this venue would also play host to U2 and the Eurythmics in the early 1980s.

Pete had been working as an A&R man and for a while had relocated to Jamaica working with Pete Tosh and Lee 'Scratch' Perry. One result of that had been a reggae song called 'Hurts So Good' with singer Susan Cadogan, which was a commercially successful reggae hit in the UK charts.

But Pete got a bit disillusioned with the record industry and came back to Coventry to re-charge his creative batteries. Having seen The Automatics, however, he put some money on the table for a recording session at a studio in Berwick Street in Soho, London. We all trooped down there and put 'Too Much Too Young', 'Concrete Jungle' and 'Jay Walker' down on tape.

Even though I regarded myself as outside The Automatics, Pete thought I was always part of the band. He saw me toasting, as I had done at the Locarno all those years before, and assumed I was their full-time toaster. But at that stage, I was still a roadie with Trevor and Rex. It would take a literal leap – on to the stage – to change my status in the band.

Pete called the songs we recorded 'great little tunes with acid lyrics'. The Automatics he described as two rude boys (me and Lynval), two grammar school boys (Horace and Jerry), a rock 'n' roller (Roddy) and a punk (Terry).

He thought we were brilliant. The industry thought otherwise. Pete became our loudest advocate and would often bring his record industry contacts to see us, but the sound just wasn't getting through to them. Eventually, sick of banging his head against a brick wall, Pete ran up the white flag of surrender. He met Jerry and explained that industry know-nothings were saying that 'punk reggae' would never catch on. He'd been as good as warned that if he kept going on about us, he'd end up damaging his reputation.

'I was even losing friends over this,' he confided to me once.

In spite of this setback, Jerry decided to press on.

In a few short months, everything would change dramatically. Our worlds would be turned upside down and the re-named band – The Specials – would be propelled to pop domination. All credit therefore to

Pete for realising the talent locked into that band before anybody else. He was just a little premature, that's all.

Jerry began to demand that everybody give the project their full commitment – even if it meant chucking in their jobs. Roddy had just taken on a mortgage but was convinced by Jerry to give up everything because The Automatics were going to be famous. You have to hand it to Mr Dammers – it was all or nothing. The band was going for broke.

This was a frustrating period for me. I found myself itching to give them more of my presence on stage. I could see the audience needed a rocket up their collective backside that only I could deliver. Either the crowd didn't get excited enough or, with some of the punks and skins, they just didn't get the ska sound. Truthfully, it needed an edgier delivery that only a veteran of the sound system scene could inject.

Eventually, however, things began to move in my direction. What happened next propelled me to the front of the band with Terry and began the transformation that turned us from a 'punk reggae' outfit into the leaders of the 2 Tone movement – the vanguard of the second wave of ska. We were about to fall into the hands of one of the masterminds of punk rock.

There were two managers credited with being the driving force behind the punk explosion. Malcolm McLaren, manager of the Sex Pistols, and Bernie Rhodes, manager of The Clash. It was the latter who crossed our path. Jerry made contact and began to hassle him to get us a support slot on The Clash's upcoming On Parole tour that would take to concert halls in mid-1978.

Eventually Bernie agreed, but not least because The Clash's Joe Strummer was interested in the band's sound. Meeting and working with him was a great experience and his death in 2002 was a terrible loss.

Joe Strummer was a friendly guy and was really into reggae – you can hear the reggae influence in The Clash very clearly. He also identified with, or at least tried to understand, black people and black culture.

I'd go even further and say that talking to Joe Strummer was sometimes like talking to a black man. I don't mean he was pretending to be black – he was just genuinely engaging with our culture.

If you'd given those boys in The Clash rice and peas or curried goat, they wouldn't have turned their noses up. And they hung out in places like Ladbroke Grove, which in the 1970s was much more black, a lot less affluent and far more street.

Having got a support slot with The Clash, Jerry now had a little problem. It turned out there was another band called The Automatics and through their lawyers, they were demanding that we change our name. There was a lot of agonising over what name to adopt – we were briefly The Coventry Automatics but then that was dropped. The Special AKA The Coventry Automatics proved too big a mouthful, so, after shortening that to The Special AKA, it was finally decided to go for The Specials.

The legend was born.

The On Parole tour was not without incident. It's hard to recall now just how much punk scared the wits out of the older generation and the establishment in Britain. But the reaction of local authorities and venues to the proposed gigs seems hilarious now.

In Liverpool, the gig was moved from the Liverpool Empire because the management were nervous about what might happen. In the end, getting moved to Eric's was great. This venue has since gone down in punk folklore and quite rightly so. Every band worth its salt played there in the late 1970s.

Eric's was a smaller venue than the Empire, to put it mildly. The walls were painted black, the place reeked and the names of the bands that had played there over the years were scrawled on the walls of the bogs – The B52s, The Pretenders, Adam and the Ants (in their more punk phase), Simple Minds (kind of electro-punk then) and Stiff Little Fingers. Our name got added, of course. Needless to say, we went down a storm.

The controversy around the tour continued. Picketts Lock Sports Centre in north-east London cancelled the gig after complaints from local residents. Outside the Apollo in Glasgow, bouncers and punks seemed to get on very badly – it was a bit of a mini-riot in fact.

We supported The Clash all over the country: Leeds Queens Hall, Manchester Factory, Aberdeen Music Hall, Torquay Town Hall, Cardiff Top Rank and Bury St Edmonds Corn Exchange, ending with four nights at the Camden Music Machine.

It was at the Music Machine that Neville Staple finally took his rightful place. I turned up as a roadie and left as a fully fledged member of the band.

The audience on our first night at the Music Machine were what we had seen all over the UK – punks, students, new wave types, rude boys – the fan base of The Clash.

In the middle of the mayhem was the stocky, diminutive figure of Bernie Rhodes.

Never showing any sign of modesty, Bernie's view was that it was his way or you could sling your hook. He'd grown up in Soho where his Jewish parents had worked hard to make ends meet. Bernie was tough to the core and believed his bands should do as they were told. The Clash sang about him wanting to shorten one of their tracks when they said: 'Now the king told the boogie men/You have to let that raga drop'. I would also sing about Bernie Rhodes in the very near future.

The Bernie Rhodes view was that he was doing the best for his acts. If they did what he said, they'd get famous. It seemed to have worked for The Clash. They would go on to fire him later that year but then re-hire him in 1981. Aside from managing that legendary punk band, he was also credited with spotting Johnny Lydon in the King's Road and getting him in as lead vocalist of the Sex Pistols. Lydon then changed his name to Rotten.

In short, Bernie believed that he had the best claim to have invented punk – and it's not difficult to see why.

The Specials went on as the support that night and the guys anticipated the usual level of spit to hurtle towards the stage as well as bewilderment from sections of the audience who just wouldn't get the ska-derived sound. The tour had been a rite of passage for The Specials, as they now were, but looking from the sidelines, I felt the only way we could win over the crowd was to give things a little vocal turbo-boost.

As they began performing and I looked out at the heaving crowd in the Camden Music Machine, something snapped inside of me. Maybe they weren't reacting that positively or perhaps I spotted a face in the crowd that looked bored or disinterested – it was a regular expression for punks at that time.

All I know is I needed to get on that stage and I needed to be there now. Without a second thought, I took one bound and found myself next to Terry. There was no going back now. Straight away I was on the mic and to song after song, I belted out my toasting. Then I'd leap about – a perfect foil to Terry's static performance. While he stood bolt upright at this mic, I bounded around like a mad man and I didn't stop 'til I could feel the audience warming up. They loved it.

The band took to it and I was in. My roadying days were at an end. It had taken the best part of eighteen months to prove my worth to the boys, but in their new incarnation as The Specials it seemed the sound system ethos was needed badly.

Bernie Rhodes became our manager and, unsurprisingly, he takes the credit for my formal inclusion into The Specials. Speaking to me recently, Bernie – or Bernard as he now prefers to be known – said the band had been way too 'heady' when he first met them. Too much head and not enough heart, he explained. He saw me as a 'rough diamond', as he puts it, and liked the way I dressed. What he hoped was that my influence would give the act a more raw, earthy feel and that the band would adopt the rude boy look.

He also points out that if this sound was going to be all about black and white uniting on stage, it made sense to have black and white lead vocalists.

Bernie believes to this day that Terry resented his move to put me in the band and that it was this that led to his eventual dismissal as manager. 'Terry was always giving me the eye,' he says. But as you'll see, there may have been other factors that led to us and Bernie parting company.

Rex, who was at the Music Machine gig and roadying for us more and more, takes a different view to Bernie. He says that Jerry had already realised I was a necessary addition to The Specials. After all, Jerry had hand picked everybody else so why wouldn't he pick me?

The experience of playing at gigs like the Steel Pulse concert in Birmingham had probably taught our leader that The Specials needed more rude boy authenticity. In other words, another black person would help – especially one that could toast and make his presence felt.

My view, for the record, is that at the start I was glad to be involved with these guys. I'd been out of borstal for two or three years and, while Jah Baddis had been a great success, the Holyhead Youth Club was winding down and I needed something new. After months on the road with The Specials, it was clear to me what I could contribute to the live gigs. But I don't think it was obvious to the others. I toasted in rehearsals and I toasted from the sound desk at gigs. But in the end, I had to take matters firmly into my own hands. With one leap on to the stage at the Music Machine, I made my point.

The rest is history.

With the tour over, we now became part of the Bernie Rhodes stable of punk acts. 'Stable' is an appropriate word because as far as Bernie was concerned, bands should be fed and watered but otherwise kept in very basic conditions. We ended up in a dingy, dank room in his studio in Camden being worked day after day and sleeping there in a dark, rat-infested hole.

Bernie's studio – called Rehearsal Rehearsals – was on the first floor of a British Rail goods yard just round the corner from Dingwalls, which was already a well-known bar and music venue. We were also within spitting distance of the Camden Roundhouse, which had played host to many great bands over the years. You can see the outside of Rehearsal Rehearsals on the cover of The Clash's first album 'The Clash', released in 1977.

To say the studio was basic was an understatement. Filthy mattresses were rolled up for use at night and there was a barber's chair in one corner. The skylights were caked in all manner of crap and there were bits of wood and scraps of paper all over the floor. The place was a certifiable health hazard.

Personally, I wasn't too fazed by all this. After all, I'd slept in equally bad places including prison cells and the floor of Baggy or Henley Gordon's flats. Some other members of the band found their new living conditions unbearable. Bernie called this his 'boot camp' for bands. It was his way of bashing them into shape.

The punk spirit was supposed to be anarchic and street-wise, so Bernie firmly believed that his acts had to be toughened up. If they didn't last the course, that proved they weren't fit to be up there with The Clash. That was his logic and he stuck to it.

By now, everybody in The Specials was basically on the dole. We were all equally poor and the only way was up. After a few weeks in the boot camp, we began to ask Bernie when he was going to release us into the big wide world. We couldn't just rot there forever after all. So he decided the best place to showcase his new talent was France.

This resulted in an episode that became a key part of The Specials' story. Off we went to la belle France – my first trip abroad apart from growing up in Jamaica. I hadn't been beyond the shores of Britain since the early 1960s and here I was in November 1978, heading off to continental Europe.

There was no plane trip. All our gigs involved endless journeys by van and this was no different – apart from the ferry of course. Bernie hired a van, we all loaded it up and off we went to Dover. Bernie, his right-hand man Mickey Foot and the rest of us. When we got to Dover, Bernie ordered us to unload everything and put the gear on some trolleys at the ferry port. Then he gave Mickey some money and, turning to us, announced that he was driving back to London and 'good luck'.

We managed to struggle across the Channel with all our gear but when we got to the other side, the fun really started. Silverton had a passport from Barbados and immediately fell foul of French work permit regulations. Although, as I found more and more, being black probably had just as much to do with it.

The van that came to meet us on the other side was way too small for all of us and the gear. So now there was the question of who would go in the van and which band members would have to find their own way to Paris – where our gig awaited us.

Lynval and me argued that given the way Silverton had been treated, two black guys were not going to be able to hitch a lift down. As this was my first trip abroad, I was beginning to get a bit freaked out with the way events were turning. And I didn't speak a word of French. Thankfully the guys agreed and, amazingly, Terry, Roddy,

Jerry and Horace were able to thumb lifts down to the French capital.

By this stage, the band's feelings towards Bernie were hardening. If he thought we were going to thank him for this experience, he was very much mistaken. And things were about to get even worse.

We got to the hotel and I just wanted to crash out and forget the last few hours. Me, Lynval and Mickey Foot got there first and the others arrived afterwards. Silverton would eventually turn up, two days later, having sorted out his little immigration issue. But now the fun was really going to start.

While we were chilling out, the hotel manager – a very French-looking lady – suddenly appeared. Were we English? Yes. Did we know that another English band had smashed up one of her rooms? Oh, that's terrible – we replied innocently enough. Turned out it was The Damned that had inflicted the damage. Then without a moment's warning, in walked some local heavies who just walked off with Roddy and Lynval's guitars. Apparently, these were now impounded until we coughed up for what The Damned had done to her hotel.

Presumably the logic ran – you are an English band, they are an English band, you must be responsible for what they did. We went from shock to anger pretty quickly. Lynval shrieked at the top of his voice for his guitar back as it disappeared down the staircase. I just got thoroughly fucked off and began to display my more aggressive side. Very soon, the police arrived.

They took one look at me and Lynval and just drew what were the obvious conclusions to them in those days. Not speaking French didn't help either. 'Jamaicans?' one of them sneered. They didn't want to know our side of the story and just stood there listening to this deranged hotel manager talking at 78rpm about how we were to blame for the wreckage caused by The Damned.

I'd never been a huge fan of The Damned and this wasn't helping.

The manager of the club we were going to play at arrived and we were told by him to get to the venue and he'd sort everything out. Somehow, he did. I don't know how, but the instruments magically re-appeared at the Club Gibus and we did the gig. Needless to say, we weren't welcome back at the hotel and ended up staying at some people's houses that I didn't know.

For me, the whole trip was deeply unnerving. I liked new experiences and I wasn't afraid of being in unfamiliar places – I'd survived prison and borstal after all. But not being able to communicate and being confronted with such a complete lack of logic threw me. Also, and I have to be blunt about this, the obvious racism we encountered straight away at immigration, but more so from the cops and the hotel, really angered me.

We came back seething to the UK but, in one of those odd twists, the episode inspired the lyrics to our first single. All of us would have an input to a song based on what had happened in Paris.

That song was 'Gangsters'.

Bernie was toast. Nobody in The Specials wanted to continue this relationship – he had put us through hell. We had been in awe of him as the man who put The Clash on the map, but now we felt we could move on.

In my view, Bernie was ultimately a good thing for us. We did get a sense of purpose and a taste of fame. But his

way of working was not the way we wanted to continue. Bernie was one step on the ladder but now we wanted a manager who was less frenetic. Rick Rogers would fulfil that role.

But before I come to Rick, there was first the small matter of Silverton. Trevor, Rex and I had known Silverton for a long time. He was a short, stormy guy from Barbados who was prone to throwing his toys out of the pram. We'd often talk in rehearsals – slipping into Caribbean patois. We'd get so animated, in that West Indian way, that I think it used to terrify the other band members.

When he had a strop, it normally involved slamming his sticks down, uttering a few expletives and stomping off in a huff. I'm afraid me, Trevor and Rex used to think this was more funny than threatening.

Trevor thinks that Silverton was less than impressed by the gradual adoption of the ska sound. Like most black guys, he thought ska was 'old man's music' – what our parents had been listening to in the 1950s and 1960s on their radiograms.

But here was Jerry, digging up the ska classics, composing some of his own songs and blending this with the punk and rockabilly sensibility. Silverton probably thought we were all mad.

He stopped coming to rehearsals and then dropped out completely. The whole trip to Paris and sleeping rough in Camden hadn't helped either. He wasn't interested in that kind of life. What he wanted was a steady income and creature comforts. I can understand but, unlike him, I decided to stay the course.

With Silverton gone, Jerry brought in his flatmate John Bradbury. Like Jerry, he was an art school product but at that stage he was working in Virgin Records in the town centre. More importantly, he'd been working with Neol Davies to create an instrumental ska/reggae number that was eventually released as 'The Selecter, by... The Selecter' – and the trombone solo was played by the owner of a local newsagent, Barry Jones.

Neol Davies, you will recall, had been gigging with Ray King but was now heading in the same kind of ska direction as Jerry. Him and Brad had been recording in the garden shed of one Roger Lomas, who went on to do sound engineering work for The Specials as well as work with me throughout the 1980s and 1990s.

Brad left Neol and came on board with The Specials. Pretty soon he'd earned the nickname Prince Rimshot. The way he played the drums was a hundred per cent reggae, always hitting the third beat, and his no-nonsense underpinning of the band's sound was a real asset.

It gave me something to move to. I sometimes felt the band could get a bit slow and ponderous, so Brad's powerful beat was to be welcomed. We needed to keep the pace going. He kept Horace moving on bass and combined with Lynval's cha-ka-ka-ka ska guitar made the audience want to dance. Even though Brad was an art student, he was down to earth and liked a good time. That gave him top marks in my books.

With a new drummer, it was time to make a single, but we didn't have any money. Through a guy I knew called Fraser, we all made the acquaintance of an Irish businessman called 'Jimbo', also known as James O'Boyle. I had no idea what his line of business was but he was only too happy to stump up the cash for our first single, which would be independently produced.

So in January 1979, we found ourselves in the Horizon Studios in Coventry recording 'Gangsters'. By now, Jerry was enforcing a rude boy look in the band. That was fine by me – I'd been wearing tonic suits, Harringtons, Fred Perry and Ben Sherman gear, as well as brogues all my life.

The song 'Gangsters' allowed us to give full vent to our frustration at what happened in Paris. It really seemed to have left a deep scar on the whole band. I kicked off by toasting: 'Bernie Rhodes knows don't argue!' That doesn't need too much explaining. We'd had our fill of his dictatorial approach to managing and I think I spoke for the whole band.

The song was a re-working of Prince Buster's 1964 ska classic 'Al Capone' and included the line – 'Al Capone's guns don't argue'. I just changed that to deal with something more relevant to us.

The lyrics also contained the words: 'Can't interrupt while I'm talking/Or they'll confiscate all your guitars' – a clear reference to the madness in that French hotel. Lynval added his own comment: 'They use the law to commit crime'.

We also recorded 'Too Much Too Young' and 'Nite Klub', but Jerry felt they didn't quite cut the mustard. So we were left with no B-side song for the 'Gangsters' single. Which was when we turned to Neol Davies. He had this instrumental track he'd done with Brad in Roger Lomas' garden shed studio – we could use that.

So on one side of the record we had 'Gangsters' by The Special AKA – that name persisted for a little longer before Jerry finally dumped it – and on the other side was 'The Selecter by... The Selecter', with the sweet shop owner doing a trombone solo and Brad on drums. Now there was the question of a record label and distribution.

As there wasn't a recording contract on the table, Jerry didn't have much option other than to create his own. This gave him the element of control he wanted. When it came to the business side of the recording industry, Jerry was nobody's fool. If anybody knew what was in the small print – it was Mr Dammers.

So although the 2 Tone record label was something we were forced into doing, it also suited Jerry's purposes. When it came to negotiating with the big record companies, Jerry was able to retain artistic direction and revenues that other bands would have had to surrender. Not for nothing does Pete Waterman say that watching the 2 Tone label launch inspired him to set up his own label in the 1980s and launch hi-energy pop on an unsuspecting world.

To show that he'd really gone for the rude boy look and sound – Jerry designed a mascot for the label based on a picture of Jamaican reggae star Pete Tosh. The so-called 'Walt Jabsco' image was born. With Walt, the black and white chequered design, and the 2 Tone logo created by Horace, this had to be one of the coolest looking singles ever made.

Chrysalis couldn't resist the package on offer – great band, great look, great label – and gave in to Jerry over the level of independence he wanted.

Having initially had to beg and borrow – not steal – to get the single distributed, we now had the might of Chrysalis behind us, and the single made a robust entry into the charts. Brad was particularly chuffed because he was drumming on both sides of the single. The deal with Chrysalis was agreed over dinner in a restaurant on Oxford Street.

Rex and Trevor were taken on as full-time roadies on salaries and were even there when we had our scoff with the big cheese at Chrysalis. For Trevor, there was no formal job to give up but he had to do less of his sound system work. Rex threw in the towel at British Telecom and threw in with us full time.

He found the dinner with Chrysalis such a momentous event, it is seared into his memory, that he even recalls Jerry ordered guinea fowl from the menu. Perhaps the oddest fact you'll ever be told about the history of 2 Tone.

Coming on as full-time roadies had an unforeseen consequence. I wanted Rex and Trevor around me. We'd always been rude boys hanging out and our presence gave the band something distinctive. Bernie saw that. Jerry saw that. What I didn't reckon on was that by making them salaried roadies, an 'us and them' mentality would develop in the band.

'Us' being the band and 'them' being the crew. I wasn't prepared to treat Rex and Trevor as second-class citizens because they were crew. In fact, I didn't recognise that distinction at all. Having come out of the sound system scene with the big crews that hung around the house of joy, I didn't think there had to be a formal membership for a band. The sound system was like an extended family but, as I would learn, bands were more rigidly defined.

For the moment though, we were all delighted with our big contract. Chrysalis knew they were on to a good thing. All the ska combos would become very familiar with that record company's offices over the years. Between 1979 and 1981, the Chrysalis walls were adorned in the familiar black and white chequered pattern of ska and the employees wandered round in tonic suits. It all made a welcome change from relying on Jethro Tull and Leo Sayer to make their millions.

As we started gigging off the back of the single and record deal, we also picked up our new manager. Rick Rogers had been managing The Damned – our friends who smashed up the hotel in Paris. Hearing our stuff and catching some of our gigs, he decided that he'd seen the future. For us, it meant return trips to a familiar part of London. Rick's offices were based in Camden, not far enough away from Bernie Rhodes' rat-infested studio.

Rick was ideal for Jerry. A born administrator, who unlike Bernie didn't stick his nose into the creative side of things. He would be our manager through the key years, but I must say that he was never close to either me or Lynval. His favourites were Brad and the sound engineer, Dave Jordan, who joined us for the first album and the infamous 2 Tone tour.

The gigs were what I lived for and we took to the student circuit and they took to us. I ran round the stage like a lunatic. Terry was glued to his mic. He was shy and I was extrovert. His delivery was sardonic and understated, whereas my toasting was in your face.

At the Colchester Institute in 1979, the BBC came along and recorded the gig for their regular *Rock Goes To College* programme (aired in 1980). The programme presenter – with long hair, beard, woolly pullover and posh voice – came up on stage to introduce us. Then we blasted the place away with a rendition of 'Do The Dog'.

Terry: *'Do the Dog'*
Me: *'Not the Donkey'*
Terry: *'Do the Dog'*

Me: *'Don't be a jerk'*
Terry: *'Do the Dog'*
Me: *'Watch who you work for'*

I didn't stop moving for a second, legs and arms everywhere. Lynval skipped across the stage with his guitar, while Terry the epitome of cool – and on a platform behind us, Jerry in what I can only call 3-D specs surveyed the whole scene from his keyboard.

At Aston University, Roger Lomas came along and recorded the gig on a Revox tape-to-tape machine. We forgot about that tape until Roger was given a cassette by a 2 Tone fan in the early 1990s. He discovered to his horror that somehow a bootleg of his recording had been doing the rounds for years. The quality was dreadful, yet people were paying good money for it. So he found the original recording he'd done way back in 1979, went to Trojan Records and released it properly in 1992.

The night Maggie Thatcher was elected Prime Minister on 4 May 1979, we played the Moonlight Club in West Hampstead in London. We had no idea at this stage how much our music would become the theme tunes for everything ordinary kids hated about the new government. From the date of Thatcher's victory to the band's split in 1981, unemployment went up to three million and more. The youth were already having a hard time in the late-1970s, but now they really felt discarded – left to rot on the dole. The Midlands and the north of England were badly hit as the factories started to close. All part of the 'medicine' the new government said the country needed.

Not that everybody disagreed with Maggie. In the south east of England, you'd have found people who thought she was just what Britain needed. In those days, plenty of well-heeled people south of Watford had no idea what was going on in the rest of the country. They called it the 'north-south divide'. For many people in the south of England, the north, with its coalmines, steel works and car factories, might as well have been a different planet.

Maggie's people were in the south east and posher bits of Britain. Our people were in the inner cities and they would very soon show Maggie what they thought of her policies.

We met a whole new breed of ska fan down in London, inspired by a band from the capital – Madness – or the 'nutty boys' as they were often called. They supported us at the Nashville Rooms in Kensington, which I think they considered to be their home turf. We were the visitors to London – this was their town – and there was no doubting they attracted a different sort of fan to us.

It's not a reflection on Suggs and the lads, but some ugly elements turned up to those gigs. As Rex says, our fans were better turned out, stylishly dressed rude boys and girls. Many of the Madness fans were from the growing minority of skins who were flirting with the far right. They didn't dress as well either. Bovver boots, bleached jeans and tight little bomber jackets – a nasty kind of uniform.

As the black man at the front, if anybody was going to get some racial abuse, it was bound to be me. It didn't happen every night, but happen it did. Either low-level stuff like coins being thrown at my feet, or on rarer occasions, an outbreak of 'Sieg Heil' chants and the salutes.

Ranking Roger in The Beat and Pauline Black in The Selecter both experienced such treatment from National

Front supporters. As Roger says now: 'You had to be brave to stand there as a black man in front of a thousand skinheads, have stuff thrown at you and say "fuck off".'

One of my rude boys from Coventry who re-emerged around this time was Bookie. He'd taught me the finer points of burglary and then we'd been caught and sent down together. Finding out I was in The Specials, he started to turn up looking very presentable, carrying a Gladstone bag stuffed with cash – loads of banknotes. In fact, Bookie was earning several hundred pounds a week, which was more than the average band member was on.

So bizarre was this sight of Bookie and his bulging briefcase, that Trevor took to calling it his 'Jack the Ripper bag'. But it wasn't body parts that were in there, but wads of the readies. Clearly my old buddy from borstal had moved on from burglary. He eventually admitted to us he'd become a trader in 'human commodities' – a pimp in other words. One girl he had working the Park Lane area of London was bringing him £500 a week.

Asked about those times recently, Bookie said that just as Thatcher's government was telling Britain's growing army of unemployed to get on their bike, he was just being entrepreneurial.

It certainly confused other members of The Specials when this street kid I'd grown up with used to buy his own plane ticket, come with us on tour in Europe and buy everybody drinks. You just never saw young black guys with that kind of money in those days.

As well as his girls, Bookie would also chaperone wealthy ladies for a few extra bob. The one thing he never did was roadie for the band. Bookie was just happy to turn up every so often, shower his largesse on all of us, then disappear off again to run his 'business'.

With several songs now nailed down in the gigging process, we felt ready to go into the studio and record our first album. The studio was under a launderette on the Fulham Palace Road. We stayed at an apartment provided by Chrysalis on the King's Road. Not very far from SEX – the fashion boutique run by Vivienne Westwood and Malcolm McLaren. This was where the punk royalty hung out, including Sid Vicious and Chrissie Hynde – who made several appearances while we were recording.

As we were arriving at the apartment, Blondie were leaving. We exchanged pleasantries – this wouldn't be the last time we'd rub shoulders with Debbie Harry.

The album – simply called 'Specials' – didn't have a duff song on it. No fillers, no second raters. There can't have been many albums in the history of pop that were bursting with that many hits: 'A Message to You Rudy', 'Do The Dog', 'Nite Klub', 'Concrete Jungle', 'Monkey Man', 'Too Much Too Young' and so on. We were creating a new ska sound that was taking over the bedrooms of the nation's teenagers.

My creative paw prints were all over the songs – both on the writing and the performance. *Smash Hits* summed it up nicely a few months later when they compared my vocals with Terry's:

'It's the contrast between his abrasive Midlands tones and the racy patter of Neville Staple that makes the whole punk reggae idea work; that makes Specials songs like "Blank Expression" and "Concrete Jungle" dramatic stories rather than mere chirpy throwaways.'

We re-worked an old ska song into 'Stupid Marriage', where I toasted at the beginning as a character called Judge

Roughneck. Sometimes I wore a judge's wig on stage when I belted the words out – which were influenced by my own courtroom experiences:

'Rude boy you have been brought in front of me and charged with smashing this woman's window/Before I sentence you what have you got to say in your defence?'

Years later, a ska band formed in Denver, Colorado, in the US, called Judge Roughneck. They're still going to this day and they've supported The Specials and Ranking Roger.

The producer of our first album in 1979 was none other than Elvis Costello. He'd come to our gigs and liked what he heard. Elvis was a huge supporter of The Specials throughout our time together.

Some other high-profile pop stars of that era sidled into our live performances to take a good look at the new ska phenomenon. Mick Jagger of the Rolling Stones included – not such a surprise, as Mick had gone to blues parties in the 1960s and had always been tuned in to the black influence in pop and rock.

Jagger was setting up his own record label – Rolling Stone Records – and having seen us play at one of the London gigs, we were told that he was interested in signing us. Needless to say, nothing came of it. Various accounts say he was 'miffed' about this but Jerry had his own game plan and clear ideas about the sort of record deal he wanted.

Back in the studio we were taking guidance from Elvis Costello. Over a few glasses of wine, he got down to work. What we tried to do was replicate the energy that we displayed on stage. But a common problem with The Specials was that in the studio, we got – as Bernie Rhodes would have said – too 'heady'. The heart lost out to the brain and it showed.

Several other pop musicians turned up during the recording, including Chrissie Hynde from The Pretenders. Chrissie was somebody you couldn't ignore, particularly as she took a shine to Charley Anderson, who was in the studio with us.

Charley was an imposing looking bloke with long Rasta dreadlocks. He was also something of a gentleman. When faced with the attentions of the lead singer of The Pretenders, Charley – who was an old school Rasta, brimming with charm and politeness – just ran a mile. Not the way I might have handled the situation.

His group, The Selecter, had originally been Neol Davies, Brad and Roger Lomas, plus the owner of a local sweet shop, who together had recorded 'The Selecter' single in Roger's garden shed. They had now expanded to a much bigger line-up, which included Charley and Pauline Black on vocals. The newly enlarged band was signed up to 2 Tone by Jerry in no time at all.

To add to the excitement of doing our first album, Jerry had managed to secure the services of Jamaican ska legend Rico – who I'd met in Bristol during my early Jah Baddis days. For Jerry, his presence in the band gave us added authenticity. It created a link from 2 Tone to the original ska sound in Jamaica.

Die-hard ska fans in England – whether Jamaican or skinhead/suedehead – would have understood the significance of Rico's involvement in The Specials. We even billed him as 'The Specials plus Rico'. But to our growing teenage fan base he was probably a closed book – some old guy on the trombone.

However, I was pleased to have him with us and when I went back to Jamaica in search of my mother –

who I'd not seen for nearly twenty years – I took Rico with me.

Rico, in turn, brought with him a musician called Dick Cuthell, whose photograph you can often see alongside us on the 2 Tone tour bus or in the hotel rooms. He's easy to spot with his handlebar moustache. Dick played trumpet and flugelhorn. The two guys always played together and I believe they are still friends. Rico, now a sprightly old man, performs in Jools Holland's band and is still going strong on the trombone.

One story that has done the rounds about the first album is that there was a move to get rid of Roddy – kick him out of the band. I can't say whether that's true but throughout the band's existence, Roddy and Jerry certainly rubbed up against each other the wrong way. Jerry didn't kick Roddy out but he didn't always take his ideas on board either.

Roddy contributed two great songs to The Specials – 'Concrete Jungle' and 'Rat Race'. His guitar style was in no way obviously ska and, as Rex would often say, he just wasn't an obvious inclusion. But Jerry brought him in and on stage – he looked the dog's bollocks.

Roddy was Mr Rock 'n' Roll. It's inconceivable to think about The Specials without Roddy Radiation. Behind the scenes though, I often felt that Jerry undermined his confidence by banging on about his playing. This wasn't quite right, that wasn't quite right and so on and so on.

I know that for years afterwards, Roddy couldn't even talk about his time in The Specials, as those run ins had taken their toll on him. But that's band politics for you – show me a rock combo that wasn't full of recrimination by the end.

To illustrate the front of the first album, we went for a photo shoot in the Coventry Canal Basin, which was then a desolate wasteland. The shot used was of us all looking upwards from a side profile. It became one of those iconic photos of rock history. The photographer was a guy called Chalkie Davies, who now runs a very successful photo agency in New York.

The album was released and began climbing the charts. At the same time, a bootleg surfaced of our gig at the Moonlight Club and it seemed to be doing very well too. For Jerry, it was time to get out on the road and take 2 Tone to the masses. So began the legendary 2 Tone tour.

The line-up was obvious. We would headline, Madness would support and The Selecter would come on first.

Madness were named after the song by Prince Buster which they covered at the time: 'Madness, Madness... they call it Madness'. The original version was released by Prince Buster way back in 1963. He was also the man who penned their hit 'One Step Beyond'. The nutty boys signed to 2 Tone after a meeting with Jerry in London and released the single 'Prince Buster' on the label. But after that number rocketed up the charts, they left for Stiff Records – a punk-era record label famous for giving the world Ian Dury, Elvis Costello and Wreckless Eric.

The line-up could have caused friction with the guys in The Selecter – being the warm up act – but such was the power of the three bands' music that the concert halls were full up from the moment the doors opened. There was no lingering in the bar for the main act. If you were into 2 Tone, you had to catch all three.

And we were all very different.

Trevor, me and Rex – the Rude Boys.
Rex Griffiths, personal collection

On tour – (*left to right*) Rex, Trevor and Terry Hall.
Neville Staple, personal collection

Rex Griffiths (*left*), Trevor Evans (*centre*) with Jerry Dammers. Rex and Trev had just become The Specials' roadies.
Neville Staple, personal collection

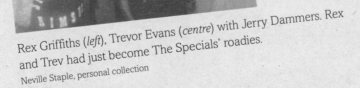

5

ON THE ROAD – SEX, DRUGS AND SKA

Me and Rex
(*foreground*).
Neville Staple, personal
collection

The Specials on stage, January 1980.
© Rex Features

Terry Hall (*left*), Jerry Dammers (*right*) and Walt Jabsco in the middle.

Neville Staple, personal collection

Me, Lynval (*behind*) and Terry (*seated*).

Neville Staple, personal collection

Roddy unwinds with beer in hand.
Neville Staple and Rex Griffiths, personal collections

A lonely breakfast on the 2 Tone tour.
Neville Staple, personal collection

The days of touring in the Luton van were coming to an end. Jerry had decided it was time for 2 Tone to hit the road and now we had our own coach, complete with Walt Jabsco logo on the back.

This intensive tour of the UK took its toll on us all, revealing the real dynamics within The Specials and possibly the reason why we eventually split. But for now, we were a big group that was full of beans. The only way was up. 'Gangsters' and 'Message To You Rudy' had been released as singles and the album, 'Specials', was out and working its way up the album charts.

This was late 1979 and a great way to be ending the decade. Rex and Trevor were now fully paid-up members of the band and were my eyes and ears on stage. They sought out women for me while I performed. The 2 Tone tour allowed me to indulge my planet-sized libido to the max.

All the clichés about being a pop star turned out to be true on that tour. Girls – and boys – followed us slavishly from one venue to the next. The girls would show me their piercings – on their nipples and pussies. I'd be asked to autograph their tits and, having done that, I'd be offered a blow job.

'Nev was like a mini-Beatle for two and a half years,' Trevor quips: 'What twenty-three-year-old man wasn't going to take advantage of everything that was suddenly on offer to him?'

After a gig, some people in the band wanted to get completely pissed (or go to bed early in one case), but I needed a good, hard shag. I was always on the lookout for women. Or more correctly, Trevor and Rex clocked the pretty girls during the gigs while I cavorted like a madman as a foil to Terry's deadpan delivery.

Trevor was on one side of the stage and Rex on the other. Ostensibly to watch out for stage invasions and help out with the instruments, but their real role was to make sure I had some fun afterwards. Trevor would spot some totty who could be 'fished out of the pool', in his words, and then I'd move in for the kill after the gig.

'He feasted on them,' Trevor says of me. As if I was some kind of sexual vampire. I eventually ended up playing a vampire for real, but I'll come back to that later.

There were other blokes on the tour who fancied themselves as pop Casanovas. Roddy and Brad would often be on the pull, along with a couple of the guys in The Selecter. I remember one bloke in The Selecter, who we called Gappa – Arthur 'Gaps' Hendrickson. One night Gappa had pulled a particularly stunning girl and she was waiting in the corridor for him.

I came off stage and, as ever, my adrenalin and everything else was roaring. When I finished my stage act, there was only thing that could calm me down – and she was standing in the corridor that evening. I turned to Trev:

'Who's that?'

Ranking Roger from The Beat was with us that night and he turned to me:

'She's with Gappa.'

'Not any more', I thought. He was on stage giving it his all next to Pauline Black and the rest of The Selecter, so I seized my chance. A little bit of chat up, got her giggling and off we went. I'm afraid I did this many times to other blokes on the tour and Trevor thinks Gappa hates me to this day over that incident. I hope he's more forgiving than that.

In Bristol, I ended up in a threesome, might even have been a foursome – who knows? But with the consent of all involved, it was taped on a video camera set up in one corner of the bedroom and I believe the tape did the rounds of the record industry for a good few years. What they got was any number of BJs, Charlie being snorted off bare skin and so on.

Outside the room was a mountain of a man called Steve English. He'd been working for security on The Clash's On Parole tour and we'd recruited him to do security on our 2 Tone tour. Steve was always up for some fun and that night was no exception. He was banging on the door begging to be let in:

'Come on lads – play the game!'

That wasn't going to happen. He got a little bit crude after that – saying through the door what he'd like to do – and that made us doubly certain not to let him in.

Down the corridor from this debauched scene was Pauline Black, lead singer of The Selecter. You might think she'd have been appalled by all this, but she told me recently she was rather disappointed she didn't get to watch. That night she'd been wandering round the hotel aimlessly and found Rick Rogers 'farting on a bed' and then heard there was a scene going on in one of the rooms.

She found out the next morning and found it amusing. What she wasn't so amused by, though, was the sight of sobbing girls in the corridor, unable to get a taxi home because it was too late. To be brutally honest, they'd have been chucked out of one of our rooms. I'm afraid male attitudes to women had a long way to go in 1979.

We all had double bedrooms – I often shared with Lynval – and Pauline would take these poor waifs and strays back to her room and let them kip on the other bed. As Pauline was pretty much the only woman on the 2 Tone tour, she had a room to herself a lot of the time. Of course, being incredibly juvenile, the rumour went round that Pauline was knocking these girls off.

'I wasn't,' she told me recently. 'I was rescuing your cast-offs.'

In the process of getting women back to our hotel after gigs, Trevor and Rex did resort to some underhand tactics. They would tell the gullible girls that they could take them to Terry Hall's very own hotel room, where who knew what might happen. With Terry being all over the teen mags, these girls came running wide-eyed to be laid by their pop hero.

But once they got to the hotel, Trevor and Rex would invent a cock and bull story about Terry being with another woman already, having fallen asleep, feeling sick or whatever. So they'd just have to make do with some-body else in the band – me for example.

'We might say Terry was already there with a girl,' Trevor says, 'and then they'd be beaten to it. So obviously they were disappointed and needed cheering up.'

Not everybody thought sex and rock 'n' roll went together. Terry was completely loyal to his girlfriend and future wife, Jeanette. If he brought a girl back – because she wouldn't take no for an answer – then he'd sleep on the

floor. A complete gentleman I suppose, but not the way I operated.

Horace was very disapproving of the sex and drugs that inevitably hovered around the band. The difference between him and me was stark to put it mildly. He was a nice boy who took his music seriously and wanted to get to bed early. Horace has said all this on the record, so I'm not being mean or taking the piss. He had no time for the coke-fuelled sex sessions that the rude boys were enjoying down the corridor.

Pauline said that Horace in those days was 'as much fun as sitting on a spike'. But he came from another world to us. I only had to look back a few short years – when I'd been sitting in a cell on remand and then in borstal, or kipping rough at Henley Gordon's pad or being booted out by my abusive father, to know that while the good times lasted, this rude boy had to seize them. I had nothing in terms of money or luxuries in my life. Now I wanted them all.

Jerry took a similar line to Horace, but from a more political standpoint. In the two years that followed, he made a point of trying to get us into the most basic hotels and if limos turned up to drive us from the airport, he'd want to get rid of them. In contrast, I'd be climbing into the back seat with Trevor and Rex.

Factions did start to form within the band, depending on how you wanted to spend the little leisure time we got between sitting in a coach all day and being on stage. Me, Trevor and Rex became the sex-driven rude boys who were like a three-man shagging posse.

Brad, Roddy and Frank Murray – the tour manager – had a similar booze and sex thing going on. Frank ran the 2 Tone tour and was a flash Irishman who had formerly managed Thin Lizzy – who must have been a handful. He also had an eye for the ladies and was in charge of our UK, US and Japan tours in the months and years that followed. I had a lot of time for Frank. He was what it said on the packet: big and brash, and straight to the point. Suited me fine.

Terry, as I said, was loyal to Jeanette throughout, even though he could have had any woman he wanted. Jerry liked a drink but was more likely to be chatting to fans afterwards than satisfying his baser passions. Lynval and Horace would be more than likely tucked up in bed by the small hours.

Lynval was very different to us three rudies. He was slightly older and a great deal more sensible. Trevor says he was 'like our dad before his time' – a very conservative bloke who didn't rock the boat and was always the conciliator in the band – or 'the diplomat' as he was sometimes called.

One night, Rex found himself in the enviable position of having a girl on either arm and was heading back to his and Trevor's room for a ménage-a-trois. At some point, he decided that he only had the energy for a twosome and decided to do Lynval a good deed. Without knocking, he marched into Lynval's room and dropped off one of the girls with him. By all accounts, The Specials guitarist looked horrified.

On the drugs front, Lynval, Jerry, Horace and Terry certainly weren't 'coked up'. I, on the other hand, couldn't get enough. Thirty years ago, cocaine was a rich man's drug. We'd never seen it on the streets of Coventry and my first encounter with the drug was watching record industry people powdering their noses – in London of course. The Midlands would remain largely free of the Bolivian marching powder for a while yet.

Our drug of choice up to then had been weed. We'd smoked it, we'd dealt it, and Trevor had briefly gone through a phase of 'reasoning' with it together with his Rasta buddies in the House of Dread. But now there were more stimulants on offer and, mixed with sex, the resulting cocktail was hard to turn down.

On the coach, we were cooped up with The Selecter and sometimes Madness – though they had their own coach I seem to recall.

We first met Madness down at the Hope & Anchor pub on Upper Street in Islington. From the outside this pub was nothing to look at, but inside was a different matter. A&R men swarmed to this boozer to find out who was playing and whether they should be signed. So it was appropriate that Madness should get recruited to 2 Tone after a conflab in that pub.

Aside from the manager of The Selecter, Pauline Black was the only woman on the tour and she was surrounded by about twenty males.

According to Pauline, she can picture Horace and Terry at the back having some sort of intellectual dialogue, while halfway down the coach some band member would more than likely be having sex 'administered' to them by 'some slapper' we'd picked up along the way. Most of The Selecter would be stoned and the rude boys might be listening to ska and reggae tracks with dirty lyrics just in from Jamaica. Madness, Pauline says, 'were like the boy scouts sitting together'.

Pauline was – and still is – fascinating to say the least. Trevor, Rex and I had never met somebody like her before. The girls we'd grown up with were a bit more passive, shall we say. Trevor used to describe her as 'facety'. A Jamaican term, which I think is clear. He also used to call her a 'pot of pepper'.

Me and Ranking Roger would often be bowled over by the way she expressed herself. If she came out with a word longer than two syllables we'd say, in amazement: 'You've swallowed a dictionary again.'

And she'd reply:

'Not what your ladies are normally swallowing.'

She was her own woman and didn't tolerate any bullshit. Unlike the rude boys present, her background wasn't in the Caribbean. Her mother was Jewish and her father was a Nigerian doctor. They'd put Pauline up for adoption at birth and she ended up being raised by a white family in Romford, Essex. A family, by her account, she had nothing in common with. Pauline was very studious for a start – a regular bookworm.

At school in Romford, half the kids came from Dagenham. A bit like Coventry in that it had a big car factory there – Ford Motors. A lot of the kids at the end of the 1960s were adapting their school clothes to look like mods. Some were skinheads and played reggae music, while others were hippies and into the emerging prog rock sound which Pauline had no time for.

She came to Coventry in 1971 to study biochemistry at the 'Lanch', where Jerry and Horace were also doing their arts degrees. None of them knew each other at that time and as Pauline stayed in Coventry to become a radiographer at the Walsgrave Hospital, it was only in 1978 that she blipped on our rude boy radar.

When she wasn't X-raying patients, Pauline was taking up her guitar to be, as she put it, 'a kind of cross between Joan Armatrading and Joni Mitchell'.

Pauline became a small part of the 1970s folk scene and sometimes performed at an Irish pub called the Old Dyers Arms on a street called Spoon End in Coventry. Not quite the brand of music you would associate with the future queen of ska.

Around the end of 1978, Pauline decided to form a band with her partner Lawton Brown and they came across Charlie 'H' Bembridge and Desmond Brown – who had been playing with Ray King – on the Coventry music scene. They got together and did a small gig at a pub called the Wheatsheaf on Foleshill Road – a road that has a lot to answer for.

At the gig, Lynval spotted them.

By this time, 'The Selecter' was on the 'Gangsters' B-side and Neol was desperate to get a band together to capitalise on the success of the record – and also to get signed to Jerry's new 2 Tone label. Lynval brought Pauline round to meet Neol and they clicked.

The Selecter was born pretty much straight away. Lawton was dropped and his relationship with Pauline ended overnight. The line-up was Pauline on lead vocals, Neol on guitar, 'H' on drums, Gappa on vocals, Desmond Brown on Hammond organ, Charley Anderson on bass and Compton Amanor on guitar.

To quote Pauline: 'Fuck, we were a good-looking band.'

Pauline changed her surname from Vickers to Black to avoid being spotted in the music press by the Walsgrave Hospital, her employer, as she was now taking more and more time off to perform. A helpful GP had written her a sick note, on account of a fictitious knee problem, but photos of her bounding round on stage in the *NME* or *Sounds* were sure to let the cat out of the bag soon enough.

The Selecter first supported us at the F Club in Leeds in July 1979. Pauline had decided to lose her pink spandex jumpsuit and Afro perm for a more rude girl look. She remembers Trevor at the F Club lending her his porkpie hat and, catching her reflection, she realised this was the image she wanted. According to Pauline, Trevor did something obscene immediately after this act of generosity but Trevor denies it vehemently so I'm leaving that story behind.

There was a big cultural gap between me, Trevor and Rex on the one side and Pauline on the other. We were Jamaicans, she wasn't. For instance, Pauline found our eating habits on the tour a bit strange. It's quite funny to hear her describe a very common occurrence:

'Why we were driving round in the dead of night looking for dumplings is anybody's guess. The amount of time we spent looking for fucking dumplings and "soul food", which I'd never heard of before.'

Nobody has to explain to a Jamaican how important dumplings are. But to Pauline, Trevor, Rex and my quest for dumplings was a complete mystery.

The Selecter was an overwhelmingly black band. It even reflected in the music with a heavier reggae beat. Some of the pop critics, notably John Peel, with his late-night show on Radio 1, seemed to think The Selecter had a more authentic feel. *Rolling Stone* magazine preferred them to us as we were sometimes seen as being almost too accessible – possibly a bit too white.

But not as white as our other 2 Tone partners on the tour – Madness. There wasn't a black face to be seen in that combo. The nutty boys came from Camden, a part of London that seemed to loom large in our lives. Home to Bernie Rhodes and Rick Rogers, it was there that they had started out, originally as The North London Invaders.

They released a single called 'The Prince' – in homage to Prince Buster. The old man of ska was getting his recognition from the 2 Tone movement, with us adapting 'Al Capone' into 'Gangsters'. The nutty boys followed up the success of 'The Prince' with another single 'One Step Beyond', which soared up the charts.

There was one thorny problem with Madness – Jerry took issue with their fans. It was clear their gigs attracted a racist skinhead element. We even had members of the audience giving Nazi salutes.

Famously, at the time, Chas Smash was quoted in the *NME*, saying 'We don't care if people are in the NF as long as they're having a good time.' Chas clearly felt the remark had been taken out of context and later responded to the article in the song 'Don't Quote Me On That'. I don't believe the nutty boys had a racist bone in their bodies but there was a growing subculture which had adopted the skinhead look and NF politics. As a multi-racial band there was no way they were going to follow us, so, sadly, they tacked on to Madness.

Pauline felt they could have done more to speak out against those skins – and eventually they did distance themselves from their original followers. But at the time it created an uncomfortable atmosphere. Maybe there was nothing Madness could have done to clear out the racist element and, ironically, 1979 was probably the high-water mark for the NF and their followers.

Three ska bands with hit singles could mean only one thing. We were all invited on to the same edition of *Top of the Pops*.

This BBC programme on a Thursday night wasn't just any old telly. This was when the nation's youth stopped whatever they were doing and sat down dutifully in front of the gogglebox to find out who was topping the charts. Bernie Rhodes says now that he hated *Top of the Pops* but until *The Tube* came along in the 1980s, this was the only weekly pop slot.

It was slightly naff. The presenters were radio DJs like Dave Lee Travis who called himself 'the Hairy Cornflake' on account of being rather hairy and presenting a breakfast show. The music varied dramatically and in one programme you might get some ultra-cool band followed by the St Winifred's School Choir. Don't laugh – they got to number one in the UK charts in 1980.

The show where we performed 'A Message To You Rudy', was broadcast on on 8 November 1979 and had Jimmy Savile presenting – a DJ famous for his gold jewellery, big cigars and corny catchphrases – and he was inexplicably wearing a fez on his head when he introduced us.

Doing *Top of the Pops* was the sign you had made it – it was broadcast into millions of homes. The Specials, The Selecter and Madness had to spend the whole day there rehearsing, recording and waiting while other bands did their bit.

Roddy and Brad got thrown out of the BBC bar for getting a bit too lubricated, while I just tried to get my head round the fact that we were in the BBC TV Centre. On that, and subsequent appearances, it was weird to find yourself sitting next to Gary Numan or Nick Lowe from Rockpile.

While we did 'A Message To You Rudy', Madness did 'One Step Beyond' and the Selecter did 'On My Radio'. Pauline and her combo had recorded that song in the Horizon studios with Roger Lomas. It went on to sell 250,000 singles, which was something of a personal victory for Pauline as the whole point of the song was a protest to radio stations refusing to play ska music.

We had already knocked together a video for 'A Message To You Rudy', which may have lacked the slick production values of today's bands but I advise you to go and download it on YouTube anyway. It's still the coolest and rudest thing you'll watch this year.

The two young black guys walking along at night at the top of the video are Rex and Trevor – of course. It then cuts to the band performing against a totally white backdrop. This same stark white backdrop was used by The Selecter to record a video for 'Missing Words'.

I'm in what looks like an equally white tonic suit (but I'm sure that's the lighting playing tricks) plus black brogues and trilby, and Rico is there on trombone with Dick Cuthell on horn. The video is interspersed with more shots of the two rude boys and some of our fans. It's a great piece of film.

After doing *Top of the Pops*, it was straight back on the coach and charging through the night to be ready for the next gig. Certain concerts on the tour stick in my mind, though not always for the most cheerful of reasons. At Hatfield Polytechnic on 27 October 1979, all hell broke loose.

The press had a field day – skinheads, Stanley knives, fascists and anti-fascists. The Selecter were on stage when things started to get nasty. But by the time we came on, the neo-Nazis were in full swing. Horace has written that he can remember our dressing room backstage being used as a 'first-aid centre' and the *NME* reported that ten people were hospitalised.

Uncharacteristically, mild-mannered Lynval snapped that night – unable to take any more of those meatheads insulting him. Off he went with his guitar into the audience as I watched slack jawed in amazement. Obviously I had to follow.

'That was like the Primrose Hill Park fight,' Trevor muses. 'The tension was just as bad. They came with the intention of causing a lot of trouble – a whole load of National Front skins. They weren't the skins doing it for the fashion. They had the Wrangler or Lee jeans yanked up and the red socks, braces and oxblood Doc Martens – you could tell them apart from the skins who were our fans in the audience – aggro merchants basically. Their clothes weren't about the fashion, they were uniforms.'

Pauline recalls National Front types on one side and Socialist Workers Party types on the other. The whole thing exploded. She felt that wherever we went there was always this friction. Politics was getting more polarised – far left and far right and nothing in between. Our music just seemed to heighten the mood, when in fact we were trying to preach a message of unity.

It just didn't get through to some people.

On a more amusing note, we were getting lots of stage invasions. That would become a hallmark of Specials gigs – a chunk of the audience climbing up with us. Sometimes Steve English would try and chuck some of them back but, in the end, the fans tended to get their way. I didn't mind. If I was surrounded by teenagers going nuts, my mission to entertain had been fulfilled.

The extra weight on stage did sometimes present problems though. On one occasion Jerry's organ disappeared through the floor. Luckily, Jerry remained poised at ground level.

Madness had left the 2 Tone label after 'The Prince' and gone to Stiff Records. They dropped the bombshell that they were leaving the 2 Tone tour early to go to the US. I've no doubt that Stiff were behind this and it caused some irritation on our side. That said, they never cracked the US to anything like the extent we did – in spite of bolting there early.

The nutty boys had their own two roadies – Chalky and Tokes. Frankly they didn't seem to strike up the obvious crew rapport with Trevor and Rex. On the contrary, one of the Madness roadies opened a can of beer in Trevor's face, which led to my rude boy buddy offering to rearrange his face for him in return. A little altercation occurred and let's just say we didn't miss them too much.

As a replacement Jerry brought in a Birmingham band we'd met on our travels called Dexys Midnight Runners. Led – and I do mean led – by Kevin Rowland, they turned up in a uniform of donkey jackets and woolly hats. They put their instruments down and picked them up at the same time. When Kevin wasn't around they were relaxed, but when he showed up, they were looking to him for what they should do next. It was like a disciplined little battalion.

Kevin even took them out on jogs, which you'd never have caught Jerry trying to do with us. The Dexys' lead vocalist had a bit of a temper and it eventually got the better of him. In some hotel reception, he was sounding off and was asked to shut up by The Selecter's roadie.

Hartford was a big black guy who was calm on the surface but, if pushed too far, revealed another more volcanic side.

Kevin wouldn't shut up. In fact, I think he got even louder. Hartford then pummelled him and didn't stop 'til he was sure Kevin was silenced. Trevor says there was blood everywhere and he looked a bit of a mess.

Eventually, the woolly hat-wearing ones left the tour. Pauline has a hazy recollection of an incident on stage which involved a guitar flying through the air and, shortly after that, we saw no more of Kevin Rowland. Though his keyboardist, Mickey Billingham, would go on to play in The Beat – Ranking Roger's band.

As Christmas 1979 beckoned, we played two gigs at the Locarno – which had now changed its name to Tiffany's. It was good to be back in the old place. Looking up from the stage, I had to allow myself a wry smile as I thought about all those shags I'd had up in the dark balconies – and Pete screaming: 'This is for Nev and the Boys'. There were plenty of ghosts from my past.

But this was now a changing Coventry – and not changing for the better. The car factories were closing and I had mates telling me how lucky I was to get my break with The Specials. Everything was going to hell in a handcart. There was high unemployment, police harassment and a government that didn't seem to care.

Our brand of music was well suited to the new climate. The lyrics talked directly about what was happening on the streets.

For my part, The Specials saved me from a life of crime. While the band wasn't paying me anything, some low-level crime – dealing in weed mainly – continued. But once I was a fully paid-up member of The Specials, I went legitimate. That had one immediate downside as Yvonne – mother of my daughter Andrea – took me to court for maintenance payments. We settled on the court steps to the tune of £25,000, which was no small sum in those days. That came straight out of my royalties.

My brushes with the law didn't come to a complete end as a result of joining Britain's top pop act. I was arrested at some point for non-payment of a fine – I can't remember the exact details – and was driven off to the police station.

Sitting in the back seat in a sheepskin coat, I had two uniformed jokers at the front singing 'Too Much Too Young' to keep me entertained. I ended up in a cell again – 'til the band busted me out of there.

When the royalties did start to flow in, I bought a few luxuries. A BMW that cost me a couple of grand, I put a deposit on a house and most importantly of all, I decided to buy myself a plane ticket to Jamaica. It was time to go back and meet my real mother.

Lynval, Rico and myself got on board that plane for Kingston and I didn't know what to expect at the other end. I was five years old when I'd come to Rugby. Like so many of us who had come over to Britain, we had left family and friends behind.

Arriving in the Jamaican capital in 1979 was a sobering experience. It was a rough and violent place, even compared to today. At first I just wanted to get straight back on the next plane to England and forget it.

Outside our hotel, people were begging for our clothes or our shoes. Either that or they wanted to rob us. I put up with Kingston for a week but didn't enjoy it at all. Rico told me how to get out and visit Mandeville and then my native

Christiana. I'd have to get on a minibus that left Kingston semi-regularly.

When I arrived in Christiana, it was a largely unfamiliar place – some dim and distant memories, but otherwise unknown to me. My mother had apparently been told I was coming but, incredibly, we passed each other on the street that day without either mother recognising son, or son recognising mother. It had been so many years.

Eventually, I got to the house. It wasn't the same house I'd grown up in – that had been a flimsier construction with walls covered in newspaper and a thatched roof. The house of my childhood had been replaced by a pleasant little house made of brick. There was running water, which we never had as kids, and an inside toilet, instead of a shed with a hole dug in the ground.

Somebody gestured to me – the woman walking towards us was my mother. Now she knew who I was:

'Oh God. My big son come back.'

I gave her a hug.

'I looked at you and I pass you,' she smiled.

We sat outside the house and I told her all about what I was doing now. But then our conversation turned to more familiar territory. We chatted about the mongoose. Me catapulting the birds. The rolling calf.

And we carried on talking 'til night fell.

Chrissie Hynde of The Pretenders offers her help at the recording of 'Specials'.
Neville Staple, personal collection

In the studio recording our first album with Elvis Costello (*centre*) and me (*right*).
Neville Staple, personal collection

Yours truly toasting and giving it some tambourine in the recording studio.
Neville Staple, personal collection

Rico Rodriguez – legendary ska trombone player.
Neville Staple, personal collection

(*From left to right*) Terry, me, Lynval and Jerry. Filming the video for 'Gangsters' at the Camden Roundhouse.
Neville Staple, personal collection

Me in my favourite place – on stage.
Neville Staple, personal collection

Bernie Rhodes knows … don't argue!
© Bernie Rhodes

6

THE 2 TONING OF AMERICA

THE 2-TONING
OF AMERICA

SPECIAL A.K.A. IN THE U.S.A.

NME front cover, 9th February, 1980.

© New Musical Express

Before going Stateside, there was Europe to contend with. Our first trip over there had been a bit too eventful for most of our tastes. However, the Paris hotel fiasco had inspired 'Gangsters', which we performed on various Euro pop shows in the summer of 1979.

Going to Europe could be a disconcerting experience for the black guys in the band. A pattern developed on the continent, where the fans loved us but our reception outside the TV studio or concert hall would verge on the hostile.

I'm not going to duck the issue. There were a lot of racists in Europe – particularly on the streets of Germany. When we drove through what was then communist East Germany to get to our gig in Berlin, Lynval and I got looks that said it all.

I seriously think some of those people had never seen a black man. There was a coldness and unfriendliness that I found totally alien.

Once we were in front of the German fans it was a completely different story. All I can say is that those who turned up to our gigs must have been the most progressive people around at the start of 1980.

It was a weird experience travelling across what was then a Warsaw Pact country – part of the Soviet Empire and all that. We even went through the big concrete wall to get to West Berlin. To add to the sense of occasion, our hotel was slap-bang in the middle of the red-light district – not something I had too much of a problem with.

Years later, we found out that our German tour had inspired some fans to set up their own ska bands. I chatted recently with a guy called Tobias Meyer who is the guitarist in the German ska band The Skaliners. He admitted that they couldn't nail down my toasting style, but 2 Tone had been a huge influence.

He told me one funny story:

'One time, I dreamt of a real cool ska song. I immediately got up and wrote down the chords and the bassline. When I was finished I suddenly realised that it was very close to "Little Bitch" by The Specials, just with a different chord. So I guess you can say that we were even influenced by The Specials in our sleep.'

Another German band that is still going are beNUTS. Organist Oliver Zenglein and trumpet player Jesko Krüger found out I was writing this book and contacted me to say that our version of the ska classic 'Monkey Man' was what originally inspired them to form their band. It's been a huge ego boost over the years to have bands and musicians come up to me and say that it was our gigs that made them take the big step to forming their own combos.

After Berlin, we drove all the way to Amsterdam where I decided to use the sauna in the hotel. Rex and Trevor came along and we stood there in skimpy towels while a health spa attendant lost the plot:

'There are some people in there. I do not know if it is right.'

He then checked and whoever was in there was happy to have us pop in as well. So into the hot box we marched to find ourselves in the company of three completely naked, stunning, blonde Dutch girls. We had to look straight ahead and cling to our towels. This was more than embarrassing – even for me.

But the women didn't seem to give a damn and carried on chatting and laughing. After a few minutes, I eyed Trevor and Rex and we gingerly removed our towels. When in Rome I suppose – or Amsterdam. Nothing happened, by the way, apart from a nice conversation, but it wasn't for want of trying.

Then it was off to sample the local dope cakes and porn cinemas. This was a whole new experience. We'd simply never been in a place like this before.

While we were sampling Amsterdam's ganga laced cookies, the band had a new road crew member – Rob Gambino. There was a reason for his arrival – Horace was keen to have a 'professional' road crew. He's written in his own book on those times that Rex and Trevor didn't quite make the grade in his eyes. So in came Gambino – who soon got the nickname 'Our Kid' on account of coming from Worksop where they use that expression a lot. This was a bit of a slap in the face to my rude boy mates.

All I can say is that Rex and Trevor slogged their guts out for the band – first with no pay and then on a modest salary. If the band meant anything, it was doing things in a different way to the monsters of rock that the punks, and then us, hated. We didn't want to be some slick supergroup – Jerry was still busy turning away limousines and making sure we stayed in the drabbest hotels.

It was when we went down the road to becoming a mainstream band, and some members of The Specials got a little too big for their boots, that the rot set in. By the way, I don't believe that Horace was motivated by any malice – but I think he was wrong on Rex and Trev. I sincerely believe we paid a heavy price when they eventually threw in the sweaty towel for the last time. Before that happened though, we had America to conquer.

The front page of the *NME* on the week of 9 February 1980 said it all: 'The 2 Toning of America'. With a picture of Terry, Jerry and Roddy at a press conference set against a giant stars and stripes that themed the whole of the front of the magazine.

An *NME* reporter, Paul Rambali, even joined us on the tour, slogging across the United States doing gigs in Oklahoma, New Orleans, San Francisco, New York and even the Mormon citadel of Salt Lake City.

Terry opened our first gig in New York in his usual sardonic style:

'This is our first ever gig in America… and we just can't say how pleased you must be to have us here."

Madness had already got to the Big Apple but it became clear to us early on that we were going to make a much bigger impact than the nutty boys. One thing that was going to help was being the support act for The Police on the first leg of their tour.

Like The Clash, The Police were a good choice for us and we formed something of a mutual appreciation society. For one thing, Sting – like Joe Strummer – had taken reggae influences on board. Ignoring the idea that white guys did punk and black guys did reggae, he

wrote songs that crossed over and incorporated both styles.

By the time we hooked up with the trio, they had released two albums – 'Outlandos d'Amour' and 'Regatta de Blanc' – as well as the number one singles 'Message in a Bottle' and 'Walking on the Moon'. Not only would I work with Sting on this tour, but we would gig together a decade on when I returned to the US. He was a huge fan of the ska sound from the word go.

We did a press conference of sorts in a club called Hurrah's in New York. It was like arriving in another world. Outside, there was a big crowd of people pressing to get in. I had to pinch myself – were they here to see us? Chrysalis really had done their work in the US ahead of our arrival and we were being heralded as the next big thing after punk.

New York was still in thrall to punk. I don't think they'd got over the New York Dolls yet and the fashions said so. We rolled up in our limos – with maximum disapproval from our leader – and got a heroes' reception. The cameras never stopped clicking all the time we were at Hurrah's – even when we were trying to set up for the gig. There seemed to be no shot the paparazzi were willing to miss.

The venue was medium sized – not huge – and we did a respectable enough gig there. Not one of our best but a good opener. I think we Coventry lads were still wrestling too hard with jet lag to give it our all.

The crowd loved 'Nite Klub' because it was marginally more punky. During 'A Message to You Rudy' I could see some confused faces. It was going to take a while to get the sound of Kingston through to our new hip fans in New York.

At the end of the gig, I couldn't help noticing that Trevor and Rex were packing up a little quicker than usual – with a real sense of urgency in fact. Of course, they'd pulled. But little did they know that on this occasion Jerry and Roddy had already made off with their girls.

In New York, we stayed at the Gramercy Park Hotel. This was something of a rock star's favourite haunt at the time. Other guests had included our old friends in The Clash, Debbie Harry and David Bowie. Trevor and me were up on the 52nd floor looking down at the little cars below, when both of us laughed.

I knew what he was thinking – the same as me. We'd both gone from prison cells to swanky hotel rooms in just a few short years. Here we were, borstal boys on Lexington Avenue, with rooms paid for by Chrysalis and all the rock star trimmings laid on – if Jerry would let us have access to them.

The press reviews of our gig were uniformly positive, with one journalist quoting a Specials song title – that it was the '(Dawning of) a New Era'.

We went off to join The Police in New Orleans – who could have viewed the reception we were getting with trepidation. Lesser bands would have gone for filler support acts, preferably ones that didn't blow them off the stage. But Sting and the boys were made of better stuff. They knew we were a class act and were happy to share the stage with us.

New Orleans was a revelation. Let's just say the Deep South was not completely politically correct. For some guys down there in 1980, black guys were people you saw pumping petrol. Certainly not driving into the petrol station in a limo and getting their driver to buy some.

When Pauline Black toured the US with The Selecter, they made an even bigger impact. After all, they were a majority black band and they dressed snappily.

'We could silence everybody at a truck stop in the southern states of America, stone dead, just by walking in to have something to eat. A big bunch of black guys and me would stroll in. Everything went quiet. There would be no talking for about ten minutes until a waitress came over to take our order,' she said.

Pauline once had a very scary experience with The Selecter outside the set of the TV series *Dallas* – the Southfork mansion in Texas. The band were having their photos snapped, sitting on a white picket fence, with the famous building behind them, when a bunch of rednecks turned up in a pick-up truck replete with baseball bats. They told The Selecter's coach driver to move the 'niggers' on.

Nothing quite that bad happened on our tour – though we had some interesting scrapes.

After a great gig in New Orleans, me, Rex and Trevor decided to take one of the limos laid on by Chrysalis and go down to Bourbon Street to check out the bars. After that, we decided to go to a party in the suburbs that a girl at the gig had invited us to. It wasn't her party, but she was sure we'd be welcome.

We drove through a very swanky part of town and ended up outside a big colonnaded mansion – like something out of *Gone With the Wind*. There were rich kids everywhere – in the grounds, on the veranda, trashing this beautiful nouveau-riche mansion. It was like a scene from *Porky's Revenge*. Needless to say every single person there was white.

We looked at each other and wondered if we should dare go anywhere near the place. I'd never been to a party like this in my life. It was all a far cry from the blues parties of Leicester. Still, we had arrived and I wasn't going to drive off now.

Full of swagger – with Trevor and Rex trying to look cool behind me – I strode up to the imposing front door and knocked loudly. It opened and a very worried white face blubbered behind it:

'No... no... I'm sorry.'

The girl who had invited us suddenly appeared and told her mate off:

'Like, do you know who these guys are?'

After a bit of explanation, the tune changed and we were let in.

'Fuck... Neville Staple from The Specials,' then turning to Trevor, 'you must be Lynval.'

Well, we do all look the same don't we? That wasn't the first time the black members of The Specials had been mixed up. I can think of at least one British journalist who confused me for Lynval.

Our gig in Norman, Oklahoma, turned out to be even more interesting, as the state seemed to be in the midst of a Ku Klux Klan uprising when we arrived. There were state troopers in the streets clashing with demonstrators. We saw all this on the television, not with our own eyes, thankfully, but the hotel advised the rude boys to stay indoors after the gig.

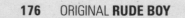

The Police cancelled their appearance, but we went on to play. At the time it felt like the Midwest wasn't our natural home. But I'd never been willing to let an audience reject me. I was determined we wouldn't end up as an east coast/west coast-only attraction.

After all, if we could appeal to kids back in England from Brighton to Glasgow and Blackpool to Norwich – why shouldn't we win over the Midwest of America? Eventually, I was proven right.

About five years after we left Norman, Oklahoma, a ska record label was set up there called Megalith Records, run by Rob 'Bucket' Hingley, the lead vocalist of American ska band The Toasters. I ended up gigging with them and some of the label's other acts in the 1990s. Far from being barren territory, Oklahoma became the unintended American headquarters of ska's third wave.

It was in Oklahoma that we found out our recently released EP 'Too Much Too Young' had gone to number one in the UK charts. Rick Rogers and Frank Murray took us into a room in the hotel and laid on some champagne. Chrysalis obviously felt their investment in us was paying off. All of us were over the moon but, looking back, that day marked a turning point for the band – and not a good one.

The very rock star mentality that Jerry hated began to seep in. Possibly it was something that was unavoidable. To give you an example of what I'm talking about, Rex recalls Brad sitting in an airport lounge shortly afterwards, waiting for our flight, flicking matches at Horace.

Flick… flick… flick…

Somebody said: 'Oi Brad – you'll have to pick them up.'

To which he replied: 'What do ya think I've got a roadie for?'

I looked across to Trevor and Rex and saw a picture of gloom and anger. Not just increasingly detached from us by the 'band' versus the 'crew' rubbish, but now treated as the servants, our hired skivvies. It wasn't a situation that would end well.

The next stop was Denver, which Trevor loved and it took his mind off the growing rift between him and some of The Specials. This part of America was full of mountain men in checked shirts. The scenery was breathtaking and we loved being surrounded by snowy mountains. The only problem was, they didn't really want to hear a ska outfit, they wanted an old-time rock band. Even I couldn't win them over.

Still, Trevor went off and scored some weed off a hillbilly and that kept us in the right mood. In fact, he got a huge bag of the stuff. I'd never have guessed you could buy such good quality gear in Colorado.

From Denver we went on to Salt Lake City and then Seattle. It was in Seattle that I think we matched The Police for stage presence and audience adulation. I don't believe anybody in that crowd was expecting the raw energy that we chucked at them.

By this time, having polished off a European tour and trekked across the US, the band was pretty wired. But when we went on stage, instead of being knackered we went into hyperdrive. It was as if we'd all gone a bit mad. None of us had slept properly for months and half of us didn't care if we ever slept again. With a steady supply of booze, drugs and beautiful women, I just wanted this lifestyle to go on forever.

In Seattle, Rex turned up for gig duty looking like the snappiest of rude boys. Sunglasses, smart tonic suit, trilby,

brogues – the lot. Trevor instantly told him to go back to his room and change. Rex, he felt, had misjudged the growing mood towards them.

Truth is, my two rude boy buddies often used to look better than the band members. They'd even get asked for autographs after gigs.

But now Trevor began to say to these fans: 'Look, I'm not in the band – OK?'

However, the girls would respond: 'We don't care!'

They'd seen Trevor and Rex up on stage with us during the performance and that was good enough for them. This undoubtedly pissed certain people off in The Specials and can't have helped the feeling in certain quarters that the lads should be cut loose.

Canada was the next stop. All we had to do was nip over the border from Seattle to Vancouver. It was at this point that me, Trevor and Rico had a spot of bother with the Canadian 'mounties' – the police at the border. Going through our bags, they chanced upon the weed we'd scored in Denver, plus a whole load of dope-related paraphernalia.

All of it was confiscated and a big ticking off was given to us – not the most auspicious start to the Canadian leg of the tour but in the finest traditions of rock 'n' roll.

There was one slot supporting The Police and then we were offered our very own date for the following night at a venue called the Commodore Ballroom. It seemed we'd already generated a lot of excitement and anticipation in advance of our arrival. One local journalist wrote afterwards that Vancouver normally adopted a sound after its time was well gone. But with us, they listened for five minutes and said 'we'll take it'.

We didn't disappoint. The crowd loved us both nights.

Back across the border a gig in Portland, Oregon, was pulled as Sting had a sore throat. This hurried us down to Los Angeles and the fantastic Whiskey a Go Go. The venue was nothing much to look at from the outside – but it had been at the forefront of the LA music scene for many years. The Byrds, Alice Cooper and Love had all played there and The Doors had some kind of residency at some point before Jim Morrison called it a day in a bathtub in Paris.

In the years that followed Mr Morrison, punk and new wave acts took over the billings. Elvis Costello had played there in late-1977 as had The Jam and now, in February 1980, we had four nights to ourselves. Our support band was the all-female Go-Go's – appropriately named – with lead vocalist Belinda Carlisle.

The Go-Go's were kind of new wave with 1960s musical influences going on. There was a touch of the B52s in there. Belinda had flirted with punk as the drummer in a band called The Germs and was then called Dottie Danger – thank God she ditched that name. She then formed the Go-Go's in 1978 and never looked back. In both the US and the UK, Belinda and the girls became a regular support act for us and were great people to be with.

Belinda eventually launched a solo career, ditched the new wave sound and went all power pop with the single 'Heaven is a Place on Earth' which went to number one in the UK and US in 1987. For now, though, they were a perfect complement to us.

Arriving at the venue, I had no idea that Jerry was about to do his nut. When we got to the Whiskey a Go Go, the whole place had been painted in black and white check both inside and out.

To be honest, I loved it. This was near enough to Hollywood and what did we expect? Some people from Chrysalis had gone a bit over the top, but that was record company marketing folk for you. To Jerry though, it smelt of cop out. He'd already told the *LA Times* that he wasn't enjoying the American tour and had preferred a school trip to the Soviet Union.

None of this carping made much sense to me. I wasn't as political as Jerry and I didn't understand all this arty angst. So what if they'd painted the bloody place black and white – as long as they didn't paint us into the bargain.

All this was symptomatic of a big difference between me and Jerry – a guy I otherwise have massive respect for. I wanted the good times and I wanted them to last. He wanted sack cloth and ashes. My heart raced at the sight of a limo, while his heart sank. Well, I'd had to drive round in a car with bald tyres and no MOT that got me stuck in borstal for a year, so I sure as hell wasn't sending any limousine packing.

As for the crassness of the recording industry – bring it on. I could cope. It must have taken the boys and girls at Chrysalis a lot of effort to get the whole building painted like that and it meant they liked us. Why throw sand in their face? But we did. They were balled out.

The Whiskey was heaving as we limbered up backstage. Outside was a seething mass of people pushing at the doors to get in. We found out that Neil Young turned up but then walked off when he saw the scene. A reporter from *Sounds* magazine wrote that Nigel Harrison – then the bass player in Blondie – also showed but got bopped on the nose by an impatient queuer.

Not only were we doing four nights at the Whiskey, but two sets each night. I wasn't too troubled but I think some band members found it hard going. Jerry said afterwards that it left The Specials drained of energy.

We started with '(Dawning of) a New Era' and then got into our stride with 'Do the Dog'. At this point, the black and white balloons laid on by Chrysalis were torn down or popped. 'Doesn't Make it Alright' went down great guns as did 'Little Bitch' and 'Gangsters'. I think we finally left the stage at around three in the morning.

I was described during the US tour as 'a cross between Joe Frazier and Wilson Pickett' with my leaps in the air and on-stage acrobatics. The Americans had no hang ups about showmanship. If you gave them a hundred per cent, they gave you their support. That was the kind of bargain between entertainer and audience that I had always strived for.

The daytimes in between were recovery periods. In LA we were staying at the Tropicana Motel on Santa Monica Boulevard and I spent a good deal of the time on my back by the pool eyeing the local talent walking past with Trevor and Rex on sun loungers nearby. Every so often exchanging knowing winks and laughs. Three rude boys still in awe of the whole experience we were having.

As I sipped my cocktail, Horace drifted past and gave Trevor and Rex his 'what are you two doing here living it up like pop stars' look. He couldn't say anything with me present. I wouldn't have tolerated it, but I think in his mind the days of rude boy roadies were numbered.

The tour continued to San Francisco where poor Dave Jordan got held up at gunpoint in his hotel room. A fact he didn't share with us immediately. In fact, he went very quiet for a few days and then spilt the beans. Back in those days none of us had handled shooters – being British and gun free.

In my youth, it was all good clean fun with a Stanley knife.

We played to a crowd in a theatre that went completely wild. This was in spite of the fact that we'd had to move venue because the original concert hall had crap sound facilities. So we'd tested the audience's patience a bit, but they were more than happy to forgive us. The *San Francisco Examiner* reported the gig in a state of amazement and were particularly taken by my antics:

'Joining Hall on lead vocals is Jamaican Neville Staple whose calypso-reggae singing style and rugged panther-like movements (leaping at times on to speaker boxes) provides The Specials with, well, something very special.'

Minneapolis brought a gig in a club called Duffy's where I made an interesting discovery. They had a strip act for the ladies earlier in the evening. This seemed like a perfect opportunity to let off some steam, get butt naked and maybe impress an American girl. Well, it certainly impressed the local newspaper, the *Minneapolis Tribune,* which wrote:

'Staple reportedly had joined the line-up of male strippers that is a regular Monday night feature at Duffy's, so apparently was warmed up even before the set began.'

Another local paper had me pictured in nothing but my briefs and sunglasses. As Rex always points out, I am an uncontrollable exhibitionist. The rest of the band – whose presence I was completely unaware of – watched slack jawed, convinced I'd finally lost my marbles.

Next stop was the home town of Al Capone – gangster inspiration for the Prince Buster hit of the same name – the city of Chicago. Completely unexpectedly, this turned out to be a city where we encountered the most overt racism. Again, I've got to say it wasn't from the fans, but there were two incidents that stuck in our minds.

Firstly, we all had to check out of the hotel that had been arranged by the tour management, after they gave me, Lynval and Rico the filthiest looks at reception and pretty much refused to let us in. Rick Rogers decided we should get out of there. We might have looked a sight for sore eyes after several hours on the coach, but everybody present knew what the real issue was.

Rex and Lynval then had the oddest experience when they walked into a local shop and the woman in charge ducked under the counter with her hands in the air, shrieking:

'Please… don't!'

Rex leant over the top of the counter.

'Excuse me love… what's going on?'

She heard the English voice and slowly stood up.

'I'm sorry. I'm really sorry.'

Clearly there were some race relations issues around at that time. Rex got over it by getting off with a beautiful local girl who carted him off to the suburbs. She then drove him back in the morning just in time for our coach which was leaving town.

Around this time there were various issues about whether Trevor and Rex should be travelling with the local crews or whether they could travel in the band coach. I hated all this. We were going from being one happy family to living up our own backsides. Trev and Rex did not have to travel third class. They'd done their time with the band, worked for nothing in the early days and I wished some people would have given it a rest.

Going back to Canada, we took on Toronto. It was here that I first met a guy called Raymond Perkins. Him and another bloke, Michael Budman, went on to set up one of Canada's biggest clothing chains, Roots. But back then, he was in charge of a venue in Toronto called the Dub Club.

Raymond was a Londoner and had experienced all the punk antics there and in Amsterdam. In his new home city he was getting more into reggae and Motown – until we came along. Like a lot of people, he was blown away by the mixed-race message and the way we had taken ska and given it a new energetic spin.

'When you saw them – the black and white, the suits, the style – punk had run its course. Seeing these guys looking sharp – it wasn't far removed from punk but cleaned up and very modern. It worked.'

From this encounter, Raymond would start providing me with outfits – clothes and shoes – for something like ten years. It was my rude boy attitude, way of speaking and demeanour that worked for him. He also referred to me as 'that complete pussy hound'.

The tour to end all tours began to reach its conclusion on the eastern seaboard of the US, with Boston then New Haven and finally Long Island. We were supposed to play a venue called My Father's Place which was then changed to another venue called Speaks because of high ticket demand.

Once more, sitting round a table, we ran into Debbie Harry. Or rather she wandered over to us. I didn't recognise her at first because the lead singer of Blondie had gone and dyed her hair black. She seemed to be going through some sort of goth incarnation.

A few minutes on, some guy approached us and slapped a big bag of cocaine on the table. I hasten to add he had nothing to do with Blondie.

'You guys... The Specials... I just love you... have this... please.'

I made my way to the gents' toilet. As I was chatting to somebody by the cubicle, an old guy with a big mop of white hair tapped me and asked:

'Are you having a toot?'

I looked straight into the face of Andy Warhol. We didn't share a line or anything. It was just rather an odd moment in my life – me and one of the artistic greats of the twentieth century in a gents' bog.

We came back from America almost convinced we hadn't cracked it. In fact, the band has beaten themselves up about this tour for a long time. The strain, the pain, the anguish. Blah, blah, blah. But in point of fact, we had touched a lot of young kids' lives out there. It just wasn't immediately obvious.

But in the near future, America would show us it had listened.

Touring the United States.
Neville Staple, personal collection

Trevor sneaks up on Police drummer Stewart Copeland.
Neville Staple, personal collection

John Bradbury (*left*) and me enjoying the latest technology.

Neville Staple, personal collection

Sting on stage during one of the gigs we supported.
Neville Staple, personal collection

The Specials – when it seemed nothing could stop us …
Neville Staple, personal collection

7

THE SPECIALS – THE RUDE BOYS LEAVE

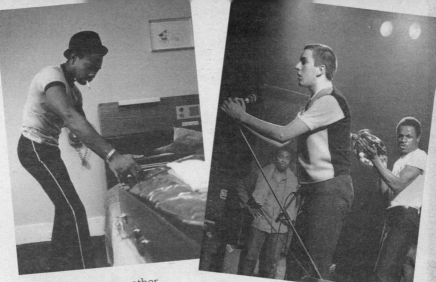

Rex unpacks in yet another hotel bedroom.

Rex Griffiths, personal collection

Terry (*foreground*), me (*right*) and Rex (*background*).

© Philip Grey

Put in a cage and pelted – the joys of appearing on *Tiswas*.

Neville Staple, personal collection

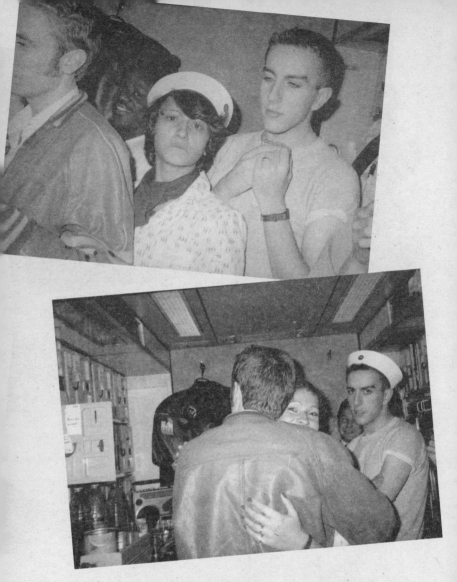

Party on a plane – note the transfer of headwear from stewardess to Terry's bonce. How did that happen?

Neville Staple, personal collection

The captain of the plane gave me his hat and the crew laid on the bubbly. This must break all the regulations!

Neville Staple, personal collection

(*Clockwise from top right*) The Captain enjoys a drink; me and Horace Panter; Jerry Dammers with a dancing steward; Dick Cuthell with full glass; Jerry pours himself another.

Neville Staple, personal collection

Paris again. This was March 1980. Rick Rogers announced that we were flying to France with The Cure in support and the money was good. As an added incentive – to a group of people who were beginning to go loco – he said we could bring our partners along as well.

Ideta never came to my performances. Instead, a girl called Jill from Coventry accompanied me to Paris. By this stage I had girlfriends in several cities, but Jill was somebody I was seeing a lot of. So off went The Specials, like a small army, to the French capital.

Europe 1 and the French record store Fnac – a sort of HMV equivalent – were presenting the show with us headlining, The Cure supporting and a band called Diesel. The venue was a place called Pavillon Baltard and the tickets would have set you back fifty francs. Certainly not small beer in those days.

Pavillon Baltard was in the Les Halles district of Paris and kids from the working-class suburbs would come in and hang around looking for fights. When we arrived, there was a growing skinhead presence in the area and, as we were to find out, they weren't necessarily our friends.

The Cure, with Robert Smith on vocals, had just scored a big hit with 'A Forest' but we were definitely the lead act. Their glory days were ahead of them. Our glory days were beginning to look like they might be behind us – the cracks in the band were starting to show.

Brad and Jerry were arguing. Horace wasn't happy with the level of 'professionalism'. Roddy felt his input was being ignored. Jerry wished everybody would do as they were told. Not only did The Specials bring together people from very different musical backgrounds – the band forced several huge talents and egos into close proximity, week after week, month after month. The hatred was starting to bubble to the surface.

The first two people to really get it in the neck were – you guessed it – Trevor and Rex.

When we got to Paris, a brand new keyboard had to be hired for Jerry. Poor old Trevor was trying to set it up but frankly didn't have a clue what lead was supposed to go where. He was still trying to figure it out when Mr Dammers arrived in a less than good mood. We were supposed to be rehearsing but the keyboard was not in any way functional. Jerry instantly rounded on Trevor and balled him out in front of everybody:

'Trev… what's going on! This is my life!'

At which point, Trevor and Rex decided to quit. They were replaced by a couple of Our Kid's mates.

The Paris gig ended up being our second bad experience in that city. The aforementioned French skinheads turned up in droves and behaved like a punk crowd in London circa 1976. Being a rude boy in a tonic suit, I didn't take well to being spat at or having beer thrown over me.

One particular skinhead caught my eye and as my blood boiled, I launched into the crowd to dispense some

Primrose Hill Park style-justice. His behaviour improved after that.

Trevor and Rex, it now transpired, had been hatching a little plan. Trevor had picked up a few keyboard tips while touring with us and Rex had been teaching himself the drums while setting up Brad's kit night after night. So they went off and formed their own combo – 21 Guns.

In no time, they had a BBC recording session with the great John Peel. Every band setting out to be both cool and famous in those days had to get a Peel recording session and I was bursting with pride when the guys got one. I set up a record company, Shack, and began managing them.

Their vocalist to start with was a guy called Richard who was very stylish but, like The Specials' first vocalist Tim Strickland, didn't quite hack it on stage. They needed a more powerful vocalist and so got in contact with a bloke called Gus Chambers.

He had taken over from Terry Hall as lead vocalist of punk band The Squad. The sound got grittier and more urban and they released a single called '21 Guns'.

On a sad note, Gus Chambers committed suicide in October 2008, but remained active in various bands right up to the end.

Rex remembers getting a letter from his bank shortly after quitting The Specials to say that his last salary cheque from the management had been taken back from his account. That was a bit brutal in my view though very 'professional' of course.

I found myself then as a solitary rude boy in The Specials. It was really the first time for ten years I'd been without Rex and Trevor around. We had built the Jah

Baddis sound system, bought and stolen more reggae and ska records than I could count and gone through the glory years of the 2 Tone era – and now they were gone.

Far from improving the band's politics, I think it was beginning of the end for The Specials. The band of brothers was more like a family at war.

Roddy wanted a new song he had written – 'Rat Race' – as the next single. We all eventually agreed. 'Rat Race' was all about privileged students at the Lanch whose parents had their whole lives mapped out for them, while ordinary kids had nothing to look forward to.

It wasn't intended to trash all students, as some people claimed, just those who didn't really need to be at university at all. It was a good number and, funnily enough, we recorded it at the Lanch in an exam hall full of students pretending to sit a test. I was in a mortarboard and teacher's cloak playing the congas. Jerry was playing at the piano dressed as an old lady!

It has been suggested that the BBC didn't give the song airplay because of his cross-dressing. They'd already taken exception six months earlier to Terry singing about contraception in 'Too Much Too Young'. The truth is that some radio DJs and TV executives fancied themselves as the guardians of the nation's morals in those days – and that could lead to some very odd clampdowns.

American TV, on the other hand, couldn't get enough of us. We were called back to appear on what is still that country's most iconic programme – *Saturday Night Live*. I didn't know anything about this telly prog so it was all new to me as we marched into the NBC building in New York. We were to be on prime-time television across the US and the band should have been thrilled.

For Jerry though, it was another opportunity to get wound up from the moment we set foot in the US. The limo – wrong. The nice hotel – wrong. By the time we got to the studio, everybody in the band was in the worst of moods. I had my usual disagreement with Jerry about the hospitality laid on by the record company. He might have felt in danger of being compromised – I had no such fears. Neville Staple knew exactly who and what he was and a suite in a swanky Manhattan hotel wasn't going to change me overnight.

Maybe because we were all at each other's throats that day the performance on *Saturday Night Live* had a certain edge about it.

When we got to the NBC studios, the band was showing the worst signs of the growing tenseness between us. Cooped up closely together on a small stage didn't help the atmosphere as we belted out 'Gangsters' – me brandishing a Tommy gun and all of us stepping on each other's toes. Let's just say the performance on *Saturday Night Live* had a certain frisson about it.

I did my Wilson Pickett leaps in a grey tonic suit, while Roddy made his guitar wail, Brad looked controlled and menacing on drums and Terry strutted backwards and forwards. After we'd finished 'Gangsters', we were invited back on stage to do 'Too Much Too Young'. We might have been grumpy as hell, but the audience in the studio was as euphoric as our fans back home. This was the tragedy of The Specials – the band was exhausted just as millions of new fans were plugging into our sound.

Watching off stage was Keith Richards – another member of the Rolling Stones who took an interest in us during our stormy career. He was very chilled and a genuinely decent bloke. Afterwards, he was full of praise for how we'd come across.

I don't think any of us saw this performance until years afterwards. It was actually a classic which cemented our place in the American pop pantheon.

June 1980 saw us go to the seaside – several seasides in fact. After the US, this was supposed to put our feet firmly back on the ground – a twelve-date reality check in sunny hotspots like Southend and Great Yarmouth. Traditional British holiday destinations that had gradually lost out to the Costa del Sol.

The big plus for me was that we would be touring with two all-female combos – The Go-Go's and The Bodysnatchers.

The gigs turned out to be great fun, apart from Roddy smashing his guitar into Jerry's keyboard and allegedly trying to push Jerry from a seafront wall or cliff, all depending on which bit of band mythology you want to believe. What was undeniably true was that relations between Jerry and Roddy were getting a bit fraught.

Jerry was not fully recovered from the rigours of the US and even thought about cancelling the seaside tour on the day before we were set to leave. But this was his baby. The accommodation was exactly what he wanted all year round. Basic seafront bed and breakfasts – no frills, no room service, no presidential suite.

He seemed to be in his element chatting to the old dears who ran these places. Then after a natter with the B&B owners, Jerry would go for a walk down the promenade in a pair of tartan trousers he'd taken to wearing.

Thankfully I had the large number of women on the tour to distract me. Belinda Carlisle was good company – even though she was a bit freaked out by the arrival of dead roses from some stalker before each gig. I have to admit that would have unnerved me after a while. We never found out who he – or she – was.

My attentions also turned towards The Bodysnatchers. The seven-piece combo had released a single – 'Let's Do Rock Steady' – and been on *Top of the Pops*. Jerry signed them to 2 Tone and there were high hopes for them. I'd already met their rhythm guitarist Stella Barker at a gig in Coventry where they had been supporting The Selecter. In Stella's own words:

'I remember Neville coming into my dressing room and he just didn't leave. Stayed there chatting to everybody. I thought – he's not shy. Charming even.'

We started seeing each other and our relationship carried on for about two years. It's going to sound odd but we split up at the same time as The Specials. I don't know if I just got in to splitting up at that time.

Stella had started out in London as a secretary at EMI and got bored. One day she saw an ad in the *Melody Maker* for female members for a ska band and the next thing she was in The Bodysnatchers supporting The Selecter and then The Specials.

For Stella, the seaside tour was a very mixed experience: 'The venues were terribly depressing – forgotten seaside towns somewhere in the north east of England, on a grey day, with an empty helter-skelter. One time in Colwyn Bay in Wales, we did our set and as we left the pier to get some fish and chips, we could feel the whole structure moving up and down to The Specials.'

Stella soon discovered that I was a less than faithful partner. She once drove up to Coventry to see me, only to discover that I wasn't even in the city. Somehow, she broke into my house and in lipstick scrawled 'you fucking cunt' on my living room mirror.

She had already downed over half a bottle of Rémy Martin and crashed out on the sofa. Waking up a few hours later in a bad way, Stella realised she had to be in London with The Bodysnatchers rehearsing. So she climbed into her car and attempted to drive down the motorway.

The cops stopped her on the hard shoulder of the M1 and, after conking out, Stella woke up in a police cell in Daventry. Unfortunately, they'd found some marching powder in the glove compartment and when they got wind that I was her boyfriend, they decided to make a rapid beeline for my house. The cops never forgot I was a borstal boy, let alone a rude boy.

I turned up at Daventry police station just expecting to pick Stella up but instead the two of us were taken back to Coventry with a heavy police escort. They went into my house, ignored the red lipstick on the mirror and, flourishing a warrant, tore my place apart.

Stella was put in one room. Me in another. I sat, powerless, as they ripped up carpets and even went through my vast record collection, shaking each one by its sleeve to see if there was anything hidden inside. On that occasion there wasn't.

Surprisingly that little incident didn't destroy our relationship and we carried on seeing each other and gigging together. Stella watched me perform with The Specials at Aylesbury when a full-on fight broke out in the audience and I waded in with one of the guitars. Roddy's or Lynval's, I can't exactly recall. Needless to say, Stella found some of the gigs very scary and unpleasant.

On a more fun note, we both appeared on a kids' TV programme called *Tiswas*. This was a very anarchic children's show where guests would be put in cages and have all sorts of slop thrown over them. Me and Stella willingly agreed to have this indignity performed on us. I seem to recall there was also a glove puppet character on the programme titled Spit the Dog which, sure enough, was a canine that gobbed.

After returning from the United States, all of us in The Specials increasingly realised that we had become a teen band. There were the obligatory interviews in the pop mags like *Smash Hits* and appearances on programmes like *Cheggers Plays Pop*. Terry and I seemed to get the teen mags to do while Horace would do the more highbrow interviews.

One place that hadn't received The Specials treatment yet – but seemed to know all about us – was Japan. So, in July 1980, we went off to the land of the rising sun. Little did I realise that this country would provide both The Specials and me with one of our most loyal armies of fans. But the tour was not without controversy.

Obviously there was no Rex or Trevor, who were busy touring with 21 Guns and had no intention of coming back. Our Kid was now in charge of roadying and Rick Rogers got us shipped over to Tokyo. A guy called Massy was the promoter.

When I got to the Japanese capital, my back felt terrible. Part of my on-stage act involved jumping off high PA stacks and this was taking its first toll. Later on in my career my knees started grumbling and I even ended up having to go on stage with a walking stick.

With the twinges in my spine getting worse and aches everywhere, I found myself in my Tokyo hotel room lying

face down with a little old lady walking up and down my back. This might have made things worse in the long run, but in terms of getting me up and running in time for the gigs in Japan, it did the trick.

We held a press conference to announce our arrival, during which there was a small earth tremor. We all looked at each other as if to say – did you feel that? The local Japanese journalists didn't seem to be at all bothered.

Many visitors from the West to Tokyo's night clubs and discos in 1980 couldn't help but notice that the 2 Tone look had arrived big time. The décor in many of these places was black and white check and kids were walking round in tonic suits and pork pie hats calling themselves mods or rude boys. They even seemed to know more about Coventry than some people back in Britain.

From the start, we would get Japanese girls on the tour coming to our dressing room and sitting around in their 2 Tone gear, all smiles and trying to chat. There was a bit of a language barrier but some of the girls had a vague mastery of English. I had no Japanese of course.

It became clear to even a randy git like myself that there were cultural differences in this country. Just because girls walked into your dressing room, that didn't mean it was a come on. This was a whole new ball game for me – talking to attractive females in an enclosed space without trying it on. But I was happy enough just to joke with the local girls, generally chill out and then take a very obliging Australian back to my room.

Our gigs in Osaka were the ones that caused all the controversy on the tour. They even led British newspapers to claim that we were on the brink of being kicked out of the country – as if we'd caused some sort of diplomatic incident. It did come close to that but we were never escorted to the airport.

The cause of all the fuss was the local fans getting up and doing a stage invasion. Just like they'd seen on TV footage of our gigs. And what was wrong with that?

What we didn't reckon with was that Japan had never really seen kids behave like this at concerts before. This was still a deeply conservative country in many ways. If you went to see a band, you remained in your seat throughout.

There had been a time when this was the case in the UK. Look at an old Cliff Richard concert from around 1959 and you'll see the girls scream but remain with bums in seats. We, however, liberated Japanese bottoms from their seats and the authorities didn't like it.

In Osaka, the manager of the Expo Hall went crazy at us.

There had been a stage invasion in Tokyo and Massy had got a bit of a ticking off from the powers that be. But in Osaka, we had some very scary looking security guards swarming in front of the stage. The idea was to allow a limited number on to the stage but then stop the rest.

As the gig went on, the kids ignored the petty restrictions and piled on to the stage with us. They were having a great time but the guards started getting heavy with some of the youth. Terry and Jerry shouted at them to stop but to no avail.

Eventually we were herded backstage and barricaded into our dressing room by the guards until somebody got them to move away from our door – where they were lined up. We were then able to do an encore.

Our promoter was told by the authorities in Tokyo and Osaka that he would not be welcome back at any time soon. In fact him and Rick Rogers were detained by the Japanese cops, but released pretty soon after.

They say revenge is a dish best eaten cold – sushi in this case – and we did manage to do another gig at the Expo in spite of everything. This time we went down into the audience and showed our solidarity with the fans.

Our tour sparked a ska explosion in Japan.

In the 1980s and 1990s, Japan spawned some great ska acts including the Tokyo Ska Paradise Orchestra – who I later worked with. I knew their front man Cleanhead Gimura. He sadly died in 1995 and drummer Tatsuyuki Aoki passed away in 1999. The band is still going strong and totally looks the part.

Other bands I got to know from Japan over the years included Doberman, Ska Flames and The Determinations from Osaka.

I also discovered that Japanese ska fans were prepared to embrace the first wave of ska that had influenced me and Jerry. They were real students of ska, not just content to stop at a knowledge of 2 Tone. Jamaican acts like The Skatalites who formed in 1963 and had a hit with 'Guns of Navarone' – which was covered by The Specials – are still welcomed today in Japan.

That welcome has also been extended to me over the years, after the UK turned its back, for a long while, on ska and 2 Tone. I know Roddy Radiation and Ranking Roger of The Beat feel very fondly about Japan as well.

In spite of the rapturous response from people round the globe to the sound of The Specials, there was a feeling that we were definitely into an end game. I felt the light was slowly but steadily going out of the band. It had started to lose its soul – the very reason for being. We were just going through the grind of gigging but without any sense of purpose.

While we bickered internally as a band, The Specials were changing lives all over the world. I often say that if you're of a certain age – you lost your virginity to 'Gangsters' or 'Rat Race' or 'A Message to You Rudy'.

I could have consoled myself with the fact that we still had the music. In this band I was keeping the flame of ska burning bright. 2 Tone and The Specials were carrying the torch lit by Prince Buster and Laurel Aitken. That alone would have kept me motivated and enthused, but unfortunately, Jerry suddenly decided it was time for a big change of musical direction.

We were gradually dropping some of the older songs from the set and bringing in new numbers like Roddy's 'Rat Race' which was a great song. Jerry dropped in some dramatic keyboard sounds at the top which were OK, but I had no idea that this signalled a move into semi-orchestral doodles and muzak.

I should have had my suspicions when John Barry albums were being played in our spare time. John Barry being the man responsible for eleven fine James Bond film themes but not many ska and reggae numbers. What we were in danger of doing was the sort of 'experimentation' that public school pomp rock bands used to indulge in during the early 1970s. A culture that was a million miles from me.

Bernie Rhodes had warned us about the cerebral tendencies in the band – the head ruling the heart. The musos getting carried away with their chord changes and arpeggios and forgetting what pop is really all about – entertaining the kids.

Now I heard Terry coming out with the new party line. We had taken Jamaican dads' music – ska – and introduced it to the kids. Now, we were going to take English dads' music and, that's right, introduce it to the same kids. This was musical masturbation in my view.

I had no problem with artists being innovative and trying out new things. But there was no integrity in this new direction. It was as if we were saying: we're bored of ska, let's go and do something different. I couldn't just walk away from the sound of Kingston as easily as that.

When we started recording some tracks in the Horizon studio in Coventry with Dave Jordan, the full horror of where Jerry wanted us to go became clearer by the day. Me, Lynval and Horace composed one of the more ska-style tracks – 'Rude Boys Outa Jail' with me as Judge Roughneck.

'Enjoy Yourself' was an old singalong originally released in the 1940s and was unobjectionable enough. But some of the other songs left me twiddling my thumbs in bewilderment.

When Jerry started turning up with a drum machine, that pissed Brad off and he stopped coming to the studio. Prince Rimshot was in no mood to be replaced by something that sounded like a biscuit tin being whacked.

Roddy was referring to Jerry as General Dammers and said years after that listening to 'More Specials' made him 'physically sick'. He also took issue with Jerry over the use of this bloody drum machine on his own composition – 'Hey Little Rich Girl'.

To quote Roddy's own website at one point he 'let Jerry admire my new James Dean flick knife'. Jerry backed off

while Roddy cooled it. This is how bad things were getting. Our leader disappeared for a while and let Roddy have his way, but then went ahead and recorded the backing vocals he wanted anyway.

I could see an album looming that would give 2 Tone an identity crisis. The picture of me on the album cover says it all. I look devastated, increasingly isolated and wondering if it was time to head for the exit. Jerry seemed to be having a big laugh and gave the impression he wasn't too bothered if the public didn't like it.

That was not what I wanted to hear.

There was also increasing unrest within the 2 Tone empire. Bernie Rhodes had famously told us never to hold meetings but most of us thought we'd turned our back on the Rhodes school of band management. We wanted to know exactly what was going on.

Everybody seemed to be in the dark about how much money they had made or were going to make out of the fame we were now experiencing. When I saw big crowds at gig after gig, it did make me wonder how this was registering on my bank account. The band now started to mutter about how the spoils were being carved up.

We'd also lost some great bands. Not that it was a complete surprise when we waved goodbye to The Beat, who formed Go Feet Records and Madness who went to Stiff.

Worst of all, the new signings weren't making the same impact that we had. Nothing near it. The Swinging Cats were one of those signings and were very much in tune with Jerry's new easy-listening sound. 2 Tone released their single 'Mantovani/Away' in late 1980 and it failed to register in the charts.

A revolt was simmering within 2 Tone. The guys in The Selecter were losing patience with the way the label conducted itself. Pauline complained repeatedly because meetings that needed to be held weren't happening. They began to question what exactly the benefit was of being part of this big family of ska bands.

They hardly ever saw us now. They'd had their own tour of the US. Guys I'd grown up with like Charley Anderson hardly crossed my path at that time. The camaraderie we'd experienced on the first UK 2 Tone tour was fizzling out by the end of 1980 and it had taken just one year to go from bright and enthusiastic newcomers to jaded pop stars.

By the end of 1980, Pauline and The Selecter had thrown their collective hands up and left 2 Tone to sign direct with Chrysalis.

Meanwhile, we went to Barcelona to put on a huge gig in a bullring – one of our more surreal performances. I still remember seeing these bulls in the pens, looking big and rough. I could just imagine those creatures and the matadors. For some reason, my days working in the slaughterhouse in Rugby came back to me as I looked at the sweaty bulls snorting angrily.

1981 started with Lynval being attacked by thugs outside the Moonlight Club in Hampstead when he was going to see a band called The Mo-dettes. He later told *Smash Hits*:

'They were National Front guys. I've never said it before but they were.'

Lynval wrote the anti-racist song 'Why?' off the back of that. The attack left him very traumatised and trying to make sense of it. During the song I toasted the words:

'With a Nazi salute and a steel capped boot

A Nazi salute and a steel capped boot
You follow like sheep inna wolf clothes
You follow like sheep inna wolf clothes…'

You wouldn't believe it if I said that at one of our last gigs in the UK, some complete idiot was Sieg Heiling to the rhythm of my toasting on 'Why?'. There came a point when I couldn't even be bothered to plant my fist in their dumb faces.

Britain was in a bad state as we welcomed in 1981. High unemployment was going to levels I never thought we'd see – three million and more. The factories were closing not just in Coventry but all over the Midlands and north of England. The youth were the worst affected with no jobs or apprenticeships. On top of all that, the police were using the so-called SUS laws to stop and search in the inner cities and this was adding to a soon-to-be explosive build-up of tension.

The gigs were a good barometer of what was happening. The stage invasions were happening earlier and they seemed to be more aggressive. Pauline Black remembers The Selecter playing a gig at Hammersmith Palais where about a quarter of the audience were giving her Sieg Heil salutes. She stopped the gig and asked:

'Why are you doing this?'

They carried on with the Hitler crap so the band walked off to the dressing room. Then the crowd pulled itself together. After all, they had parted with money to get in. Even they could work out it was going to be their loss if The Selecter didn't reappear. Eventually, when things seemed calmer, the band came back on.

But within a few minutes, the Nazi thing had started again.

Pauline says she tried to engage some of these skinheads – even talking to a rather menacing example who had a big swastika tattoo on his head. She saw it as her role to get through to these kids who were being misled by the National Front and other far-right organisations.

One skinhead she cornered got very apologetic and started blurting:

'Oh sorry, Pauline, it was my mate made me do it.'

A lot of these kids just needed to hear another voice apart from the National Front or the British Movement. They didn't have a job and some poisonous snake had told them that black or Asian people were to blame. We had to counter that poison and we thought the weapon that would work was ska music.

Our mates in The Beat had similar hassles at some of their gigs. Ranking Roger used to take to the mic and single-out the people who were being racist. They'd get booed by the rest of the crowd.

'If there was a fight, we'd say – what are you doing? This is a peace and love concert.'

But peace and love was going out of fashion.

As early as October 1980, we got a strong flavour of the anger that was about to spew out on to the streets of every major city in Britain through the long summer of 1981.

We played an outdoor gig in Cambridge to a crowd of about 4,000 people. Local residents' associations and other busybodies had warned that there was going to be trouble and the gig should be stopped.

At the university, they had talked for years about a divide in Cambridge between 'town and gown'. The 'gown' were the well-heeled students with their academic gowns and the 'town' were the local ruffians –

or skinheads and mods in this case. Kids who had no degrees and no chance of ever going anywhere near any of those ancient colleges.

The concert was on Midsummer Common. Midsummer madness more like. I looked out at a very angry crowd. Not only had a mass of skinheads bussed in from every county around Cambridge, but there also seemed to be a big squaddie contingent from a barracks somewhere. This was all going to go pear shaped – I could feel it.

I didn't have to wait long to be proved right. One of The Swinging Cats got thumped on stage as they played support. From that moment, the whole event descended into the sort of brawl you see in a Wild West saloon.

We tried to keep people calm but it was total anarchy. Terry and Jerry tried their hardest to calm things down but there was nothing they could do.

Afterwards the promoters turned up backstage – with the cops. Jerry and Terry were arrested for a 'breach of the peace'. I'd never held the police in the highest regard but this was a new low. From memory they both got fined something like £400 each. We wouldn't forget Cambridge in a hurry.

On a brighter note, we released 'Do Nothing', which went to number three, and did a tour of Ireland with The Beat. This was at a time when Northern Ireland was still a war zone but we did our bit to unite Catholic and Protestant kids behind the 2 Tone banner.

Touring with the Beat gave me the opportunity to get to know front man Ranking Roger that little bit better. In fact, it was the beginnings of a working relationship and friend-ship that's endured to the present day.

It amazed Roger that I could end each gigging session with a three-in-a-bed romp and still be able to perform the next night.

'I got to know Neville, the rude boy. A real ladies' man. He'd always be telling me about some woman he'd shagged the night before and there'd be two in the audience and he couldn't separate them so he'd have to go back with both. I don't know where he got the energy from.'

Back on the other side of the Irish Sea things were getting more not less divisive. The growing violence at the gigs and the way the country was going gave me the inspiration for the words I would toast in our big hit of 1981.

'Ghost Town' was the high point for The Specials but it would also be our swan song. Watch the video or listen to my voice summing everything up:

'This town is coming like a Ghost Town
Why must the youth fight against themselves?
Government leaving the youth on the shelf'

I wrote earlier that toasting was a way in which Jamaican artists would comment in a matter-of-fact way about events that were happening – a sort of singing newspaper. I saw our cities dying, the youth being left to rot, people turning on each other, a mean spirit descending everywhere and increasing crime.

'No job to be found in this country'

We filmed a video for 'Ghost Town' in a Vauxhall Cresta driving round London streets in the early hours of the morning. I don't know anybody who hasn't seen that bit of film. Me in the middle singing gloomily until Terry pipes up sardonically with:

'Do you remember the good old days

Before the Ghost Town?
We danced and sang
And the music played inna de boomtown'

There are songs that capture the mood of a people at a certain point. Like a photo snapshot. 'Ghost Town' did that brilliantly. We released the song on 20 June 1981 and it went to number one for three weeks. During that time, Liverpool, London and Manchester burned.

The news bulletins on the BBC and ITV covered the scenes of rioting every night. Scenes that had never been seen in Britain before. Kids going crazy, riot shield-wielding cops, Molotov cocktails being thrown, shops going up in flames and faces full of hatred and despair.

In the Brixton area of London – where I used to buy my dubplates for Jah Baddis – it transformed into a war zone with Railton Road referred to as the 'front line'. The Toxteth area of Liverpool witnessed the first use of CS gas against civilians in the UK and there were little copycat riots around the country.

As we released that song, The Specials decided to play an anti-racist gig in Coventry in the wake of two race-motivated murders in the city. One had been the unprovoked killing of a twenty-year-old Asian student Satnam Gill, which had disgusted everybody. It was a symptom of a sickness on the streets.

The National Front had seen their vote fall so they were trying to recruit thugs at gigs, football matches and anywhere they could find working-class young people to get their claws into. They'd given up trying to be respectable and reverted to type.

I was told that some of the far-right nutters who came to our gigs now referred to us as 'The Specials plus two'. The

'plus two' being me and Lynval. How stupid was that? The whole point of 2 Tone was black and white united, but these thick gits didn't get it.

Jerry moved mountains to organise the Peaceful Protest Against Racism gig at the Butts Athletic Stadium in the Earlsdon area of Coventry. We were supported by, among others, Hazel O'Connor who had a string of hits around that time.

While we sang, fascists and anti-fascists clashed in a small riot down at the Pool Meadow Bus Station. A riot policeman was knocked off his horse and the cops chased a load of black and white kids into Hillfields. We had become a society at war.

I needed a break from all this and was lucky enough to be able to get on a plane and fly out of Britain. I found myself back in Toronto a few weeks on, supporting The Police, with Killing Joke and Iggy Pop, as well as The Go-Go's. The gig was one of our finest, but my heart wasn't in it anymore. It was Terry who planned our next move. Three of The Specials were about to hand in their cards.

I'm not somebody who likes to lead a double life. When I knew what Terry had in mind and that me and Lynval were part of it, I just wanted to make a clean break. Being dishonest or two-faced to Jerry was not what he deserved. If we'd decided to go, then I wanted to tell him as soon as possible.

I went to see Jerry and our manager Rick Rogers and told him that the three of us were leaving to form our own group. At first Jerry was totally deflated – it was like I'd hit him in the stomach – bent over with the life pulled out of him. I hated seeing him like that.

Then he remonstrated with me. Things would be different, we didn't have to leave. He had loads of ideas. I couldn't do this to him. We talked for a while and I realised how much I admired the man in spite of our occasional differences. But I'd had enough.

I wasn't the only person looking for the exit. Everybody in the band wanted to do their own thing. Brad was off setting up his own record label and Roddy was forming a new rockabilly band. Horace had joined some positive-thinking cult called Exegesis and his preaching on the subject drove us bonkers.

The band was slowly hollowing out. Jerry had done his best to create one of the best pop acts this country had ever seen – in retrospect he'd succeeded – we just didn't fully appreciate it at the time.

I walked out and left Jerry behind me, totally crestfallen. For me, the future looked more encouraging. I'd honed my performance skills in The Specials and built up my confidence. Now I could take things further with a new band.

Pop was changing but, as I was to find out, not necessarily for the better.

Roddy Radiation and me with our Japanese crew.

Neville Staple, personal collection

Press conference – Horace (*in front of table*), me (*looking back*), Lynval (*next to me*), Terry (*far right*).

Neville Staple, personal collection

Me and Horace share a bed with two local ladies; (*bottom*) I tuck
into some local food.

Neville Staple, personal collection

Terry Hall (*top left*), Jerry Dammers (*top right*), me (*bottom left*), Lynval Golding (*bottom right*).

Neville Staple, personal collection

Me (*top left*), John Bradbury (*top right*), Terry Hall just visible inside the restaurant (*bottom*).

Neville Staple, personal collection

Terry Hall tunes up on stage (*left*); the band fill a taxi boot (*top right*);
I take the strain (*bottom right*).

Neville Staple, personal collection

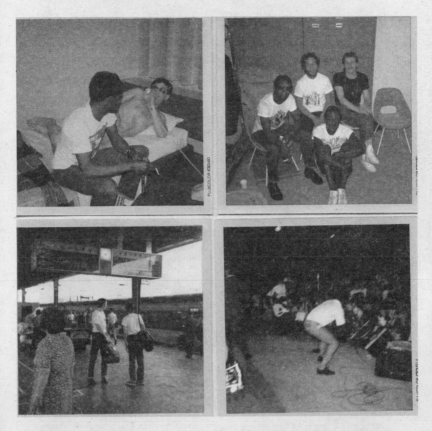

'Our Kid' Gambino takes a call (*top left*); me, Rico and Lynval (*top right*);
Jerry waits for a bullet train (*bottom left*); Lynval and I relate to Japanese fans
(*bottom right*).
Neville Staple, personal collection

'Our Kid' Gambino, me and Roddy Radiation in traditional
Japanese garb (*top*); Japanese technical support (*bottom*).
Neville Staple, personal collection

The Specials head to the seaside, June 1980.
Neville Staple, personal collection

8

FUN BOY THREE – BUBBLEGUM POP RULES

THE FACE

NUMBER 24   APRIL 1982   65p

The Fun Boy Three.
Madness. Lou Reed.
African and
Bolshevik Chic.
Heaven 17/B.E.F.
Associates. Higsons.

Fun Boy Three . . . bubblegum pop triumphant?
© Redferns/Getty Images

Fun Boy Three and backing 'girl band' Bananarama.
© Redferns/Getty Images

These pictures were taken when I lost my voice in Fun Boy Three. The operation was successful – thankfully!

Neville Staple, personal collection

'**S**ka fell off a cliff. Fell off the ionosphere. Just stopped.' That was how Pauline described the death of 2 Tone. Not that it officially kicked the bucket in 1981 – it struggled on 'til the mid-1980s – but something happened in the summer of that year. The record companies didn't want pop with a serious message anymore. Maybe the riots had scared them or there was just a change in the air.

Pauline went down to the Chrysalis offices that summer and got her first inkling of what was going on. For two solid years, the walls at Chrysalis had been covered in black and white chequered designs. Like the way those Chrysalis executives in Los Angeles had painted the Whiskey a Go Go.

The staff had wandered round in pork pie hats and tonic suits – everybody from the post boy to the board directors. The Chrysalis HQ had been a temple to 2 Tone but that was no more – any hint of ska had been removed and chucked away.

Chrysalis chairman Chris Wright was walking down the stairs and said hello to Pauline. Behind him were some men in kilts and scarves with flamboyant haircuts.

'Have you met Spandau Ballet?'

Tony Hadley and the Kemp brothers stood before her – the vanguard of the new romantic movement. They'd just released the single 'To Cut a Long Story Short' and done

Top of the Pops. The whole new romantic phenomenon was a million miles away from what we were about.

2 Tone reacted to the grim times the country was facing by singing about the issues. We talked about violence on the streets in 'Concrete Jungle', the hopelessness in the inner cities in 'Ghost Town' and gritty, funny commentary on clubbing and getting pissed in songs like 'Friday Night, Saturday Morning'.

But the new romantics wanted to create a sort of glamorous world where boys and girls dressed up as pirates or Regency dandies and wore stacks of make up. It was a cross-dressing, hedonistic universe that centred on clubs like the Blitz. Steve Strange of Visage was on the door of that club and if you didn't come up to his high standards, you didn't get in.

There was an elitism and contempt for those who were deemed not fashionable enough. This was in complete contrast to the 2 Tone approach. We'd reached out to working-class kids and tried to be as accessible as possible. Now, it was all about creating an exclusivity – 'we'll let you in if we like the look of you'.

The music was mainly synthesiser based and influenced by German pop bands like Kraftwerk. When we supported The Clash, there was another band called Suicide which was one of several outfits pioneering electro-pop. They often had a rough reception from the skinhead audiences in 1978 but now, their kind of sound was moving mainstream.

Even the drum machine, much beloved of Jerry Dammers and hated by the rest of us, became a mainstay of this new generation of pop acts.

As Pauline went up the flights of stairs at Chrysalis to the A&R department, she could see the fickle staff at the

record company had swapped their tonic suits for the over the top garb of the new romantics.

The head of A&R didn't seem to want to discuss Pauline and The Selecter's contract. Instead he popped a record on and insisted she listen to it – of course it was the Spandau Ballet hit and Pauline smiled weakly.

'I remember sitting there thinking – "this is going to be a tricky meeting".'

Never one to mince her words when she reported back to us, Pauline described the record company guys as 'wankers'. She loathed the new romantics too. This new sound was all about trying to have fun instead of challenging what was going on. Now all pop stars wanted to sing about was making loads of money, Pauline believed.

New romanticism was a style perfectly attuned to the new political climate. Margaret Thatcher had been in power since 1979 – the night of our gig at the Moonlight Club.

Two or three years before, people thought she'd fall flat on her face in no time. Her policies were too extreme and she'd be chucked out of office by her own side or by popular opposition. This was all proving to be very naïve and way too optimistic. We'd underestimated the strength of the beast. Maggie had no intention of leaving 10 Downing Street any time soon.

As those political facts of life became all too clear, it seemed like the media and music industry didn't want protest pop anymore. They were falling in line with the new status quo.

That was illustrated by what happened to The Beat when they released their political protest single 'Stand Down Margaret'.

The Beat brought out the single and announced the proceeds would go to Greenpeace and CND. They went on to a BBC kids' show and told the rather gullible and ill-informed producer that their new hit was an innocent little calypso song – nothing that would offend anybody.

Taking to the stage, they soon had all the youngsters enthusiastically singing 'Stand Down Margaret' – much to the horror of the TV executives.

The radio airplay for that number dried up instantly. Radio 1 was completely off limits, even though the band tried to reason with the station's controllers. The DJs weren't interested in that kind of message going on air. From now on, it was anodyne ditties and nothing else.

Ranking Roger says they were still able to make £40,000 out of the single and that helped CND open a London office. But the incident did a lot of harm to The Beat and ultimately led to them departing for the United States.

Though they'd left 2 Tone early on, The Beat had been part of our ska movement from 1979 onwards.

Their symbol was the Beat Girl in contrast to our Walt Jabsco logo. That piece of imagery and their hit single 'Hands Off She's Mine' led them to have a massive female following. Also, Roger is not without his charms and was a regular pin-up in the teen mags and the new fashion bible of the 1980s – *The Face*.

It was hard to believe that just a few months before, Chrysalis had asked The Beat to perform at a party in their offices in honour of our old friends Blondie. The walls had still been covered in 2 Tone imagery and we were all still their most bankable acts.

Backstage, before Roger went on in front of the assembled record company executives, some guy in a suit racked up three hefty lines of cocaine. Roger had never actually taken cocaine in his life before. As I said, it was never a substance we saw in working-class neighbourhoods back then.

Not knowing how much he was supposed to take, but very enthusiastic as he always is, Roger snorted one entire line up one nostril and the second line up the other nostril. Then he did the remainder and asked if he could have some more. The guy in the suit was a bit nervous by now and asked:

'Are you sure you're OK?'

With half of Colombia's annual gross product racing round his system, Roger charged out among the great and good of the music industry. In the middle of the throng was a large Christmas tree – as it was that time of year. Babbling away and making little sense, Roger turned a little too quickly and walked straight into the forty-foot tree covered in baubles and decorations.

The whole crowd went: 'Wheeeeeaaaay!'

Then fled in all directions as the tree came crashing down sending baubles flying and skidding in all directions. This was the last time he touched the white powder for a long while. When he took to the stage, his usual liveliness had left him. The comedown was obviously kicking in and he gave a very subdued and slightly contrite performance.

Those were the good times for Ranking Roger. But as The Specials faded, so did The Beat and everybody else associated with 2 Tone.

Try as hard as he did, Jerry couldn't get the newer signings up the charts. The Swinging Cats made no impression and The Bodysnatchers struggled to make an impact. Their song about date rape – 'The Boiler' – was a good

number but airplay was getting harder for this sort of material. Jerry's song 'War Crimes' about events in the Lebanon was roundly ignored by the nation's DJs.

He was still getting new bands that wanted to be on 2 Tone, though. One of Jerry's signings after we quit were The Higsons. They formed at the University of East Anglia and featured one Charlie Higson on vocals and Terry Edwards on guitar.

They were often accused of being the 'English Talking Heads' and two or three years earlier might have gone on to great things. But the singles released with 2 Tone didn't chart very well. Their most respectable chart entry came with 'Music to Watch Boys By' released later on Upright Records.

However, success of a different kind came to Charlie Higson who ended up being one of the writers and actors on the BBC's *Fast Show* in the 1990s. Terry Edwards went on to work with Nick Cave, Julian Cope and Tom Waits.

Just as we thought nothing could possibly be worse than the new romantics, their star began to fade. But the worst was on its way – we had no idea how inane pop was about to become.

The person who seemed to realise we had to go down a new path was Terry Hall. A chameleon who had gone from punk to ska and on to mainstream pop without a second's thought. He could change his musical colours effortlessly.

Terry always said that leaving a band was easy. To me, it was a painful and ultimately unfulfilling wrench to leave The Specials, ditch ska and go for this new sound. A type of music I didn't really believe in and by kidding myself that I did, I think a little bit of me died inside.

I had undoubtedly been the bearer of the bad news to Jerry. But I hadn't plotted to break up The Specials as some people have suggested. Terry showed me and Lynval a way forward and as the band politics worsened, we went for it. There was no point sticking around when Jerry was playing with drum machines and Roddy looked ready to murder him.

Staying in the madhouse that had become The Specials wasn't an option. We left on a high having got 'Ghost Town' to number one. Looking back, I can see that was a truly unique moment in pop history. A year after, it would have been inconceivable to get a song as political and edgy as that into the charts let alone the top slot. We had captured a moment.

As Roger says, we were the theme tune of the riots. He spoke to John Peel, the Radio 1 DJ, many years later at the Custard Factory in Birmingham and Peel said that a song like 'Ghost Town' would never be allowed into the charts again. He thought it was incredible that 2 Tone had ever been allowed to get those sorts of messages across. That was a year before Peel passed away.

Once that summer and its violence died down, people wanted something a bit more upbeat. Our new band was ready to give it to them.

Me, Lynval and Terry formed Fun Boy Three and set out to completely change our image. Gone were the tonic suits, Ben Sherman shirts and brogues and in came Terry's big, fluffy hair. Out went the trilbies and in came the white jump suits.

Other casualties from The Specials hopped on board with the new combo. Rick Rogers had been fired by Jerry in the US and both he and our sound engineer Dave Jordan came and joined us.

Terry talked about our split with The Specials to the *NME* in their 13 February 1982 edition:

'It was planned in advance, but there was no real point in telling the others when we started thinking about breaking away. It would only have caused friction. Some of them probably knew it was on the cards anyway.'

In the same interview to the *NME*, we all had a good moan about the lack of credit we had been given in The Specials for our contribution to the song writing. I was to spend years in a legal battle with Jerry over one song in particular.

Rex and Trevor had sworn affidavits in my defence. But eventually I backed down. The choice was between keeping up with child maintenance payments or paying huge legal bills. This left a bitter taste in my mouth for a long time.

Our first single as Fun Boy Three was 'The Lunatics (Have Taken Over the Asylum)' which charted respectably at number 20. But as 1982 dawned, we started to make a much bigger impact as we fully embraced the emerging bubblegum pop ethos.

Teaming up with the all-female trio Bananarama, we released a 1939 jazz song called ''Tain't What You Do (It's the Way That You Do It)' but with a 1980s pop twist.

As if we were unable to completely shake off our immediate past, there is a small section of the video where we are seen driving at night in the front seat of a car. The imagery is eerily reminiscent of the 'Ghost Town' video we had recorded just months before. Only now we had our names – 'LYN', 'TED', 'NEV' – across the windscreen.

There was still a little hint of ska in there but I felt my original influences were disappearing rapidly. Strangely,

Pete Waterman says that he can hear the faint strains of songs we used to play at the Locarno in the hits we were producing at this time.

That song got to number four and was a big hit. So then we changed places for the next single and Fun Boy Three were backing vocalists for the Bananarama hit single 'Really Saying Something', which got to number five. That was an old Motown number sung by a 1960s all-female combo called The Velvelettes.

There was Terry in the video, in blue dungarees and shades, with Bananarama in spiky gelled hair doting on him. Me and Lynval appear from behind what looks like a yellow Christmas tree intoning:

'Really saying something…bap…bap…shooby…doo aaaah'

The only redeeming part of the video, which shows my old rude boy ways had not been completely snuffed out, is when I pinch Keren Woodward on the behind and smile cheekily.

Bananarama were lovely girls and we got on well with them. The trio – Keren Woodward, Sara Dallin and Siobhan Fahey – sent teenage boys' pulses racing for several years. They couldn't really sing but they looked good. In answer to the question that might be going through your mind – no, I didn't make out with any of them.

I had just broken up with Stella. She had already called time on The Bodysnatchers after their failure to register any hits under the 2 Tone label. There was no point flogging a dead horse as far as she was concerned. So together with Sarah-Jane, Miranda, Penny and Judy, plus a couple of new recruits, they formed their own bubblegum pop combo, The Belle Stars.

In my view – and you can accuse me of bias – they were better than Bananarama. Their biggest hit was in January 1983 with 'Sign of the Times', which you would know instantly if it came out of your radio. It was one of the most catchy numbers of that year. They also had a hit with the song 'Iko Iko' which featured in the Tom Cruise and Dustin Hoffman movie *Rain Man*.

Signed to Stiff Records, I don't think they were marketed hard enough. They should have enjoyed the same success that Belinda Carlisle and The Go-Go's went on to have in the United States. But that's spilt milk and I'm not going to cry over it.

Bananarama went on tour with us, as did The Go-Go's. If I was perfectly honest, this very large female presence, and the absence of my rude boy buddies, meant I had to tone down my womanising. Maybe there was also a changing attitude to that sort of behaviour. Radical feminism was very much to the fore at that time and I had to mind my step – for the moment anyway.

After a brief dip in their fortunes in the mid-1980s, Bananarama fell into the arms of Pete Waterman. The Stock Aitken and Waterman Hit Factory was now up and running. Pete was Britain's leading pop mogul and was busy churning out chart toppers one after another.

He achieved his first successful single with Dead or Alive doing the electro-pop number 'You Spin Me Round' in 1985. The girls recorded their first single, 'Venus', with him in the following year, which got to number eight in the UK and number one in the United States and several other countries. Pete then went on to give the nation Rick Astley and Kylie Minogue.

Trevor and Rex had been enjoying some success on the college circuit with 21 Guns and had a couple of singles through my Shack label. But with no big breakthrough looking imminent, the two decided to part company.

Rex wanted to finish off his education – and when he said he wanted to do something, he meant it. In just a few years, he'd got a degree in material sciences and a masters in computing. He now teaches at a college in Brixton. But Trevor was determined to stick with the music. It was his first and greatest love and he wasn't ready to bow out yet.

So – bubblegum pop it was. Trevor teamed up with an ex-girlfriend of his, Kim Shields, and her sister Debbie – Franklyn had been seeing Debbie at some point. A girl called Sarah came into this new band on keyboards and I'd been seeing her for a while. Then a guy called Johnny St John was recruited as a vocalist and together they became Splashdown.

The gritty urban look of 21 Guns was exchanged for white shirts and trousers, with red bow ties. Like us, they also had to surrender to the inevitable beach shorts. Wham! had a lot to answer for.

Produced by me, they signed to Red Bus Records and released a single with the songs 'To Your Heart' and 'Actions Speak Louder Than Words'. This was the same label as funky dance floor band Imagination who had hits with 'Just An Illusion', 'Body Talk' and 'In and Out of Love'. No disco escaped an Imagination single being plonked on the turntable in the middle of this decade.

Trevor pretty quickly found that it was a very different kind of venue that wanted to book his new bubblegum act. Splashdown went on tour and found themselves playing

gay bars and clubs from Blackpool to Brighton. As Trevor says:

'We had girls in the Splashdown for the girls to fancy. And boys for the boys to fancy.'

Trevor recalls an atmosphere on the 1980s gay scene not dissimilar to a Frankie Goes To Hollywood video – rather decadent and quite a lot of amyl nitrate getting sniffed. Standing there in his white beach shorts, the former Specials roadie got his fair share of unwanted attention – all a far cry from wearing a tonic suit on stage with The Specials on the look out for my aftershow entertainment.

In contrast, Jerry had not surrendered to the bubblegum pop wave. He bravely soldiered on with The Special AKA – as the band had now reverted to being known – and kept true to his own vision. Jerry wasn't going to put on a white jump suit or multi-coloured Lycra for anyone.

His refusal to water down the political message of the songs was eventually rewarded with the hit 'Free Nelson Mandela' in 1984. But by 1985, with Chrysalis losing patience and money, the band folded. After that Jerry got more deeply involved in politics and in 1988, organised a benefit gig for Nelson Mandela's 70th birthday.

Fun Boy Three might have created a good clean living image for this rude boy, but I couldn't escape from my past so easily. Two events brought home to me where I had come from. Both happened in Coventry.

It's been well documented that when the single ''Tain't What You Do…' came out, Fun Boy Three picked up the acetate from the offices of Chrysalis and waltzed off to Coventry with it. We also stole a bottle of vodka from the directors' drinks cabinet while we were at it.

When we got to Coventry, Terry went to bed while Lynval and I went to the local radio station and, in flagrant breach of the record company's instructions, got it played live on air. It was all supposed to be under wraps but we were both drunk and excitable. We then thought it might be a good idea to get it played on a big PA so we went off into town to find a club that would oblige. We wanted to gauge the reaction from the punters live.

That night saw an old face re-emerge. Banacek, the guy Ray King had banned from the Holyhead Youth Club, had become quite a flash git in the years that followed. Always seen going round the grubby streets of Hillfields in a smart car – something like a Bentley – with beautiful women on his arm and different ladies on different nights. None of this endeared him to the local gangs whose noses he seemed to be putting out of joint. Here was a black man who was making money and flaunting it more than the rest of us.

Banacek wasn't a man you could be indifferent towards. We put up with him, but plenty of people wanted to take him down a few notches.

One night, Banacek dropped off one of his many girl-friends at her house and shortly afterwards some white guys tried to kick her door down. In a complete state, she contacted Banacek to tell him what had been going on. He got together with Rex and they were able to identify one of the blokes.

Quite why these people had taken such a big dislike to Banacek and his girlfriends, I have no idea. But Rex decided it was time for an old-style lesson to be administered.

Together with Bookie and Banacek, Rex found one of the men drinking at a local pub. Waiting for him outside, they saw him leave and let their fists and feet fly. A good pummelling was meted out. As far as Rex, Bookie and Banacek were concerned, that was an appropriate way of dealing with a thug who had terrorised a woman late at night in her own home.

Now at that time in Coventry there were two particularly notorious families. They were both white, they both lived on the same estate, and people knew not to mess with them. Let's call them the 'Wattses' and the 'Mitchells'. Unfortunately, Rex and the guys had beaten up a Watts.

A few days on, Banacek narrowly escaped from a pub where they turned up in force to beat the living daylights out of him. He then phoned Rex to give him the bad news – they were now marked men.

Rex decided that the only thing they could do was show their faces out on a Saturday night. We had never cowered in the face of this kind of thing in our lives. If you didn't stand up to the bad guys, then you could never leave your house again. So Rex went out to meet me and Lynval in a local night club called Shades. The same club we'd chosen to play our acetate.

Shades was something of an institution. A well-known late-night venue in Coventry, that had previously been called The Cottage and Reflections but was now going through a new incarnation. The clientele were quite mixed. Ironically, today the venue is called Club Release and the patrons are almost all black.

Back on that night in February 1982, our new single was getting some unauthorised airtime. I was soon distracted by some nice-looking ladies. Lynval, meanwhile, was on the other side of the club from me talking to Rex – who failed to mention his ongoing adventures with Banacek, the Mitchells and the Wattses.

While they talked, Rex spotted some members of the Wattses and Mitchells arriving at the club entrance. The bouncer gave them an unconvincing frisk and they strode in with murderous looks on their faces. Initially they walked past us – several well-built white guys – but then reached towards their backs and brought out knives and God knows what.

I had no idea what was going on. Rex fled, just suffering a cut to the eye that need stitches. As Lynval had nothing whatsoever to do with Banacek's local difficulties, nobody would have predicted he would get hurt. But just being in proximity to Rex was enough for these psychos. One of them plunged his knife into Lynval's neck. He later described what he felt at that moment in the 13 February 1982 edition of the *NME*:

'I was conscious all the way through it… I remember just staggering around. It was like walking across a tightrope, trying to balance yourself. I could feel myself going… falling over… but I just kept thinking that I had to pull myself together.'

Through the night, doctors struggled to save Lynval's life. The next morning, the national papers were full of reports about the attack on him. To add insult to grievous injury, Lynval was burgled while he was in intensive care.

Shortly afterwards, one of the Watts brothers came out of prison and a member of the Mitchell family ran him through with an ornamental sword. The thug who attacked Lynval was eventually tracked down in Scotland and sent down.

Lynval was a total innocent – he'd never been a street rude boy like us. For this to happen to him was sickening.

In an interview with Fun Boy Three, *The Face* magazine talked to us about this incident and summed it up:

'The Specials guitarist and singer Lynval Golding was always the most open, direct member of the group. Now it seems perhaps as though this accessibility and humanity exposed him to the wrath of some terrible, malicious force desiring to destroy such honesty.'

The attack on Lynval – and an operation I had to have on my vocal chords – put The Fun Boy Three out of action for a couple of months. Our album launch on 5 March 1982 also had to be delayed.

Lynval's sight was affected for a while and he had to keep going back for medical tests. Mentally, he was scarred as well. One of the experiences he talked about afterwards was the feeling in hospital that he was going to die. He was so terrified that every time he started to fall asleep in his hospital bed, he'd wake himself up again. Lynval convinced himself that the moment he shut his eyes, he could be a goner.

While we reeled from that, another ghost from my past came back to haunt me. A rival sound system called Sound City. Years before, we had competed with this multi-racial sound system to see whether they or Jah Baddis were the best in Coventry.

As I said, these battles could be quite heated. Frankly, our Jamaican patois from the mic ran rings round their attempts at toasting and they knew it. The success me and Trevor enjoyed over the years that followed only made them more bitter.

So one night, they came up to Trevor in a Coventry pub called The Queens and stuck a broken bottle in his face. He felt a darting pain and then blood spurted everywhere.

As he took his palms away from his now moist face, they came back into view covered in crimson. He was bleeding badly and somehow managed to stagger out of the pub and get home.

After cleaning himself up, Trevor realised his injuries weren't as bad as he'd initially thought, so there was now only one course of action open to him. He had to go back to that pub.

First though, Trevor gave me a ring. I was beyond furious. I got the rude boy crew together and we tooled up – I had knives, iron bars and an old starting pistol under my coat. As an added bit of protection, I grabbed a short piece of pole from a scaffold as we walked towards the pub. I wasn't prepared to be run off Coventry's streets by a failed sound system.

Franklyn was with me, as were Trevor and Dennis. We stood outside The Queens and I sent word in that I wanted Sound City to come outside and explain themselves.

We knew the names of all these guys. We'd grown up on the same streets, played the same clubs. Sadly, two of them are now dead: Leonard, who was a big stocky white guy; and Glen Ford, who was mixed race.

That night they came out of The Queens – five of them, all told, and cocky as hell. I put a stop to that by pulling my coat back and showing them my armoury. This seemed to reduce Leonard to a blancmange.

'Leonard – is this finished or what?'

'Yeah... yeah... sure.'

And that was the end of our trouble with Sound City. They could see I meant business and I had the tools to make the point. It's hard to believe I was purvey-ing bubblegum pop to the masses while engaged in rude boy battles like this. But that was the reality on the street.

Just to update you on my sex life in the mid-1980s – in case you think I'd slowed down a bit – I had a paternity suit served on me around this time.

While handling that little legal conundrum, both my neighbours decided to turn on me as well. They took out private summonses complaining about the racket coming from my house. It wasn't music. This legal action was in relation to the noise coming from my incessant sex romps at all hours. The story made it to the *News of the World* and the pop mags.

In between my bedroom-related episodes, I was starting to feel adrift in Fun Boy Three. I was barely a backing vocalist, just a kind of ornament on stage. It was as if all my energy and verve had been neutered. Even though we made a respectable amount of money out of Fun Boy Three, and enjoyed a level of financial security I'd never known before, this couldn't be a long-term proposition.

Pauline Black thinks that Fun Boy Three finally lost the musical plot with our version of 'Summertime'. I think she's got a point. It's pretty nasty and the late George Gershwin must have been spinning hard in his grave. Still, we ended up back on *Top of the Pops* for the umpteenth time and there I was beating my tom-toms.

I was painfully aware that something had gone wrong with my pop career. If you want, I knew that I was living a bit of a lie. Where was the man who had set up the gritty urban street sound of Jah Baddis? The toasting maniac at the front of The Specials? Fame had surely come at a big price for Neville Staple.

The record industry liked Fun Boy Three because we had a photogenic white guy singing at the front. I had always realised that we would never have got signed with a black lead vocalist.

If you don't believe me, look at the struggle that had to be fought to get MTV to play black music in the early 1980s. The problem wasn't imaginary, it was very real. Teen pop was, with a very few exceptions, about white faces – the sort of pop stars that most mums would have been happy to have their daughters bring back home.

This left the thorny problem of what exactly to do with all these talented black musicians that 2 Tone had thoughtlessly left behind. The industry simply had nowhere they wanted to put us. Pauline Black said that we were 'the black edges on the white envelope of pop'.

Sooner than I could have ever expected, I was about to find out that without a white front man I was surplus to requirements.

Fun Boy Three did a short, eight-date tour of the United States. Then Lynval and I went on holiday to the Caribbean to recharge our batteries. Now that I'd gone back once to see my real mother, I found myself going over and over again. I still go to Jamaica regularly now.

The holiday was exactly what we needed – the sun on our skin, swimming in the sea, drinking by the pool and seeing my family and the growing number of friends we had over there. Even Kingston seemed to be improving, but that might have just been growing familiarity.

Once we were back in the UK, we were in for a shock. We both received a phone call curtly informing us that Terry had left the band. Fun Boy Three was finished.

Me and bubblegum pop were over.

From 21 Guns . . . a gritty
urban sound . . .
Neville Staple, personal collection

. . . to Splashdown . . . and
bubblegum pop.
Trevor Evans, personal collection

The Higsons. Charlie Higson (*second from left*) was later to become
a star on the BBC's *The Fast Show*.
Supplied to Neville Staple by the band

Me and what guys might have 'tooled up' with back in the day –
maybe not the handcuffs!

Neville Staple, personal collection

9

BHANGRA HOUSE – DANCE MUSIC TAKES OVER

The short-lived
Sunday Best.
© Chrysalis Records

So began a fifteen-year rift with Terry Hall. We hadn't said a huge amount to each other in either band, but we'd always got on. I'd often walk down the street with him and deflect some of the unwanted attention he got. Terry really was as shy as people thought. If somebody shouted 'Oi... Terry!' from the other side of the road, he would stare bleakly at his shoes, wanting them to shut up or disappear.

He once said in an interview: 'People who don't know me think I'm miserable... people who know me – they know I'm miserable.'

But after the way Fun Boy Three folded, I was in no mood to talk to him. I felt I'd been kicked in the teeth. Jerry and I were now similarly estranged. There really wasn't much to say any more. He carried on with The Special AKA for as long as was bearable. Rhoda Dakar had joined him on vocals from The Bodysnatchers, Brad stayed on drums and Jerry drafted in a talented young vocalist called Stan Campbell who sang the lead on 'Free Nelson Mandela'.

When success didn't come Stan's way, he disappeared off the radar. The Special AKA fell apart shortly after. Brad, for his part, had already formed a band called JB's Allstars.

Ranking Roger went off to the United States and The Beat were hugely popular over there – though they were known as The English Beat as I think there was another band of the same name. They toured with David Bowie and REM, among others, before Ranking Roger and guitarist/vocalist Dave Wakeling split off to form General Public.

They had quite a bit of success on MTV as the music channel broadened its horizons. They were a pop band with telegenic black and white guys up front doing reggae-influenced pop. Again, not as cutting edge as what we had all done previously but I wouldn't write it off as bubblegum pop.

They didn't enjoy any chart success in the UK but they did well in the United States and Canada. Their single 'Tenderness' got to number 11 in Canada and 27 in the US.

Horace – now liberated from The Specials – took up the bass with General Public. One other surprise addition to that combo was Mick Jones who had now parted company with our old friends The Clash. He'd been their guitarist. Mick would later form Big Audio Dynamite, which Ranking Roger was also in for a while.

As for the remaining members of The Beat – guitarist Andy Cox and bass guitarist David Steele soon found fame and fortune in the late-1980s. They teamed up with a very distinctive voice in the form of Roland Gift and became the Fine Young Cannibals. In 1989 they had chart-topping hits with 'She Drives Me Crazy' and 'Good Thing'.

The ska sound we had brought to the United States had infected many young people, but we had no idea what was bubbling under the surface in that country by the middle of the 1980s. Only at the end of that decade and in the early 1990s would the full extent of what we had achieved with The Specials' US tour become clear in the so-called 'third wave' of ska. The 2-Toning of America would become a reality.

After the split of Fun Boy Three and the winding up of The Selecter, Chrysalis tossed me, Lynval and Pauline a bone. At least that's how it felt.

In 1984, we formed a band called Sunday Best and put out a single called 'Pirates on the Airwaves' – a Pauline composition that celebrated the heroes of pirate radio.

'If you're bugged with radio pop
Time for you to stop the rot
All night long'

I suppose we shouldn't have been taken aback when Radio 1 proved unwilling to give it airplay – even though many of their DJs had started on pirate radio stations. Not long after this single went nowhere, Chrysalis and me said goodbye to each other.

In the years since I'd leapt on stage at the Camden Music Machine, I'd steadily put more money in the bank. During Fun Boy Three, I'd got a Lotus to speed round in, then an Alfa Romeo. For three weeks I was the owner of a Bentley, before deciding it wasn't me and traded it in for a Porsche.

Round about 1983, I might be seen round the streets of Hillfields in a white Renegade Jeep and I was one of the first people in the city to have a car phone – then seen as the height of yuppie extravagance.

Ranking Roger says we were probably classified as 'buppies' at that time – black yuppies. There weren't many of us, that was certain. We had nice cars, owned our own homes and had beautiful women. Not many black men made their way to the upper ranks of the working class, let alone the middle class. In the factories of Coventry, black guys had done the worst jobs. Our pay was lower and our prospects in life were generally shit, so lads like me and Roger had done extremely well.

I wasn't ready to fall into an abyss of poverty quite yet. The question was – with no recording contract and no pop band, what was I going to do next? The answer came from the most unlikely quarter.

I owned a house in Broomfield Road and when doing some DIY, I popped into a builders' merchants in Wyken – a suburb of Coventry. The place was run by an Indian family and I went in occasionally. On this particular morning, their son was singing away to something on the radio while looking for nails or screws for a customer.

Short of saying 'Hey kid, let me turn you into a star', I did invite him down to my studio. There was a certain quality to his voice and the way he was interpreting the song – a kind of Asian take on a European song – I liked what I heard.

My aim wasn't to create something brand new. I wasn't about to start listening to John Barry albums and playing with drum machines, but in my mind, I was already thinking about the possibility of fusing this guy's voice to the sort of sounds I preferred.

Anyway, Tarsame Singh Jamail – as he was then called before his makeover – came to my studio and we messed around with some ideas. There was something instantly likeable about the bloke who would eventually be launched as Johnny Zee. From the start, I found him easy to work with and had the gut feeling this could go somewhere.

What I didn't realise was that I'd tapped into something of a movement within the younger generation of Britain's Asian community. They wanted to break into the mainstream but also wanted to maintain their cultural identity.

We talked about this and realised we could create a new type of music that would fuse Western and Asian sounds. I obviously had plenty of reggae, ska and pop sensibilities, while Johnny Zee had very broad tastes – from George Michael and Prince through to Punjabi singers like Gurdas Maan and Kuldip Manak.

So we got started on some tracks and very soon were putting together a debut album. I roped in a producer called Tom Lowry – who became very important to me in the years ahead.

There was already a bhangra music scene with bands playing to Asian audiences round the UK. We decided that Johnny Zee was going to burst into all this with our new 'bhangra base fusion' sound. We had no idea how it would go down but, the more we blended reggae rhythms with Johnny's vocals and Asian harmonies, it just grabbed my ears.

So in 1989, we released the album. It spent thirty-six weeks at number one in the Asian pop music charts and, in that same year, Johnny was voted Best New Artist at the Asian Music Awards. I hadn't expected this kind of recognition so quickly – he was even being described by the music press as the 'pioneer of pop fusion' and the 'prince of crossover music'. All this came from me listening to him chirping away in a builders' yard.

But not everybody was happy with this incredible and rapid success. The more traditional bhangra bands that had been slogging away for years and had – what they thought were until now – loyal audiences now turned against us. Johnny Zee was playing to packed venues. He also had hundreds of girls all over him as if he was an international pop star. As Johnny explains:

'There was a lot of animosity, primarily as the female fans went completely nuts and frenzied wherever me and Neville travelled. These kinds of scenes were never witnessed or seen before so the Asian guys used to look on with a great deal of hatred.'

Even though they hated us, they were blasting Johnny Zee's music out of their car stereos as they drove round town. It wasn't long before I was at the receiving end of some of these guys' wrath.

I made it my mission to coach Johnny Zee. For me, it was almost therapeutic to pass on to a new young protégé everything that I had learnt with the two bands – and also with Jah Baddis, Ray King and the older sound system generation. How to whip up an audience, catch their attention and never let their spirits flag throughout your whole performance.

I told Johnny that he had to look good. Like a rude boy, he always had to be turned out well – there was never any excuse for dressing like a slob.

We discussed how he would handle interviews with the music press and look after his money – a subject close to my heart. But most of all, as Johnny recalls well, my main message was to humble himself before his fans. I'd never agreed with the attitude of some of the punk bands all those years ago that had scorned their audiences. I respected anybody who had paid for a ticket to come and see me – and I still do.

I showered him with fine words and lectures. This felt good. It must have been what Ray King felt like when he took Jerry, Lynval, Silverton, Neol and me under his wing

– the old man of soul giving us his wisdom. Now I was doing the same.

A few months before my trip to the builders' merchant, I'd met a 'dub poet' – as Tom Lowry described him – called Kendell Smith, or DJ Kendell. He had been trying to find a producer for his album and his first choice was Charley Anderson. Instead, he ended up with me.

We put together a few tracks and sent them down to Ariwa – a new dub music record label that had just been set up by the leading dub producer, Guyanese born Mad Professor. He wasn't interested in our offering, so we went back to the drawing board.

With no sign of movement on his album, DJ Kendell offered to be a road manager of sorts on Johnny Zee's proposed UK tour. I needed the company. He was a bit of a rude boy at heart and very soon we were in my BMW smoking the requisite amount of weed and talking about whatever came into our heads.

One of Johnny Zee's gigs was the Leicester Palais. This was where we discovered just how much some people resented the success of my new up-and-coming star.

Kendell and I arrived at the Palais and parked in a side street. We couldn't take the weed inside with us so I popped it under the driver's mat on the floor. It would be safe there and ready for duty when we came back. Then we both got out and I locked up the car.

A few hours passed and we were doing the sound checks in the venue, when a very concerned promoter waddled up to us. He looked totally flustered. Apparently there had been a phone call for me from a group calling itself Sheer Punjab – some local militant group that I'd never heard of. The upshot was – they were going to blow up my BMW.

I had to make sure my ears were working properly. The promoter repeated himself and when I tried to laugh it off, he got even more agitated. This group, he explained, was fighting for the rights of Punjabi youth – at least that's how they saw it. He said they were big round the Midlands and we had to take this very, very seriously.

'Why would they put a bomb under *my* car?'

It seemed that our friends in Sheer Punjab resented black guys getting involved in the bhangra scene. My suspicion was that what they really resented was Johnny's success.

'But they're not really going to blow up my car?'

'This is for real', the promoter went on. He'd already phoned the police, who were on their way. Kendell and me both looked at each other and had the exact same thought: Our weed was still under the driver's mat.

We were going to be in deep shit if the car was searched. After all, I had a bit of a track record as far as the police were concerned. So we walked back to the side street and turning into it, were greeted with the spectacle of my car surrounded by cops. They were keeping a respectful distance expecting it to explode into a fireball at any moment.

We moved gingerly towards my BMW. But a cop said something like: 'Is that your car?.'

'Yes', I said.

'Don't go near – there may be an explosive device – we need to check.'

This was not a good situation. I had to make a split-second decision. Retrieve the weed and risk being blown into the skies above, or do nothing and risk the cops finding it.

So I reached for the door handle.

'Please don't do that sir!'

Too late – I'd opened the door. Somehow I managed to slip the weed up my jacket sleeve and then stood up facing a very concerned looking police officer.

'It's all yours,' I said to him calmly. Then strode off trying not to look as guilty as sin.

We had a few more encounters with Sheer Punjab – on radio stations mainly. We'd be with Johnny Zee on some call-in programme and they would phone to ask why black men were involved in bhangra music. Johnny asked us once if we took this stuff seriously and we said no.

I'd gone through the whole skinhead thing with The Specials and these guys were a walk in the park in comparison.

Kendell ended up touring as a two-man act with Johnny. They called themselves Johnny Zee & DJK. In 1994, they produced the album 'Spirits of Rhythm' and caught EMI's attention. The record industry was waking up to the huge potential in the Asian music market and wasn't going to miss this act off its roster.

After the EMI signing, they became Stereo Nation and Johnny Zee became Taz. The fusion of bhangra and reggae continued, and the most impressive thing was the huge following that Taz found in India. Inevitably, his songs ended up in Bollywood movies with the hit 'Oh Baby Don't Break My Heart' featuring in the soundtrack of the gigantic Bollywood movie *Mohabbat*.

While I was producing Johnny Zee, I also worked with my daughter Sheena Staple who was keen to make her first

record at sixteen years old. She ended up on vocals with an Indian pop star called Bindu and Multitone released their single 'We've Got Feelings Too' – a song composed by me, Sheena and Bindu. It still does the rounds on compilations and was featured on 'World of Indian Pop' a few years back on the ZYX label.

Taz, meanwhile, went from strength to strength and you can see him playing to vast crowds of screaming girls on YouTube. His 2000 album 'Slave II Fusion' shifted three million copies in India and won Best Selling Album of the Year at the 2000 UK Asian Music Awards. He went on to perform at the Indian Oscars in 2001. Not bad for the boy from the builders' yard.

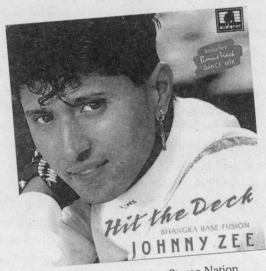

Johnny Zee – later Taz from Stereo Nation.
© Taz Singh

Johnny Zee's first stage image.
© Taz Singh

10

THE THIRD WAVE –
AMERICA REVIVES
SKA

Back in Japan – this time with Special Beat.
Me (*left*) and Ranking Roger.

Neville Staple, personal collection

Ranking Roger was in for the shock of his life. He'd been asked to go and do a gig in San Francisco, at the Greek Theatre, performing in a line-up that called itself International Beat.

Back in 1983 when the original line up of The Beat had gone their separate ways – Ranking Roger and Dave Wakeling forming General Public and two of the other guys becoming the backbone of Fine Young Cannibals – that left behind veteran saxophone player Saxa as well as drummer Everett Morton.

Saxa, like Rico, was one of the grand old men of ska. Born in 1930, he'd played with all the greats like the godfather of ska himself, Laurel Aitken, Prince Buster and had also been involved with Desmond Dekker. Having made his mark on the first wave of ska, he went on to be a key figure in 2 Tone. Saxa joined The Beat and you can hear his playing all over tracks like 'Mirror in the Bathroom'.

But in 1983, he was left high and dry by The Beat's split. However, Everett and Saxa weren't left licking their wounds for too long. They bumped into a young song-writer called Tony Beet – not to be confused with The Beat – and as they all shared the same ska and rocksteady influences, the trio decided to form a band.

They started playing in a way that was reminiscent of the old band, but with new songs. Beet and the boys formed a band called The Elevators but in 1988 changed the name to International Beat.

Former Dexy's and General Public keyboardist Mickey Billingham hopped on board and they all approached Ranking Roger and Dave Wakeling to see whether they'd like to join them on stage every so often – to relive the glories of ska one more time.

Ranking Roger was quite amenable to gigging with the guys. General Public had folded but he was still hungry for the limelight – a disease I also suffer from. So in 1990, he agreed to play with International Beat at the Greek Theatre in San Francisco. Nobody had particularly high expectations for this concert.

The band was touring to promote their new album called 'The Hitting Line', which Buster Bloodvessel of ska band Bad Manners released on his label, Blue Beat Records. Ranking Roger produced it and loved the songs that Tony Beet had penned.

That night at the Greek Theatre was when we all woke up to what had been happening in the United States since our Specials tour back in 1980. We had unknowingly sown seeds back in those days.

Our music had inspired young kids, who had gone straight back home from the gigs, formed bands in their garages or clubs and started playing ska.

They all wanted to be The Specials or The Beat. I recently spoke to Eric Din, a Berkeley High School graduate who was typical of many ska fans. He saw The Beat play back in 1980 and formed a band called The Uptones. They ended up touring throughout the 1980s, getting a recording contract and supporting Madness. But we were completely unaware of the scale of this activity even by 1990.

When International Beat walked out on to the stage at the Greek Theatre, there was a sea of people. The band started playing, then turned to the screaming crowd and said two simple words: 'Ranking Roger!'

Roger danced out and it took a while to get the raucous throng to calm down. Then he belted out 'Ranking Full Stop' – his famous song with The Beat. Thousands upon thousands of kids were jumping up and down – about 15,000 people in total – this was a sight that none of us had seen since the glory days of 2 Tone.

It was a very excited Roger that I encountered back in England days later: 'We've got to do something. They're going mad for ska over there.'

I still had bhangra rhythms in my head, but Roger wouldn't let the matter drop. America had gone bonkers for ska. The surfing community in California were all into 2 Tone and in New York there was a massive scene. Boston had some great bands and even Texas had its network of ska fans. We had blinked and missed all this.

To understand what had been happening in the US since our 2 Toning of America, take one example of an American ska band that I still know well today – The Toasters.

After The Specials fell apart in 1981, the whole 2 Tone movement and those bands that had been associated with it were pretty much written off by the fickle British music press.

Some of us ran up the white flag, put on the white jump suits and made plinky plonky pop. But while Britain turned its back on the Coventry sound, America was gradually adopting it.

Robert Hingley had seen The Beat play in 1981. At the time he was working in the Forbidden Planet comic book store on the Lower East Side of Manhattan and got together with some of his co-workers to form The Toasters.

They played some gigs and the audiences grew. Before they knew it other ska bands were popping up in what they call the Tri-State area – New York, New Jersey and Connecticut. So Robert formed Moon Ska Records in 1983 and put out a compilation album of all these bands called 'New York Beat: Hit and Run'.

Then it came to his attention that there were similar ska bands all over California. Not one to miss a trick, Robert released a compilation of these bands and called it 'Skaface'. Both albums did well and he knew he was on to something.

One band he included on his compilations was a brand new combo called No Doubt. At that time they were a twelve-member ska band from Anaheim, California. No Doubt included a bloke called Eric Stefani and his sister Gwen. She went on to be referred to as the 'Queen of Ska' in America and still enjoys – as I'm sure most of you are aware – a hugely successful pop career.

Like The Specials, No Doubt gigs became famous for their stage-diving fans. Audience participation was alive and well in the third wave of ska – a term made popular by my old friends Tazy Phyllipz and Albino Brown, who set up a radio station called Ska Parade in the US, which is still on air. They helped to promote many of the bands that Robert was recording including No Doubt.

Moon Ska Records carried on through the 1980s and 1990s, before closing its doors in 2000. In its time, the label, and the man behind it, promoted loads of third wave ska bands but also released records by Bad Manners and me. Moon Ska released my EP entitled 'Skanktastic' in 1994.

In all this time, Robert's band – The Toasters – were touring and found themselves part of this ever-growing American ska family. In 2002, he set up a new label called Megalith Records and decided that the ethos should be to nurture grassroots talent and maintain the highest quality threshold. He decided to base the company in a town called Norman, Oklahoma.

For Robert, it gave him the opportunity to look at the burgeoning ska talent in Texas to the south, Florida to the south east and then in the more familiar stomping grounds of California and New York.

In 1990, Ranking Roger was insistent we get out to the States as quickly as possible and start playing regularly to these mega audiences on the east and west coasts. The question was – what would our group be called? And who would be in it?

We answered the first question pretty rapidly. The band had to be what it said on the tin. We would be doing Beat and Specials numbers so the band name was to be Special Beat.

In time, we'd start adding in our own new compositions, but this was the starting point. Brad agreed to come and join us on drums – it would have been unthinkable at that point not to have Prince Rimshot keeping us to the old familiar rhythm.

Then we phoned Horace. Whatever differences of opinion I'd had with him about having rude boys as roadies, Horace Panter was the only person we would consider on bass. He'd played with General Public so he knew Roger well. At the time, I think he was working for a transport firm so I can't believe he didn't find the phone call a welcome development. A few months after, Lynval also joined us.

Ranking Roger was an ideal person for me to work with. The first time I'd shared the same stage with him was when The Specials did the short tour of Ireland a few months before our eventual split. Roger and I had similar backgrounds, though he was a bit younger and grew up in Birmingham – the big city down the motorway from Coventry.

Our roots were in the Caribbean and we had experienced all the skinhead stuff on the streets in our youth. We had also both been lead vocalists for two of the top bands of the 2 Tone scene.

Over the next four years, we were in each other's presence day and night. Far from making us sick of the sight of each other, it created a very deep bond – blood brothers if you want. If my performance wasn't one hundred per cent, Roger would think nothing of turning round to me in his Brummie accent and opining:

'Oi Stapes – what's wrong with ya man. You were crap tonight.'

He'd tell me that I was singing out of tune or whatever and, whereas I might get very defensive with other members of the band, I'd take it from him. I knew he wasn't point scoring or trying to put me in my place.

Roger knows what makes me tick. He thinks I've been misunderstood by a lot of people. The problem apparently boils down to the look on my face. I just come across as a bad boy, a rude boy – the kid who was constantly shouted at by his teachers or picked up by the cops in his teens.

As my musical soul mate knows, all I've ever really wanted is to be able to live well. I've always been generous to family and genuine friends, and I'm a loyal person. Trevor, Rex and all the other rude boys from my childhood are mostly still in contact – I couldn't imagine it any other way.

There have been lots of stories in the press over the years suggesting that I'm a less-than-legal chap, which has been true. But ultimately, I've not wanted to lead a life of crime. I've wanted to be financially secure and on stage making people happy. Though there is a mean streak. As Roger puts it: 'You've got a rude boy side which can be quite violent but it takes a lot of provocation.'

There was one guitarist we used in Special Beat – a session musician – who gave me the required level of provocation to display my rude boy tendencies. A regular smart arse who took to taking the piss out of me. I can't remember what he said but I didn't like it one little bit. As far as I was concerned, I'd earned the right to be respected.

He finally saw my darkest side when we were on our second Special Beat tour of Japan. The dumb comments kept coming and I told Roger: 'I'm going to deal with him.' I was true to my word.

Backstage, he pepped up again with some idiot remarks and it was as if I found myself back in borstal having to defend myself. Knowing that if I let another bloke ridicule me in front of other people, I'd be unable to hold up my head. I watched this guitarist's mouth opening and closing but I wasn't listening to what he was saying anymore.

He was a lot taller than me but that wasn't going to present an insurmountable obstacle. In my hand was a dressing room towel and with one leap – like the ones I make on stage – I shot up and wrapped the towel round his neck. Then dragged him to the ground all the time tightening the towel. He was now quite red in the face.

'You little fuck – you had enough!'

He thought this was a joke.

'No.'

So the towel gripped a little harder round his neck and his face went a little redder. Now he couldn't answer at all and his eyes were popping. I could see he'd had enough.

'That'll teach ya to fuck with me.'

Another incident that brought out my rude boy side was an over-zealous security guard at a Special Beat gig in Florida. As I sang on stage, I watched him roughing up the audience. It brought back to me all those times in The Specials when we'd stop gigs and demand our fans be treated properly – not smacked round the head and thrown around like rag dolls.

I stopped the band and made my point. Then we started playing again. But this time, I just couldn't sing. There was so much anger inside me at seeing that sort of behaviour again that I just stared furiously at this one particular security guard. He was left in no doubt that I was harbouring some murderous thoughts towards him. It took all my self-control not to plant the mic stand in his head.

As I set off to play with Special Beat for the next four years, one woman in my life had decided she needed a big change. Ideta had been living in my house for about ten years but now that Byron and Melanie were grown up and she was seeing nothing of me for weeks and months, it was time to move on.

We met in 1972 at the Locarno – which had now been demolished and a public library built in its place. Where

Ideta and I had once smooched and danced, and Pete Waterman had played the latest Jamaican sounds, there were now people shuffling round quietly thumbing through novels. Where I had shagged in the dark balconies, books were now being stamped – the only noise allowed.

Ideta and me had been an item for twenty years. But we'd lived apart – I'd been on tour with The Specials, Fun Boy Three and Taz, and I'd been less than faithful. However, she was the one woman who really had a handle on what Neville Staple was all about. Our time together had often been difficult but she knew me inside out.

After all, Ideta had been with me when I was just a rude boy on the streets: 'He got famous and I wasn't happy. The relationships with other women. Felt like a fool.'

I should have treated her better. Ideta had visited me in borstal and she came to see me when I was on remand in Brockhill. No matter how terrible my life had been, she was there for me.

For a long time, Ideta hadn't really been happy. She's even said she wished she'd never met me. Back in the 1970s, Ideta found herself in the unenviable situation of meeting Yvonne who was not only another girlfriend, but mother of Andrea. At first, Ideta didn't know there were other women I had children with. When she found out, she tolerated it for a while and buried the pain. But eventually – though it took two decades – she walked out.

Ideta has tried hard to forget me but, unfortunately, those bloody songs from The Specials keep popping up everywhere. At the moment, there's a crisp advert that uses one of our songs. 'When I hear that commercial, I start remembering Neville and it really hurts.'

I'm sorry Ideta.

In 1991, we began a forty-five-date tour with Sting across North America. It seemed like the US and Canada couldn't get enough of Special Beat. Roger thinks that both Jerry Dammers and Dave Wakeling, his fellow member of the original Beat, could not have been over-joyed by what we were doing.

But we got Dave along to star in the gigs every so often and that seemed to bring him round.

The one thing we didn't want to be was a tribute band. Brad's interpretation of The Beat's songs was quite differ-ent to their original drummer Everett Morton and it gave the songs a whole new feel. Having both Ranking Roger and me on vocals also created a new powerful dynamic.

If Roger and I had got the original line-ups of The Beat and The Specials back together again I'm sure we could have trousered even more money. But frankly, we were happy working with the more chilled line-up in Special Beat. After the miserable band politics I'd experienced at the end of The Specials, it was still a relief to be in a sane environment.

As word got out about the big gigs we were playing, there were reunion rumblings among the other ska combos. Pauline reformed The Selecter in 1990 and a couple of Bad Manners members teamed up with her and Neol Davies to go on tour in the UK.

Finding themselves playing sell-out gigs, they then packed their bags for the States. And what do you know? They had the same experience as us – big concert halls full of a new generation of ska fans.

Gappa climbed on board in 1991 and they recorded three albums throughout the decade that followed. For all of us, coming back to the US this time round was an uplifting experience – we were treated like legendary figures.

Touring with Special Beat, we met American rude boys and skinheads who had got 2 Tone tattoos back in 1980. Their skin was slightly more wrinkled now, but there was Walt Jabsco skanking on somebody's forearm. These fans' hair may have receded a bit and the midriffs might have been a bit porkier, but the belief in ska was undimmed.

One guy who had been at high school in the early 1980s and into 2 Tone was a fan from Denver, Colorado called Rolf Reitzig. He told me that he got so obsessed with 2 Tone that when he got to college, he'd bought a 1963 Vespa and painted it with a black and white chequered pattern. He drove round in tonic suits, skinny ties and had a rude boy tattoo on his shoulder.

At college, he met a black punk called Byron Shaw and the two of them decided to set up their own 2 Tone style band called Judge Roughneck – after the toasting character I created in The Specials. They played some of our old songs and some of their own. Not only did the band take off, but Judge Roughneck and me have played together many times over the years.

Talking to the fans, I began to get a clearer idea of why this third wave of ska had taken off in the States. Between our departure in 1980 and the end of the decade, there seemed to be a dip in interest in ska. But the movement was growing in garages and clubs all over the country.

On the surface, the 1980s were all about power pop, heavy metal and the beginnings of the Seattle grunge scene. But like lava building up under the surface, ska was about to pour out creating hundreds of bands in California, New York and Boston in paricular.

Nirvana's exit left a gaping hole, which bands like No Doubt, Unwritten Law and Rancid quickly filled. In the same way that we had crossed ska with some punk and rockabilly infuences, the American bands cross-fertilised ska with stuff that was going on around that time. But the end result was, like 2 Tone, a brand of music that had serious messages, but you could also dance to it. It was pop with a conscience.

A guy named Nigel Knucklehead formed a ska band called The Allstonians in 1992. He went through a musical journey that I think a lot of these guys experienced. At the start of the 1980s, he was listening to The Clash, Sex Pistols and Elvis Costello. Some of his mates knew about Jamaican ska but none of them thought about playing it.

They used to have what were called 'black and white' parties where they wore... well... black and white. They listened to music that wouldn't normally get airplay on US radio. One night, Nigel heard our version of 'A Message to You Rudy' and he was floored. The Jamaican ska sound with a dose of punk was life changing.

'I ran out as soon as I had the money, and could find a store that carried The Specials, and picked up the album.'

Most of his friends didn't get 2 Tone. But he loved the songs and my voice, which he calls 'lazy yet authoritative'. He couldn't describe what moved him about The Specials' sound, but it touched him somehow.

As ska began to make waves again, it was only a matter of time before the record companies sat up and took notice. In 1993, Trojan Records asked our old friend Roger Lomas to do a record with Desmond Dekker. Roger had recorded the original version of the song 'The Selecter' in his garden shed, if you recall, and acted as our sound engi-

neer in the very early days of The Specials. He'd also worked with The Bodysnatchers.

Trojan Records had set up in 1968 and they had an impressive roster of ska, reggae and dub acts including Lee 'Scratch' Perry (who Pete Waterman worked with), Nicky Thomas (whose gig sparked a riot at the Locarno) and of course, Desmond Dekker.

What Trojan wanted was a new spin on Desmond Dekker. With that in mind, they told Roger not to use Desmond's usual backing band – The Aces. To get a different tempo and feel, they would have to be left out of the project.

So Trojan and Roger hatched the idea of getting Desmond together with The Specials to do a covers album. That was all well and good, but it couldn't be assumed The Specials wanted to sit together in the same room, let alone communicate. It hadn't been long enough for the wounds to heal.

Terry didn't want anything to do with this or The Specials, so we could forget him immediately. The whole thing didn't work for Jerry either. He took legal advice over us using The Specials name but, with a majority of the band eventually coming on board, we kind of outvoted him.

Four out of seven of The Specials signed up – Lynval, Horace, Roddy and me. Roger tells me that Trojan continued to fret about the use of The Specials name and went to some lengths to check it would be OK. In the end, we were able to proceed as Desmond Dekker and The Specials.

Desmond had adopted the rude boy ethos a quarter of a century before with singles like '007 (Shanty Town)'. That had been a hit in the UK in 1967 and he followed

it up with 'Rude Boy Train' and 'Rudie Got Soul'. His big breakthrough was with the single 'Israelites' which shot to number one in the UK charts in 1969, just as I was showing up at my first Saturday matinees at the Locarno.

When we met him during the recording of this album, he really didn't seem to have changed at all.

In the intervening years, he never went out of fashion and even signed with Stiff Records in the late 1970s. The third wave ska bands doffed their caps to him with several mentioning him in their songs. Rancid name check Desmond in their track 'Roots Radicals':

'The radio was playing
Desmond Dekker was singing…'

When it came to working with Desmond, he was a quiet and very reserved man. He chose the songs he wanted to cover and we all laid down our tracks. Desmond and I didn't meet during the actual recording of the album, only afterwards, when we did the video.

There were no discussions about how to fuse our differing styles. Desmond showed up and sang the songs exactly how he wanted. We then showed up and recorded the backing in our own 2 Tone style. Then Roger mashed the two together.

Most people who listen to the album now think it's got a real energy to it – Desmond's voice is incredible – but the record didn't shift as many copies as Trojan had hoped.

However, Desmond Dekker's agent rang Roger to say that Desmond Dekker and The Specials had been noticed in Japan. He'd been rung by a promoter over there asking if The Specials had now reformed – he assumed they had after seeing the band name on the album cover.

This Japanese guy said it would be easy to get a tour fixed up for The Specials in Japan because, as with the United States, ska had not only survived but prospered. There were plenty of bands and plenty of fans.

Roger Lomas rang the four of us individually and explained what the Japanese were putting on the table. The money looked very, very good. It was difficult for any of us to turn our noses up at what was on offer. It seemed the Japanese didn't want any new material – just the old songs – everything from 'Gangsters' to 'Ghost Town'.

That left open the six million dollar question – did we want to reform The Specials on an ongoing basis? Being musicians and temperamental types, there was some bellyaching about whether it was the right thing to do. But for me, if the Japanese were itching for us, my suitcase was already packed.

I'd been working with Horace and Brad in Special Beat, though Brad had bowed out to become an IT specialist – what some people might call a real job though not my cup of tea. I knew that Roddy and Lynval were gagging to blast out 'Rat Race' and 'Guns of Navarone' to appreciative fans.

Jerry and Terry were not going to join us. Terry had put a distance between himself and his 2 Tone days and Jerry was off our radar at this time.

We needed somebody on sticks so we drafted in 'H' from The Selecter. Mark Adams joined on keyboards as our Jerry replacement and Adam Birch played trombone. Then there was a slog of rehearsing. We were almost relearning the songs and then working out how this line-up would gel. As it turned out, we sounded much more energetic than we ever expected.

In more of a leadership role than I had before, I steered us – The Specials mark two – on to a secure ska footing. There would be no muzak or John Barry influences where we were going. I had every intention of taking global audiences by the scruff of their collective necks and giving them a good shake.

With more confidence and self-belief than I had back in the old days, I started to grow as a front man. With no Terry or Jerry, or Ranking Roger for that matter, it really was up to me to be the person communicating directly with the audience. The Specials mark two would live or die on my ability to entertain.

For a short period, we called ourselves The Coventry Specials but, inevitably, concert halls billed us as The Specials, so after a while we just gave in. Nobody issued any writs or complained so we stuck with the old band name.

Anybody who went to the gigs we did in the mid-1990s across Japan, Europe and the United States will tell you how electrifying they were. Roger Lomas became acting tour manager and made sure the arrangements for our touring would minimise the risk of rows breaking out. For a start, all of us would have our own hotel rooms – none of this sharing nonsense we had with the original Specials. We were older guys now and really needed the luxuries that Jerry had once denied us.

My daughter Sheena came out to see us perform in Washington DC and when she turned up got the warmest of welcomes.

The guys in the band looked after Sheena like they were her uncles. She calls them her 'ska Dads'. They would sit there telling Sheena not to do drugs and to stick on the straight and narrow. They'd come to me and say: 'I think

Sheena's wearing a lot of make-up today.' Or turn round to her and say: 'Are you going out wearing that?'

She saw the lively gigs we were doing from New York to Los Angeles, where old ska fans would come up and say: 'Oh my God, you're Neville Staple.' She thought it was great to see her old man being treated like this.

Her so-called ska Dads were a little longer in the tooth than they had been and I had to deal with a certain amount of moaning about wanting to go home, see their families, go to parents' evenings at the schools, etc – not very rock 'n' roll. This eventually torpedoed us but to start with, some members of the band still showed a bit of the old spirit.

Roddy was still keen to sow his wild oats, as was I. This time though, he wasn't prepared to tolerate me running off with what he took to be his women. One time we were on the road to Pomona in California to do a gig. We stopped at a roadside café and started chatting to some of the locals. I instantly spotted two girls and asked if they were coming to the show.

Not to be left empty handed, Roddy came over and started to natter as well. I would have one girl, he would have another. But when they turned up to the gig, Roddy was in for a big let down. They came up and both of them asked him where I was. Later that evening, another of my infamous three-in a-bed romps ensued.

I thought Roddy had taken this on the chin but I was going to be proved very wrong. He had a few drinks before our next gig and went on stage cursing away. Fuck this and fuck that. The mics were off so the audience weren't treated to his display of anger. Then he came over and muttered something to me about stealing his girl.

The atmosphere on stage throughout the gig was pretty lousy. Afterwards, we all took it in turns to calm him down. I suppose my attitude was: if they wanted to go with me, that was their decision. But that didn't wash with Roddy one bit.

Next thing he was trashing the dressing room in true jaded rock star style. Then he moved on to the tour bus where the driver had to beg him to stop sticking the boot in. This was one of the problems we had with Roddy. A brilliant guitarist with fantastic stage presence but when he was moody, you knew it.

His way of relaxing was to knock into the Jack Daniel's. Mine was to smoke weed. That meant he could get pretty mean after a gig if he was in a bad mood, whereas I was more likely to mellow out as the night wore on.

Kendell came and joined us on the American tour. He was going to work with me on The Specials mark two album I wanted us to start recording. Ironically, Kendell had dismissed the original Specials. He branded our songs a 'sacrilege' against Laurel Aitken and, like many black guys, stuck to hardcore reggae and ignored 2 Tone. In his own words:

'I grew up being chased by skinheads in Birmingham. When The Specials happened I thought – hang on – Terry Hall is a skinhead isn't he? This looks dodgy.'

Kendell heard songs like 'Skinhead Moonstomp', which had originally been performed by Jamaican bands but then became a boot boy anthem. Like a lot of black musicians, he just scratched his head in confusion. This was our music being patronised by the sort of blokes who used to kick the crap out of him. It didn't make sense.

Worse still, he came to one of the Special Beat gigs we did in the UK playing alongside white reggae artist Judge

Dread and was confronted by a sea of skinheads – masses of them. I kept trying to explain that plenty of skins were OK – they weren't all racist. In fact, most skinheads were into the music and having a good time – just like us. But Kendell couldn't be convinced and was still happier to keep his distance.

During the course of working together on the Johnny Zee/Stereo Nation project, I felt I started to win him round to 2 Tone. But it was a short-lived victory. His relationship with the new Specials was to take a bit of a nose dive during the recording of our first album.

In 1996, we went into the studio back in the UK, with Tom Lowry as producer, to put together 'Today's Specials'. A lot of the stuff on the album was never really intended to be released to the general public. They were cover songs that I just wanted hawked round the industry to get some interest in the band. But after some arm-twisting, I agreed to put these numbers on that album – a decision I've come to regret.

We signed a deal with a new label called Kuff Records set up by UB40's Ali Campbell. This got a lot of publicity. It was his big signing and our first album as The Specials since the early 1980s. Sheena and Kendell got involved doing vocals and some rapping.

The covers were a mixed bag with numbers as diverse as 'Take Five', 'Dirty Old Town' by The Pogues and Desmond Dekker's '007 (Shanty Town)'. 'Hypocrite' was released as a single with a picture of then Prime Minister John Major on the front. But I wasn't sure this album had been well conceived. In hindsight, we'd rushed into it flush with a record deal and thinking we had to get something out there quickly.

The critics hated it. We would make amends with the second album – 'Guilty 'til Proved Innocent!' – but it wasn't good to disappoint the music press with our first offering.

Lynval had come to me and asked whether I would do Kendell's rapping bits at the gigs. When Kendell found out, he went ballistic. During a rehearsal, he decided to tear strips off us four original members of The Specials. He stood there and screamed – 'I know you're trying to save money on the tour. Those lyrics are mine. I performed them. You can't ask Nev to do them without asking me first. I don't want to be in your band anyway. Don't want to be an eighth member of The Specials.'

The band apologised profusely and asked him to come on tour – which he did.

Kuff Records, incidentally, was a short-lived business venture. The label had been created for Ali Campbell by Virgin, but ultimately had little impact on the charts. Not long after Virgin negotiated UB40's new recording deal Kuff seemed to get wound down. The only other significant signing to that label was Bitty McLean, a reggae artist who started life as UB40's engineer. His album never saw the light of day.

In spite of the less than stellar reception for our first album in twenty years, Trojan were back on the covers trail again – they couldn't get enough of the giants of 2 Tone.

Roger Lomas was asked to get The Selecter to do two covers albums from the Trojan back catalogue. Then we were asked to pick some tracks and do our own versions of them. We did it, enjoyed the experience of covering some classic ska numbers and then Trojan asked for a second album from us.

Poor Roger was tasked with getting us all back into his recording studio to lay the tracks down. But the second covers album revealed that Today's Specials were not to be a long-term proposition. The strains of domestic life were beginning to show among my middle-aged musical comrades.

With only two weeks to go before recording Lynval pulled out. He had a girlfriend in Seattle with a baby and was more interested in being a house husband than a recording artist. Luckily, Roger was able to replace Lynval with Neol Davies and the whole thing went ahead. The first covers album was called 'Skinhead Girl' and the second was called 'Conquering Ruler'.

This growing domesticity in the band was something I found intolerable. It wasn't that I didn't love my family. But being on the road as a musician was my job. Horace had already done teacher training and Brad had gone off to work in IT, but I had no intention of doing an office job. This rude boy was never going to be chained to a desk.

Tom Lowry, Kendell and me once sat round talking and Tom said – 'Nev, Horace is a teacher, what are you?' I said: 'I'm a musician. Gigs are my work'.

Music wasn't a hobby. It had been my life since childhood – the sound system, The Specials, The Fun Boy Three – non-stop music. I'd turned forty but I was in no mood to retire. Now I was getting earache from the band about missing their wives and kids and I just wanted to stick my hands over my ears and scream – 'stop!'

To me this talk was idiotic. We were back in demand. From 1995, for example, the Warped Tour became a huge US rock festival sponsored by Vans – the youth fashion business. The billing was a roll-call of the best in American punk, hip hop, reggae, emo, hardcore and so on – and we were headlining! It was never going to get better than this.

1998 saw us record 'Guilty 'til Proved Innocent' with MCA Records. I'd gone and negotiated the deal and the record company had liked the material I was writing.

It was important to start getting my own work recognised. Like other members of The Specials, I felt that I'd been given insufficient credit for the contributions I'd made to some of the classic 2 Tone numbers.

Now I was going to put out tracks that were indisputably written by me and see what the critics and public had to say. It was time to put my neck firmly on the block, as it were.

The other guys contributed songs as well but MCA picked my stuff to be the released singles. This kicked off a bit of a whispering campaign against me in the band. Then the whispering ceased because it switched to being in my face. The insults flew thick and fast: apparently I had angled to make my songs the singles and MCA and me had some sort of underhand relationship. I was 'ignorant' anyway and I even 'sang out of key'.

Everything was hurled in my direction and I got very defensive at this time. It was hard not to feel bruised when guys I'd known for so many years were sticking the boot in like this. For the first time, I started to realise what Jerry must have felt like – the hated leader. In effect, without Jerry or Terry, I was the leader of this motley crew. So I was taking all the flak.

The pressure got to a stage where, at a show in Chicago, I flipped. We arrived at a venue called the Metro and some jobsworth was making my life as difficult as possible. The report in *Rolling Stone* said that I began arguing with a production crew member and then hit him with a bar stool and grabbed his throat.

So on 29 April 1998, I found myself being charged with a 'simple battery misdemeanour' and told I faced either jail or a fine. The *Rolling Stone* article amusingly went on to detail how I had influenced American ska bands like Operation Ivy, The Mighty Mighty Bosstones and The Toasters. The article's headline was appropriately:

'Specials Singer Gets Rude & Arrested in Chicago'.

I suppose the rude boy was still untamed.

The officer who arrested me was a little embarrassed and confessed to being a huge Specials fan. The court case dragged on until eventually, there was a no-show by this production crew member and the whole thing was dropped. But it left me drained and can't have improved the internal band politics.

To cheer ourselves up, we played in front of 7,000 skiers and snowboarders at the Board Stiff festival hosted by Seattle radio station KNDD.FM. The stage was next to the snowboarding jump and the crowd were wrapped up in ski gear – it was arguably one of the most surreal gigs we ever played.

Supporting us were California's finest third wave ska band Rancid. Their music was a kind of ska/punk fusion and two of the blokes in the combo – Tim Armstrong and Lars Frederiksen – made appearances on our second album and in return, I collaborated on their fourth album, 'Life Won't Wait'.

Back on the ski run, we were in danger of getting pneumonia. Teeth chattering and with blue fingers, we went on after Rancid and I had to move around more than usual just so I wouldn't die of hypothermia.

Our new material from 'Guilty 'til Proved Innocent' went down a storm and I felt we had finally buried the ghost of album number one. Then when we kicked into 'Gangsters' and 'A Message to You Rudy', the roar from the thousands of skiers and snowboarders almost triggered an avalanche.

But by the end of 1998, the moaning had reached a crescendo. A tour of Japan was full of recriminations and proved to be the last straw. The guys were fed up of being on the road and wanted to go home. They were like an army that had been on campaign for years.

I was forced to sit back and watch Horace, Lynval and Roddy leave. Truthfully, this gutted me. For the first time in my life, I had a genuine breakdown in my own self-confidence. Maybe everything I was doing was a waste of time. Could the others be right? Should I move away from the microphone stand and take up the pipe and slippers?

Fortunately, there were now enough American ska bands around that I realised we had achieved something. There were plenty of good reasons for me to carry on. Roddy, Lynval and Horace might be hanging up their instruments, but I hadn't finished 2 Toning America.

Shaking off the blues, I set up base in California and decided to work doubly hard. The Americans had taken us to their hearts and I was not going to desert them. Band after band looked me up to work with them and I sniffed around for every challenging opportunity.

Together with Sheena, I got involved in a tribute project called 'Searching for Jimi Hendrix' which came out on Capitol Records. I got my daughter signed to V2 records, part of Virgin, and then the guys from No Doubt – Tony Kanal and Adrian Young – recorded with her.

Then I dived into a collaboration with John Avila of Oingo Boingo to produce 'The Best of The Specials and Fun Boy Three' performed by yours truly and released on Cleopatra Records.

Oingo Boingo was a ska influenced new wave band set up by, among others, Danny Elfman who went on to compose the theme tune to *The Simpsons*.

John Avila hooked up with Sheena on my next, rather bizarre, project. They composed a song called 'Stone Cold Love' and recorded it in something like fifteen minutes. This rapidly inspired number joined a series of tracks I wrote and produced for a horror film called *Vampires Anonymous*.

I suppose it was inevitable that living within driving distance of Hollywood, I'd eventually get roped in to the film business. This was a completely tongue-in-cheek – or fang-in-neck – shlock movie released in 2003.

I even featured as a black vampire alongside Michael Madsen who had just starred in Quentin Tarantino's *Kill Bill* and became a household name through *The Sopranos*. There was nothing remotely highbrow about this film. It had a completely goofy plot line in which a vampire tries to reform himself through a twelve-step programme which begins:

Step 1: Admit that you have a problem

Step 2: Take the test

Step 3: Deal with the sun

And so on to step seven, which asks vampires to apologise to people they've maimed or killed, and step eight which is simply 'no necking'. The film was a good laugh and therapeutic after the stress of being on the road with The Specials mark two.

My next port of call was recording on tracks for Unwritten Law's 2002 album 'Elva'. One of the songs off that album, 'Seein' Red' soared to number one in the US modern rock charts. Vocalist Scott Russo, myself and Sheena became firm friends. Scott says of me:

'Neville has done so much for us and other artists. His music is inspirational and The Specials were a huge part of my youth and identity. Being able to work with Neville on music was a magical experience and one I will cherish for the rest of my life.'

What I least expected at this time was to discover that 2 Tone had reached Latin America. So I nearly fell off my chair when I got a letter from a band in Venezuela called Desorden Público, asking if I would collaborate on their fifth album 'Diablo'. Being something of a devil myself I couldn't refuse. Always an impulsive type, I travelled from Los Angeles to Miami to meet them off a plane.

It was the crack of dawn and we all headed back to a hotel where I slept 'til the late morning. Then I recorded a vocal track with them for a song called 'Black Market Man'. The guys had written it especially for me, which was very touching. I asked them how they'd come to know about us. Caplis, the guitarist, answered for the band:

'You, Terry, Jerry, Horace, Roddy, John and Lynval are our own Beatles.'

Then Caplis, drummer Dan and vocalist Horacio talked to me at great length about the glory years of 2 Tone. They wanted to know everything. What they kept repeating was that ska had become a 'big world family'. Or as Caplis put it 'a big community of good vibes' – I couldn't have put it better myself.

Venezuela has a lot of political issues and the band have never shied away from singing about them. Keeping alive the ethos of ska as that singing newspaper talking about current events to the masses.

Other bands have sprung up across South America in Brazil, Chile and Argentina. I even discovered a ska festival in Peru recently against domestic violence. The logo – get this – was Walt Jabsco hitting the Beat Girl!

Canada remained a favourite destination for me with my old friends at Roots always happy to put some hip clothes on my back. So it was only a matter of time before I hooked up with a ska combo there. I recorded the single 'Explosive' with Quebec-based band The Planet Smashers. The video, which is still on YouTube at my time of writing this, featured a lot of scantily clad ladies. I raised no objections.

Matt Collyer was the lead singer of The Planet Smashers and went on to set up Stomp Records in Montreal, a very successful indie label modelled on Jerry's 2 Tone.

For about eight years, I made California my home, hanging out with the guys in bands like Rancid, Unwritten Law and No Doubt. These guys had come of age in the 1980s, but there were bands now forming with members that hadn't been alive when we originally 2 Toned the States.

In 1997, a twelve-year-old called Adam Tilzer came to the Vans Warped Tour and saw the reformed Specials playing. He wasn't to know that we were crabbing at each other backstage 24/7. To him, we were incredible performers who played a unique sound that changed his life.

He'd known some of the newer ska-influenced bands like Reel Big Fish but, having only been born in 1984, us

boys from Coventry were a mystery to him. Like a lot of young Americans at that time, he was coming out of grunge and hard rock and to quote him: 'I thought music was supposed to be pissed off.'

He arrived back in his home state of New York and, for years, couldn't get ska out of his head. With some mates, the garage jamming sessions started and continued throughout his teens. Steadily, he converted his friends to 2 Tone and the end result was impressive. Adam is now lead singer of the east coast-based Avon Junkies and one of many in a new generation carrying the flame.

While I was living Stateside, Sheena wasn't the only one of my kids making music in California. My son Darren was also making an impact, but not through ska. He had gone back to the roots of reggae and was lead singer of a band called DreadStarr.

Darren's mum was Carmen, who I had been seeing at the same time as Ideta during my earliest years in Coventry. She left Coventry many years before, married a GI from a US Air Force base and went to live with him in America – partly to get away from me I think.

During my time in California, I was sure that Darren – who has a slight resemblance to his old man – was pretending to be me to get some gorgeous women in the sack. I even told one newspaper as much – said I wasn't talking to him because of it.

But I'm sure being lead singer of DreadStarr is what really gets him the ladies. He's a presentable enough bloke I suppose – taking after his father of course.

For the briefest of times, I tried to go respectable in my new home state. The rude boy met and fell in love with a beautiful Japanese woman called Summer. Maybe I kidded myself that I was calming down at long last and could make a go of domestic bliss.

Some hope. In no time I was back on the road and then divorce papers were filed. But as Sheena always says of me, I can't let any relationships go. We are still in contact and she sees Summer all the time.

Married life was to elude me. While other members of The Specials stuck their slippers on and crashed out on the comfy sofa with a mug of cocoa, I couldn't leave the stage. Any stage. And that didn't bode well for a steady private life.

Earlier in my life, I'd burgled to afford good clothes. Now I thought about setting up a fashion label to sell rude boy clobber. Once I got this idea in my head, I couldn't get rid of it. So in 2003, I teamed up with music industry executive Barry Sanders and fashion experts David Gold and Neil Wiseman to launch Rude Wear Fashions.

The idea was to celebrate twenty-five years of ska with the clothes that we had been wearing back in 1979 and which had never gone out of fashion.

In November 2003, I launched Rude Wear at the MTV Europe awards standing alongside Lynval, Roddy and Jerry, as well as Ranking Roger and 1960s singer Donovan. There we were, promoting my new line of tonic suits, polo shirts and T-shirts.

Donovan and I had struck up a friendship and his son-in-law, Jason Rothberg, was now effectively my manager. He introduced me to a company called Alchemy Entertainment who helped me set up a new record label. Not since Shack had folded in the 1980s had I been a record company boss and this seemed like a good direction to go in. So Rude Boy Music was formed at the same time as the clothing company.

Things got off to a good start on the talent-signing front. Rude Boy Music proved to be a good way of hunting down new ska talent. We took on psychobilly, punk and reggae outfits like Ictus, Jah Waggie, Mishka and Harry The Dog – all experimental bands pushing back boundaries. Plus I got to promote Roland Bolan, son of the late and great glam rocker Marc Bolan.

However, I'm no accountant and with both ventures, the sums didn't add up. They both went bust. The main lesson of that very public episode was just to concentrate on making and performing music. I knew that my Rude Wear company and an earlier foray into branded clothes had irritated some members of The Specials, so maybe it was just better to let that idea go for now.

Up to 2004, I gigged with various musicians and line-ups including Neville Staple & The Hitmen. But I got the sense that something was pulling me back home – back to Coventry in particular.

At the turn of the millennium, my mum left Jamaica to go to Britain. Adassa had died and my father finally agreed to marry my mother. She lived with him for four short years, before he died.

In all honesty, my mum pined for Jamaica throughout their brief marriage. The colder climate of Britain wasn't to her liking and moving to the UK quite late in life was too much of a break from her daily routine in the Caribbean.

Getting the news that my dad had gone, I decided to pack my bags and return from California. My time in the United States had been something to cherish, but the third wave of ska could survive without me.

Ska legend Desmond Dekker on *Top of the Pops* in 1970.
© Redferns/Getty Images

Street Talk   BY JAMES FLETCHER

Back in business . . . The Specials sign a new deal

COVENTRY'S chart-topping ska stars The Specials are back with a brand new record deal.

The former Two-Tone band have recorded a new single to be released in the autumn followed later in the year by an album of new tracks.

Street Talk revealed exclusively in February that the band had reformed and were working on new material.

The band spent two months working in secret at Coventry's Ramp Studios in Far Gosford Street.

Now the band have teamed up with UB40 front-man Ali Campbell and signed for his new record label, Kuss.

The re-birth of the '80s super-group has been led by four original members — Lynval Golding, Roddy Byers, Neville Staples and Horace Panter.

Absent

Former front man

LINKING UP: UB40's Ali Campbell (third from right) watches The Specials sign up

Four of The Specials reunite under Ali Campbell of UB40's record label.

© Coventry Evening Telegraph

In Las Vegas with Megalith Records label manager Jeremy Patton at the 2003 Ska Summit Festival.

© Jeremy Patton/Megalith Records

Me recording in Miami with Venezuelan ska band Desorden
Público.
© Desorden Público

Life in the sunshine state.
Neville Staple, personal collection

11

THE SPECIALS RETURN – JERRY AND ME

Theatre Royal | 1979 - The Specials SKA NIGHT!
STRATFORD EAST | 1984 - Fun Boy Three
2004 - The Rude Boy Returns

NEVILLE STAPLE
& the ALL STARS

with special guests Saint & Campbell
DJ: Andre Shapps (Big Audio Dynamite)
SATURDAY 20th MARCH 7.30pm

Performing in Australia.
© Jason Doyle, Studio Commercial

The start of the UK comeback.
Neville Staple, personal collection

Me and Ranking Roger share a stage in Australia.
© Jason Doyle, Studio Commercial

Jerry had sat there looking at me like I'd just told him he had five minutes to live. What I'd actually said was that I was leaving The Specials.

For a few unbearable moments, we exchanged all sorts of glances which said all sorts of things. For my part, I was sorry to be doing this to him. It was almost as if I was kicking over his train set and stamping all over it. For his part, the look was all one of betrayal. But at least I'd had the decency to come and tell him straight out what was going on.

That must have been the worst day of his life, back then in 1981. As a combo, we were a fractious bunch of argumentative sods, but together we'd stormed the charts and with 'Ghost Town' we'd created one of the greatest numbers in British pop history.

The animosity, though, had grown to such a level, that getting out was the only option. I took one last look at Jerry – at that gap-toothed mouth, half-open and searching for the right words to make me stay – but I'd had enough. Mumbling something incoherent and totally forgettable, I sloped off.

So began the long freeze between me and our former leader. He went off and sang about Nelson Mandela. I joined Fun Boy Three, swapping a tonic suit for a jump suit, before putting Coventry behind me and embarking on a new life in America and the various ska line-ups of the 1990s.

As the twenty-first century dawned, however, my sunny exile in California began to dim and I found my way back to Britain. Facing an underwhelming reception, I set about forming a solo band. Even if re-capturing those past glories looked impossible, I still couldn't keep away from a stage. I'm just a man who has to perform.

Reunited with Jason Rothberg, I took a good look around for some musicians and soon found a group of individuals who'd make an ideal backing band for me. The only problem was that they were all in Bad Manners, and between me and my new stage buddies stood a formidable obstacle in the shape of lead singer Buster Bloodvessel.

Buster was a giant of a man with a tongue that was ox-like in size and length. A fact known to millions of people as he frequently stuck it out during his many appearances on *Top of the Pops* in the 1980s. Produced by Roger Lomas, Bad Manners had enjoyed a string of hits with sing-a-long numbers like 'Lip Up Fatty' and the 'Can-Can', but they'd always been the Joker in the ska pack.

Jason set about mining the talent out of Buster's band including one Bad Manners veteran of ten years' standing, Warren Middleton. 'Wazza' would go on to replace Jason as my manager as well as play trombone in the Neville Staple Band for most of the decade that followed. After Warren defected, the rest of Bad Manners soon flocked in my direction – or at least the best ones did – which left the big man hopping mad.

I'm not especially proud of leaving Buster bereft of his backing band, but I was a man in a hurry to make some money. In the music business, you can't sit around for too long twiddling your thumbs. I knew those guys were the right people for me and I went for them. I was back, I needed a band and I realised there was a steep wall of scepticism still to climb.

It was like having to crawl out of the dustbin of pop history and beg for acceptance again. But needs must and there was only one way I could see to get back on top and that was to belt out the 2 Tone classics. By 2004, I felt confident enough to stick out a new album and teamed up with Mick Jones of The Clash and Rat Scabies of The Damned to make 'The Rude Boy Returns' – a pretty accurate expression of how I viewed my own homecoming.

Fearing, as I neared my fiftieth birthday, that I'd be due some flak for this album from the critics, I sat back and waited for the reviews. I needn't have lost any sleep – it got a big thumbs-up. The *Guardian* wrote: '"The Rude Boy Returns" has an air of nostalgia but also sounds rudely contemporary as bands like the Libs (Libertines) pillage The Specials.'

The reviews were great but the touring proved to be more of a problem. After being mobbed in the States for years, it was a bit humbling to have to hustle for gigs in Britain. Warren, as my new manager, became a booking warhorse, but he came up against the same doubts over and over again. Neville Staple? The Specials? Blimey, he's a bit of a throwback! As I'd learned twenty years before, the British music industry just can't wait to throw you out with yesterday's trash. So I had to fight to prove I was a going proposition.

For the next four years, I trudged tirelessly from venue to venue playing to the loyalists: middle-aged fans, students, bikers, skinheads and 2 Tone obsessives from all over the world. Gradually, the audiences built up and the stages got bigger. A dormant army of ska fans began to stir, seeping out of the brickwork and flooding into the concert halls – and as they did so the venue managers started changing their tune. Suddenly I was flavour of the month.

I gigged with the Neville Staple Band round the UK doing festivals and college bashes almost non-stop. I also kept touring with Special Beat, or sometimes Roger would share the billing with me in his newly reconstituted line up for The Beat, minus Dave Wakeling.

One interesting addition to the new Beat was Roger's son Ranking Junior, who also featured on the 2005 single 'Boys Will Be Boys' by the The Ordinary Boys – a new band who many had high hopes for at the time, and who had more than a hint of ska in their music.

The lead singer of The Ordinary Boys – a guy called Preston – created headlines by becoming a contestant on Channel 4's *Celebrity Big Brother* programme, and later marrying its 'ordinary girl' winner, Chantelle. But unfortunately their marriage didn't last and the band never managed to deliver a chart topping single – a great shame.

My next set of gigs would take me to the other side of the world. Special Beat were to prove very popular in Australia when I went to perform there in 2005. We had never taken 2 Tone Down Under but I discovered that they loved their ska in Sydney, Melbourne and Perth. Our support band and organisers of the Australian gigs were a combo called Backy Skank. Their vocalist, Simon Smith, was overwhelmed by the crowd response to Special Beat:

'Neville held the Australian audiences in the palm of his hand. He was well aware that the audience of both young and old had been starved of the 2 Tone ska sound. The crowd loved him and he loved the Aussie audiences.'

Since 1981, there had been a very vibrant ska scene in Australia with bands like The Porkers leading the way. They had been just one of several ska artists to release a tribute album to The Specials in 2000.

The album was called 'Spare Shells' and brought together some very diverse groups from across the globe who wanted to give a 'modern interpretation' of our songs. The bands included Voodoo Glow Skulls, Citizen Fish and my friends from Caracas, Venezuela – Desorden Público.

In the same way that I had worked with or guided America's third wave ska bands, I now reached out to some of Europe's up-and-coming talents. Groups like Fratelli di Soledad in Italy – who went on to support the Neville Staple Band. As vocalist Giorgio 'Zorro' Silvestri explained to me, The Specials introduced them to ska and rocksteady music. Without 2 Tone, they might never have got to know about the music of Jamaica – let alone Coventry.

After so many years of touring, I've now found myself being forced to ease up a bit with the stage antics as my knees have gone on strike. They've basically had enough of me bouncing up and down and jumping off PA stacks.

I suppose I haven't shown them much mercy. I'm often unaware of the pain I'm causing them when I'm on stage but when I'm sitting back at home, the agony can be something else.

By the time I was gigging at the now knocked down Astoria in London in July 2008, one of my knees had swollen up like a football. A great big lump of aching flesh. But that night there was a big enough distraction on hand to banish the agony from my mind. Backstage I could see a large, bearded man, chuckling away at this and that. Every so often he'd open his mouth and I'd get a glimpse of that familiar gap in his teeth. Because Jerry Dammers, his impressive and very varied collection of records in tow, was now turning up at my gigs to do a supporting DJ set.

This had been going on for several months – in April we'd played the Shepherds Bush Empire where I'd also performed alongside Pauline Black and Ranking Roger – and, being older and more chilled about life in general, I was glad to make the grand old man of 2 Tone feel at home. Also, by that time, both of us had already been at the receiving end of feelers put out from our former colleagues in The Specials. A reunion was on the cards.

The first meeting had been back in September 2007. All of us had been present, including Jerry. He'd declared that if we did reform, there would have to be tracks from both Specials albums and some new material. The Specials should be moving forward, he insisted, not just doing the classics. Unsuprisingly, this diktat didn't go down very well among a bunch of grown men who were in no mood to take orders anymore.

Needless to say, when I played with Jerry that July, he was already unhappy about the way things were going. We chatted about it backstage and then I put it to the back of my mind, as it was time to go out and play to the big crowd at the Astoria.

Jerry had done his DJ set earlier and agreed to play keyboards alongside the Neville Staple Band. I felt honoured and pleased to have the great man next to me tinkling the ivories. But hardly had we walked out on stage when he grabbed hold of a mike and vented his spleen against Terry Hall and his manager.

I looked out at the ska fans who had little idea what was going on behind the scenes. Thank God they didn't. They

just looked a bit confused and I felt a bit embarrassed. Little did these fans know that they were only getting a dress rehearsal for the verbal fireworks ahead.

While we gigged at the Astoria, Lynval was doing his diplomatic shuttles between the other members of The Specials, trying to get them back together. He was the real dynamo behind the reunion, working tirelessly to set the band on its feet again. Lynval repeatedly stretched out his hand to Jerry, who he'd always got on well with, only to have it bitten in return. Well, Lynval was always the 'diplomat', as Horace called him. But now even that relationship was breaking down.

By December 2008, Jerry had released a statement to the press saying that he was dismayed the rest of The Specials only wanted to play stuff from the first album and that his own suggestions had been largely unwelcome. He went on to accuse the band of holding 'secret rehearsals' without him, although towards me he had nothing but kind words, saying: 'Neville Staple is the only former member who demonstrated real commitment to Jerry's involvement'. And so I did – at the time.

Jerry's statement also made clear that he did not believe the reunion represented 'what the real Specials stood for, politically, or in terms of creativity, imagination or forwardness or ideas'.

It seemed only I was speaking to Jerry anymore, but inevitably Lynval and Terry reached out to me and it was time to make a decision. Did I throw in my lot with them or remain on Jerry's side?

After much soul searching, I did decide to go with the majority.

I'm not going to deny I had mixed feelings to start with, but for very different reasons to Jerry. The Neville Staple Band, Special Beat and my other projects were doing well, and after years of gigging I'd proved both to myself and to the crowds that I could hold my own as a front man. I might even say that for the first time in my life, my performances were shot through with complete self-confidence. Even the mighty Jerry himself told me he'd never heard me sing better.

The idea of reuniting without the great man didn't make me very happy either. Look at it from my perspective – whatever my differences with him, Jerry had invited me into The Coventry Automatics. He'd worked hard to make the original Specials successful, forcing us to give up our day jobs in the hope of something better and getting us on to the Clash tour – The Specials, with Jerry, had made us part of pop history

Most of all, going back to The Specials line-up reawakened some old demons inside Neville Staple. Would I feel as if I was playing second fiddle on stage? Would my contribution be valued? Was I going to feel happy? The only way to answer these questions was to sit down and talk to Terry, Brad, Horace, Lynval and Roddy and see how I felt. If the vibes weren't right, then I wouldn't be part of this reunion.

But when I started going to meetings and then the first rehearsals, I made an incredible discovery. Where we'd once been frenetic youths with king-sized egos and tempers to match, we were now a bunch of fifty-something blokes with families and a more reasoned outlook on life.

All we wanted to do was get on stage and see the ska Mums and Dads – even grandparents – enjoying them-

selves for an evening. Jerry was right about it being a nostalgia trip in some ways, but with things in Britain going downhill in terms of the economy and politics, the old songs had suddenly acquired a brand new relevance.

When we appeared on *Later With Jools Holland* on BBC2 in 2009, Jools quipped: 'When you had a lot of success in the 1980s, there was a recession. You've got back together and there's a recession. Do you think it's you?'

Once again, we were providing the soundtrack for desperate times. The credit crunch and the loss of hundreds of thousands of jobs across Britain made 'Ghost Town' a song with real power once more.

As I threw in my lot with the lads, Jerry moved into hyperdrive to pour scorn on the reunion tour. Down in his Brixton home, the seething Mr Dammers wasn't shy about telling anybody who wanted to listen what he thought about us.

For example, when we played our set on the Jools Holland show, there was a revealing chat between Jools and Horace, Lynval and Roddy.

Jools: 'Why no Jerry?'

Horace: 'We asked him to join and it didn't work out – let's not talk about that.'

Jools: 'He rang me up you know. Said he's not very happy about it and said when I introduce you could I just say your names and not say The Specials which is why ... ' Jools gestures up to the big band sign above the stage, ' ... you've got such a huge ... '

The only way to answer Jerry and those who thought we shouldn't reform without him under any circumstances was to get out there and perform. April 2009 saw the start of the tour in Newcastle – and we put on the tightest gig I've ever been a part of. Billing the concerts as a thirtieth-anniversary tour, we reduced grown men to tears. Lynval saw one forty-five-year-old bloke repeatedly hitting a wall and wailing: 'Why has it taken so long?!'

The *Guardian*, reviewing the gig, pronounced that our songs spoke to today's problems: 'Picking any song at random from their glorious 1979–81 run of seven consecutive hit singles gives a running commentary on 2009 Britain, from binge drinking (Stereotype), teenage pregnancy (Too Much Too Young) to knife crime (Why?).'

This wasn't just the orgy of nostalgia that Jerry had feared. People felt we were talking to them about the here and now as much as during the events of thirty years ago. I knew that just by looking out at the sea of two-thousand faces in front of me. As I toasted on the mic, I could make out not just guys my age in extra large Ben Sherman shirts but young kids as well. Maybe some of them were dragooned in by their dads but they were having the best of times. I can't do it justice in words but there was a powerful positive energy in our performance that matched anything we'd done in the past. The fans and the press were both in agreement on that.

When we stormed the Birmingham Academy a couple of days later, the moans about our absent former leader were receding rapidly. The tour tickets had sold out and the *Daily Telegraph* said of our decision to play the old numbers that we were a band that 'deserved to be preserved in aspic'.

By the time we found ourselves at the Brixton Academy, on Jerry's home turf, celebrities like actor Jude Law had joined the audiences, gaping in awe at their childhood heroes. Any sense I'd had that this might not be the right decision now disappeared.

What cheered me even more than our performances was having Trevor as support. Warming up the crowd before we charged on, my oldest friend took to doing a DJ set with Felix – Terry Hall's son. I have to confess, I think we've infected Felix with the rude boy ethos. He definitely wants to be one of us; all kitted out in classic clobber and stylish as fuck.

Getting myself kitted out didn't prove too difficult either. Ace Face provided the band with their very stylish mohair and wool mix tonic suits, a far cry from the suits we wore the first time round. I also took to modelling a range of heritage suits from Burtons. On our first visit to their headquarters off Oxford Street me and Trevor were offered a suit each – of course we walked off with six, and a Harrington jacket, some shoes and a few shirts to boot. We repeated the same old rude boy trick at the Vans store in Carnaby Street where me and Mr Evans stripped the place of whatever our eye took a fancy to.

Although I seemed to be wowing the music writers with my ability to charge around the stage like a madman, Trevor was sometimes worried I was over-exerting myself. At Brixton, Lynval and I would run the whole length of what was a pretty big stage and to some younger people, it seemed incredible we could manage it. But I have to confess it took a bit of a toll on me and when we took the tour abroad, my knees began to let me down again.

'We had to rebuild Nev in Japan,' Trev says.

It's true that my knees and ankles were in a mess out there. The only solution was endless massages which I didn't find completely unendurable.

Inevitably, as seems to happen in my life, the rude boy once again had a little run in with the forces of law and

order. In seventh heaven with how the tour was going, I decided to take a break in Jamaica during July, 2009. Seeing my family out there has become more and more important to me in recent years and leaving them again is always hard.

This time though, it was even harder than usual. Sitting on the plane for London and waiting to take off, I suddenly found myself being manhandled off by the local cops and carted away to be both strip searched and X-rayed. As the press back in Britain later reported, I was yet again being accused of drug possession. Unfortunately for my accusers, nothing was found on me.

I returned to England spitting blood about the whole affair and only gigging again with The Specials put the humiliation out of my mind. It seems that there are a few people in this world, often uniformed, who are intent on stopping this rude boy enjoying the quiet life he thinks he now deserves.

The high point of our UK tour was, of course, the gig at the Ricoh stadium in Coventry. Nine thousand fans equalled a brilliant homecoming. It might not have been our best gig in terms of musical performance but there we were before our own people, like prodigal sons returning. We'd made our fellow Coventrians wait a long time for that night and as we belted out 'Gangsters' and 'Too Much Too Young' the whole place erupted.

At the packed after party, I briefly bumped in to Liam Gallagher who growled something to the effect that it was 'the best fucking thing he'd seen all year'. Then he left because he was getting too much hassle. Liam's thumbs-up was followed by an even bigger endorsement from Amy Winehouse.

Backstage at that summer's V Festival – while sitting on Trev's lap, as I recall – Amy agreed to join us during

'You're Wondering Now'. Then she stayed on for 'Ghost Town' and as we exited the stage she was still encouraging the huge crowd to keep on clapping. The *NME* later paid us a massive compliment by declaring that our set put younger bands to shame, but we weren't intentionally point-scoring; things just turned out like that.

Now that I've found myself, with the rest of the guys in the reunited Specials, creating a global ripple of excitement, it's clear that Jerry has burnt his bridges with us. So where do I stand on that?

First of all, none of us are getting any younger. I've had my ups and downs with the guys – say what you want about The Specials, when it comes to having a bust up, we're without equals – but I'm prepared to let bygones be bygones. We've all got families to support and there's nothing wrong with trying to make a living from your music. Jerry can't and shouldn't stop us from doing so.

I held out as long as I could, waiting for him to compromise – to find a way forward with the rest of The Specials. During that time, I carried on touring with the Neville Staple Band. Just being my own man. Not having Jerry dictating to me. I realise I've kind of got to like that. I suspect that's how the rest of the band feels.

After touring the world again with Horace, Lynval, Brad, Terry and Roddy, I can see we're all fed up with our former leader. We had this freeze in our relationships for a quarter of a century and a thaw was long overdue. Brad and me get on better than we ever did the first time round. Lynval goes round to Trevor Evans' place for tea. Horace and Roddy are more chatty with me than I ever imagined – though I reckon the two of them still think I'm a bit of a tosspot. The same no-good rude boy who can't play an instrument.

If I'd stuck it out with Jerry, I wouldn't have moved on. Nobody wants to stand still in their life, and this seems the right way forward.

Jerry's main problem was that he didn't realise he was dealing with a group of fifty-year-olds. None of us were young men anymore who would just do as we were told. We'd all experienced long journeys since 1981 and trying to rewind the clock back to the way things were done back then wasn't going to wash with the band. None of us wanted a leader anymore.

I can't see me doing any new creative work with the guys. The reason to get back together with the rest of the Specials was to please the crowd. Nothing else. This was our pension – simple as that.

We were riding a thirty-year wave of nostalgia – a lot of people wanted to be transported for a single night back to 1979. They wanted to hear me toast 'Bernie Rhodes knows, don't argue', Roddy's guitar soaring over the crowd, Horace's bass thumping out that ska rhythm, and Prince Rimshot and Lynval getting the punters skanking to the music.

For too many years, we had been a contradiction. We talked about unity, about black and white. But we couldn't unite ourselves. A quarter of a century had passed without the full line-up being seen by the public. However, there were now solid reasons for us to bring our sound and message back.

Probably our most surreal appearance as a reunited combo came in early 2010 when the BBC rang up and asked if we'd perform on the thirtieth-anniversary edition of the programme *Newsnight*. Not what you might call a traditional pop programme – more used to booking government ministers and top business people than ageing rock stars. But it turned out that when the first programme went on air in 1980, The Specials were coasting up the charts with 'Too Much Too Young' at the very same time.

Newsnight presenter Jeremy Paxman, famous for being a bit of a rottweiler when interviewing politicians was a puppy dog with us backstage. All photos and backslaps. I thought he was a very nice bloke, but then I don't run the country.

Then, in front of a terribly serious panel of guests, we played a song about what happens when you don't use contraception. A song that some BBC disc jockeys back in 1980 had been pretty squeamish about giving airtime at all. Three long decades after teaching a nation how to skank, there we were on a small stage in Television Centre – almost as small as the one on *Saturday Night Live* all those many years before in New York. That singing newspaper we call 'ska' had made a comeback.

In Britain, and the world, the good times have come to an end. An economic boom and easy credit have all dried up. It's as if we've all got into a time machine and gone back to the bad old days – sky-high unemployment, kids with nothing to do. Strikes are back in fashion, the far right is marching up and down English high streets and some people even think riots are just round the corner.

Our return has reminded the country that pop music was once a lot more relevant – that it could move minds and hearts. I hope that in taking to the stages of the UK and beyond this eclectic bunch of people called The Specials has helped inspire new bands – groups of young kids who will have new things to say. And more importantly, who will move the ska sound forward.

Roll on the fourth wave!

The influence of The Specials lives on.
© Sound System Records / Pete Cooper

Jerry Dammers shares the stage with me a Neville Staple Band gig at the Astoria, London 2008.
Tony McMahon, personal collection

The Specials reunited at Bestival, September 2008.
Neville Staple, personal collection

Back on stage with the reunited Specials at the Hammersmith Apollo, November 2009.
© Getty Images

All of us, giving it everything we've got at the Brixton Academy, May 2009: roll on the fourth wave!
© Getty Images

EPILOGUE

A STAPLE FAMILY ALBUM

Me and my sister Elaine.

Me and my grandson Fidel.

My daughter Sheena.

My brother Manny.

Tianna and her granddad.

Tammy, Darren and Carmen.

Me and my brother Jimmy.

Just after Christmas 2008, my mother passed away. She'd been ill for some time but it still came as a shock. I was gigging in Ireland with the Neville Staple Band when I got the news, but cut it short to fly to Jamaica straight away.

I'm so grateful that I had enough time to get to know Mum again after being separated from her throughout most of my childhood and teenage years. I never stopped journeying backwards and forwards to Christiana to see her — and the rest of my family — over the past twenty-seven years.

Earlier in 2008, my grandmother also died at the impressive age of ninety-eight – just missing her centenary. Even in her last months, she was still talking about that time she saw a mermaid in the caves all those years ago. I would regale her in turn with the time I saw the rolling calf.

I'm not just a father now, but also a grandfather. As I get older, my family means a lot to me – and I have a bigger family than many people. In between the never-ending schedule of gigs, I make as much time as I can for my kids, grandchildren, cousins, brothers and sisters – whether in the UK, United States or Jamaica.

Friends have always been important to me as well. Nobody can accuse me of disloyalty or not spending time with my fellow rudies.

I don't see as much of Rex as I used to. He went off to study at university and became a lecturer in south London. Rex has a family and a very nice house. Trevor does too, only he remained in Coventry and is still making music with Sir Baggy, who is going strong.

Ray King is another of that generation of arrivals from the Caribbean who seems to be in the rudest of health. He looks the same now as he did when we were building the Holyhead Youth Club. There must be something in those dumplings that keeps us all going.

I am a rude boy. I need to say that loud and clear. No matter what I do in my life, I'm still a bad man in the eyes of the law. Look at that hassle with the police kicking down my door, ripping up my skirting boards and carting me off to a cell only a year ago. To them, I'm definitely a rudie.

My life started in Jamaica where the rude boy culture originated. With the sharp-suited, well turned out 'bwoys', with pork pie or trilby hats who spent their time dancing at blues parties – out all night and sleeping all day.

I didn't have to become a rude boy or learn it. I was a rude boy from day one – it was in my genes.

Me, Trevor, Rex, Franklyn, Bookie, Johnny Stevenson, Banacek and the rest of our gang – we fought to exist on the streets. There was no alternative. If we didn't stand up to our enemies, they'd walk all over us. To meet Rex today, you'd never know what a mean and keen fighter he was when the chips were down.

Unlike Rex, Trevor and I knew what the inside of a prison looked like – and the boredom and random violence that we encountered every day inside. We were punished because we wanted the good things in life that we hadn't been born with – rude boys who would risk incarceration just to be dressed in the best tonic suits and brogues.

In between all the violence I have detailed – lashing out with our fists against hostile skinheads – we were addicted to the music of our home country. We brought the sounds of Kingston to the streets of Coventry – Prince Buster, Laurel Aitken, U Roy, Dillinger – these were our musicians, our heritage. They created the tracks we loved to listen to – all those dubplates I bought or stole and played in the hope of winning one sound system battle after another.

The many nights I spent at the Locarno are forever etched in my memory – a place that almost defined us. Looking up on a Monday night to Pete Waterman at the turntable, he was a godlike figure who was able to get his hands on all the latest sounds from Jamaica – a country I didn't have the money to return to until I was in my mid-twenties.

'Quite a life,' Trevor commented to me recently.

Yeah, but it's not over yet. This rude boy is nowhere near retirement. I've fought boot boys, sabotaged sound systems, burgled houses while their owners snored fitfully and made love to more women than I could ever count or remember. It's certainly been action packed.

But I suppose if a day sticks out in my mind more than any other in this life of mine, it has to be the one where I pushed open a door at the Holyhead Youth Club to find a bunch of blokes calling themselves The Coventry Automatics. And no matter how many harsh words we were determined to trade with each other over the years – I can't deny, they changed my life.

ACKNOWLEDGEMENTS

Three Rude Boys: (*Left to right*) Rex Griffiths, me and a glimpse of Trevor Evans on stage before a gig by The Specials.

Rex Griffiths, personal collection

The following people have co-operated with the writing of this book and given insights never before seen in print about the 2 Tone era, the American third wave of ska and the life of yours truly, the original rude boy.

The rude boys:
- Trevor Evans – fellow founder of Jah Baddis, more than a roadie in The Specials, keyboards in 21 Guns and friend
- Rex Griffiths – more than a roadie in The Specials, drums in 21 Guns, friend
- Dennis Willis aka 'Scuff the Hustler' – friend
- Cedric Bogle – friend
- Bookie – friend

2 Tone artists:
- Pauline Black – lead vocals in The Selecter
- Ranking Roger – lead vocals in The Beat (English Beat in the US), Special Beat and General Public
- Stella Barker – rhythm guitar in The Bodysnatchers and The Belle Stars

Family and friends:
- Pete Waterman – founder of Stock, Aitken and Waterman, judge on ITV's *Pop Idol* and DJ at the Locarno in Coventry in the 1970s

- Bernie Rhodes – manager of The Specials and The Clash
- Ray King – lead vocals, Ray King Soul Band
- DJ Baggy Hi-Fi – sound system DJ
- Roger Lomas – sound engineer, The Specials
- Tom Lowry – sound engineer, Today's Specials
- Sheena Staple – my daughter and singing artist
- Kurt Soto – Vans
- Raymond Perkins – head of communications, Roots (http://canada.roots.com)
- DJ Kendell – musical collaborator and friend
- Albino Brown – producer, Ska Parade Radio
- Taz from Stereo Nation
- The Higsons – 2 Tone signed band
- Warren Middleton – the Neville Staple Band
- Ideta – my former girlfriend
- Fay – my sister
- Melanie and Byron – my daughter and son
- Paulette – my girlfriend, mother of Tara and Chance
- Yvonne – my girlfriend, mother of Andrea
- Dawn – my sister
- Franklyn – my brother
- Alvin – my cousin and sound system DJ
- Sue Blackburn – friend

International ska bands:
- Adrian Young – drums, No Doubt
- Scott Russo – lead vocals, Unwritten Law
- Caplis – bass guitar, Desorden Público – Venezuela's top ska band
- Matt Collyer – lead vocals, The Planet Smashers – Canadian ska band

- Nigel Knucklehead – keyboards and vocals, The Allstonians – Massachusetts ska band
- Brendog – guitar, Mephiskapheles – New York ska band
- Adam Tilzer – lead vocals, Avon Junkies – New York ska band
- David Kirchgessner – vocals, Mustard Plug – Michigan ska band
- Jeremy Patton – manager of Oklahoma-based Megalith Records
- Dan Cuetara – Beat Soup – Boston ska band
- John Pantle – United Talent Agency
- Tokyo Ska Parade Orchestra – Japanese ska band
- Pete Porker – vocals, The Porkers – Australian ska band
- Simon Smith – lead vocals, Backy Skank – Australian ska band
- Giorgio 'Zorro' Silvestri – Fratelli di Soledad – Italian ska band
- Quique – vocals, Skatala – Spanish ska band
- Tobias Meyer – guitar, Skaliners – German ska band
- Jesko Kruger – trumpet, beNUTS – German ska band
- Oliver Zenglein, organ, beNUTS – German ska band
- The Valkyrians – Finnish ska band

Thanks to all those who filled the gaps in my memory.

The Coventry Automatics: (*left to right*) Silverton, Terry, Horace, Roddy, Jerry, Lynval and me.

Neville Staple, personal collection

Later as The Specials performing 'Stupid Marriage' at the Hammersmith Palais, 1979.

© Gerard McNamara

The Beat – Ranking Roger in the middle with hat and dazed expression.

Neville Staple, personal collection

The Selecter – Pauline Black (*right from middle*) sporting her trademark trilby.

Pauline Black, personal collection

The Nutty Boys.
© UrbanImage/Adrian Boot

Dexy's Midnight Runners in jogging gear – led by Kevin of course.
© UrbanImage/Adrian Boot

DISCOGRAPHY

ALBUMS

1979 Specials – The Specials (2 Tone/Chrysalis)

1980 More Specials – The Specials (2 Tone/Chrysalis)

1982 The Fun Boy Three – Fun Boy Three (Chrysalis)

1983 Waiting – Fun Boy Three (Chrysalis)

1984 The Best Of Fun Boy Three – Fun Boy Three (Chrysalis)

1991 The Singles Collection – The Specials (2 Tone/Chrysalis)

1992 Live – Special Beat (Receiver UK)
The Specials & Friends (Receiver UK)
The Specials Live – Too Much Too Young (Receiver UK)
Dawning Of A New Era – The Coventry Automatics AKA The Specials (Receiver UK)
The Specials Live At The Moonlight Club (2 Tone/Chrysalis)

1993 King of Kings – Desmond Dekker and The Specials (Trojan)

1994 Skanktastic – Neville Staple (525 Music Productions)
Shack – Neville Staple (Receiver UK)

1996 Today's Specials – The Specials (Kuff Records/Virgin)
Too Much Too Young – The Specials (EMI Gold)

1998   BBC Sessions – The Specials (EMI)
Guilty 'Til Proved Innocent! – The Specials (Way Cool Music/MCA)

1999   Blue Plate Specials – The Specials (Big Ear Music)
Ghost Town: Live At The Montreaux Jazz Festival (Trojan/UK)
Searching For Jimi Hendrix – Various (The Right Stuff)

2000   Skinhead Girl – The Specials (Receiver/Trojan Records UK)
The Very Best Of The Specials and Fun Boy Three – performed by Neville Staple (Cleopatra Records, Los Angeles)

2001   Conquering Ruler – The Specials (Receiver/Trojan Records)
Archive – The Specials (Rialto)

2002   Ska Au Go Go – Special Skank (Cleopatra Records)

2004   The Rude Boy Returns – Neville Staple (Rude Boy Music)

2005   Stereo-Typical: A's, B's and Rarities – The Specials (Chrysalis)

2006   The Best of The Specials and Fun Boy Three (Pegasus)

2008   The Best of The Specials (EMI)

SINGLES

1979   Gangsters – The Special AKA (2 Tone)
A Message To You Rudy – The Specials (2 Tone)

1980   The Special AKA Live! EP – The Special AKA
(2 Tone/Chrysalis)
Rat Race – The Specials (2 Tone/Chrysalis)
Stereotype – The Specials (2 Tone/Chrysalis)
Pearls Café – The Specials (2 Tone/Chrysalis)
Do Nothing – The Specials (2 Tone/Chrysalis)

1981   Ghost Town – The Specials (2 Tone/Chrysalis)

1981   The Lunatics (Have Taken Over The Asylum) –
Fun Boy Three (Chrysalis)

1982   T'Ain't What You Do… – Fun Boy Three
(Chrysalis)

1982   Really Saying Something – Bananarama with Fun
Boy Three (Decca/London Records)

1982   The Telephone Always Rings – Fun Boy Three
(Chrysalis)
Summertime – Fun Boy Three (Chrysalis)
The More I See (The Less I Believe) – Fun Boy
Three (Chrysalis)

1983   Tunnel of Love – Fun Boy Three (Chrysalis)
Our Lips Are Sealed – Fun Boy Three (Chrysalis)

1984   Pirates on the Airwaves – Sunday Best (Chrysalis)

1995   Hypocrite – The Specials (Kuff Records/Virgin)

1996   Pressure Drop – The Specials (Kuff
Records/Virgin)

INDEX

Neville Staple's family and his girlfriends are filed as subheadings under Staple, Neville.

Records by the Specials are filed under Specials, The. Other records are filed under their titles.